W9-CUX-727

Corporate Capitalism in Japan

Classics in the History and Development of Economics

General Editor: **Michio Morishima**, Emeritus Professor of Economics, London School of Economics and Political Science

In the postwar years the discipline of economics has become highly advanced by focusing upon issues which can be expressed in mathematical terms and ignoring issues upon which it is difficult to make axiomatic analysis. This series aims to make available in English texts which might well have played a major role in the development of a more balanced – not exclusively mathematical – economic theory but for the fact that they were written in a language other than English. However, the series' interest will also embrace mathematical and English-language works where these appear to have been unduly neglected. The series will also seek to make available in English important works that present the experiences of non-English-speaking economies; it is hoped that these will contribute greatly to making economics more comprehensive and more widely applicable to a range of world economies in the future.

Titles include:

Marco Fanno
A CONTRIBUTION TO THE THEORY OF SUPPLY AT JOINT COST
THE MONEY MARKET

Hiroshi Hazama
THE HISTORY OF LABOUR MANAGEMENT IN JAPAN

Hiroshi Okumura
CORPORATE CAPITALISM IN JAPAN

Alfonso de Pietro-Tonelli and Georges H. Bousquet
VILFREDO PARETO
Neoclassical Synthesis of Economics and Sociology

Joseph A. Schumpeter and Yasuma Takata
POWER OR PURE ECONOMICS?

Yasuma Takata
POWER THEORY OF ECONOMICS

Giulio La Volpe
STUDIES ON THE THEORY OF GENERAL DYNAMIC ECONOMIC EQUILIBRIUM

**Classics in the History and Development of Economics
Series Standing Order ISBN 0–333–71466–0**
(*outside North America only*)

You can receive future titles in this series as they are published by placing a standing order. Please contact your bookseller or, in case of difficulty, write to us at the address below with your name and address, the title of the series and the ISBN quoted above.

Customer Services Department, Macmillan Distribution Ltd, Houndmills, Basingstoke, Hampshire RG21 6XS, England

Corporate Capitalism in Japan

Hiroshi Okumura
Professor of Economics
Chuo University
Japan

Foreword by
Michio Morishima

Translated by
Douglas Anthony and Naomi Brown

First published in Great Britain 2000 by
MACMILLAN PRESS LTD
Houndmills, Basingstoke, Hampshire RG21 6XS and London
Companies and representatives throughout the world

A catalogue record for this book is available from the British Library.

ISBN 0–333–57532–6

First published in the United States of America 2000 by
ST. MARTIN'S PRESS, LLC,
Scholarly and Reference Division,
175 Fifth Avenue, New York, N.Y. 10010

ISBN 0–312–23083–4

Library of Congress Cataloging-in-Publication Data
Okumura, Hiroshi, 1930–
[Hojin shihon shugi. English]
Corporate capitalism in Japan / Hiroshi Okumura ; foreword by Michio
Morishima ; translated by Douglas Anthony and Naomi Brown.
p.   cm. — (Classics in the history and development of economics)
Includes bibliographical references and index.
ISBN 0–312–23083–4 (cloth)
1. Corporations—Japan—Finance. 2. Capital stock—Japan. 3. Industrial
management—Japan. 4. Capitalism—Japan. I. Title. II. Series.

HG4245 .O4813   2000
338.7'4'0952—dc21

99–053113

This book is printed on paper suitable for recycling and made from fully managed and sustained
forest sources.

10   9   8   7   6   5   4   3   2   1
09 08 07 06 05 04 03 02 01 00

Printed and bound in Great Britain by
Antony Rowe Ltd, Chippenham, Wiltshire

Contents

General Editor's Foreword

Hiroshi Okumura has influenced a number of Japanese economists well known in the Western academic world, such as Professor Masahiko Aoki of Stanford University and many others including myself, through his works on Japanese enterprise groups, parent company–subcontractors relationships, the Japanese type of takeover bid, the main bank system, and so on. Based on these concepts, Okumura has characterised the Japanese economy as a type of 'corporate capitalism'. He has shown that the famous familistic management, the permanent employment tradition, the bonus system, etc. are all natural properties attributable to corporate capitalism. He has powerfully illustrated that even work ethics in such an economy differ from those in usual capitalist economies presumed in the orthodox textbooks.

In spite of these achievements Okumura is very critical of the Japanese economy viewed in his way. He has recognised the vulnerability of corporate capitalism; especially its inconsistency with contemporary Japanese society. We may describe corporate capitalism as a state of affairs where employees of big firms are forced to do everything they are told by their bosses. However, it imposes a big burden upon individual workers as well as small firms, and if workers quit from their present companies, especially in the case of large firms, they severely suffer economically. The economy was considered to deserve admiration while the Japanese still maintained the virtues of feudal days, but as soon as those who had gone through the old education system were retired from the business world, corporate capitalism began to stagger, as Okumura foresaw.

In spite of his warning, such great names of Japanology as Ronald Dore and Hugh Pattrick supported the Japanese way of business management. This may perhaps be because where Okumura saw feudal evil practices the Westerners observed oriental gracefulness. In any case, it is of course true that corporate capitalism must be examined to reveal its non-optimality.

Okumura is a surprisingly prolific writer. Besides the present volume there are many others which are concerned with various aspects of corporate capitalism, though none are available in English. They include:

1   *Six Biggest Enterprise Groups in Japan* (Diamond Sha, Tokyo, 1983)
2   *The Structure of Corporate Capitalism* (Nippon Hyoron Sha, 1975)
3   *Bank and Enterprise* (Toyo Keizai Shinpo Sha, Tokyo, 1978)
4   *Merger and Acquisition* (Iwanami Shoten, Tokyo, 1990)
5   *Irresponsible Capitalism* (Toyo Keizai Shinpo Sha, Tokyo, 1998)
6   *Will Corporate Capitalism Collapse?* (Iwanami Shoten, Tokyo, 1992; German translation, 'Japan und seine Unternehmen', R. Oldenboung Verlag, 1998)

Okumura was born in 1930 and graduated from Okayama University, Faculty of Law and Literature, where he specialised in the history of the western world. He served as an economic journalist for the *Sankei shinbun* (1953–62), was appointed to the post of senior economist at Japan Securities Research Institute (1972), and became Professor of Economics at Ryukoku University, Kyoto (1984–93). He is currently Professor of Economics at Chuo University, Tokyo.

MICHIO MORISHIMA

Introduction: Banking and Industry in Japan

Michio Morishima *

I

In this Introduction I review the history of the Japanese economy since 1931, concentrating on the following points. First, during this period of sixty years the Japanese economy was converted from a free enterprise economy to a controlled, planned one and then after the war returned back to a free enterprise system. The transformation to the planned economy was quick and rather easy because of the existence of a powerful, despotic government. The military forces were very strong. It was impossible for the general public and businessmen not to follow the military's will, especially after the majority of journalists and academics had surrendered themselves to the opinion guided by the militarist-ultranationalist power. However, although Japan was put under a new strong power (the occupation forces) at the beginning of the post-war period, she was provided with a weak government in the period of self-governing democracy after independence. Democracy created chaos. Therefore, the reverse course from the planned economy to the free enterprise system was slow because of bureaucratic resistance against losing vested rights to meddle in private business and other difficulties. This was especially true in the monetary field.

The process of transformation to the planning economy and the reverse process back from it, will be studied in sections II and III of this

*This paper was discussed at Covegni Internazionali, Salone della Banca, Assicura 92, held in Torino, Italy, 22–27 October 1992. In writing it, I have benefitted from various books by Professor H. Okumura, as well as *Nihon Ginko 100 Nen Shi* (The Centenary History of the Bank of Japan), 6 volumes (The Bank of Japan, 1984). I am also grateful to Professor S. Yoshida, Musashi University, for his comments.

introductory chapter. It may particularly be emphasised that throughout most of the post-war period, Japan adopted Keynesian monetary policy, fixing the rate of interest at a low level; city banks lent as much money to the industrial companies as they demanded. Where commercial banks could not satisfy all the demand directly, they satisfied it by borrowing from the central bank. Of course, this easy supply of money created a number of bouts of inflation; on several occasions they were very severe. In the trade-off between inflation and economic growth, Japan obviously chose the latter rather than minimising the former, and she was then clearly rewarded greatly.

Secondly, after the war, *zaibatsu* families were prohibited from running their own business; they had to sell their companies' shares and retire from the business world by order of the occupation forces. Thus the main problem of post-war Japan was to find out how a free enterprise economy would be workable without the money from these rich families, that is to say, how a capitalist economy is possible without dominant individual capitalists. After the peace treaty, the businessmen devoted most of their effort to this problem of restructuring the economy. The answer they came up with was to establish a system of 'mutual shareholding' which will be explained in section IV below. On the basis of this organisational innovation having been carried out in 1955–60, Japan paved the way to flourish in 1970–90. (In fact, if I were asked what element had most contributed to the success of the Japanese, I would without hesitation mention their ability to make organisational innovations, which the reader will observe in various places throughout this chapter.)

Thirdly, it will be seen that behind this system was the power of professional managers. It was higher education in Japan which enabled her to achieve this organisational innovation. Accordingly the analysis of the cliques of university graduates in the Japanese business world is very important. It is seen in section V below that the dominance of university graduates in the sector of big business was already obvious in pre-war Japan as early as the 1920s. Among the most powerful cliques has been and still is that of graduates of the University of Tokyo. They succeeded the *samurai* group which formed the central government after the Meiji revolution and dominated the other cliques in the government until now. Therefore, in the business world too they were extremely powerful, because the company would have a great advantage by establishing within it a power structure similar to the one in the government, in order to maintain good relationships between them. Of course, it is without doubt that cliques of any kind are a big source of corruption. Nevertheless, a country dominated by selected university graduates, though I personally dislike it, would be a more bearable and more productive society, compared with the usual plutocratic, capitalist countries where cliques formed by the rich families let nepotism prevail among them. The cliques in the big enterprise group and in the financial sector are examined in section VI below.

The market in Japan connecting the firms as demanders for money capital with the commercial banks as the suppliers is not competitive but collaborative. The 'main bank system' which originated during the war (see section II) formed couples, of demander and supplier, in which the latter took the responsibility of providing the former with the money capital it needed. In many cases the couples were in a 'one to many' correspondence in the sense that several banks formed a consortium which collectively took the responsibility of supplying the funds. Because of this system, it has seldom happened in Japan that at some point in the construction of production facilities (say, a channel tunnel) the money is exhausted and the construction work is stopped, as has often occurred in the case of the construction of the Euro-tunnel. 'Once it was decided, it should go ahead as planned.' This iron rule was very rarely broken in Japan as far as the financing of investment projects was concerned, thanks to the main bank system.

The main bank relationship is usually formed within the enterprise groups, between the companies in a group and the city bank in the same group, so that the bank naturally plays the part of the headquarters of the group; it is the pivot for unifying the group. We discuss, in section VII below, quantitatively how the city bank grips the industrial companies of the group, that is to say, an index is given for quantifying the bank's control of the enterprise group. In any case, having city banks supplemented by industrial and other special banks, Japan never felt a shortage of money in supporting ambitious industrial innovations in the 1970s and 1980s. It is not an exaggeration to say that this banking system is another example of the organisational innovation made by Japan; it smoothed the channelling of money required for investment from banks to companies in these two decades remarkably. It was indeed a great achievement.

In that section, technical innovations of the 'Japanese type' which were carried out especially during the years of the oil crises and after are also discussed. It is seen how the rapid progress of the real sub-economy inevitably induced the development of the monetary sub-economy, as it happened in the midst of the long continuing process of economic growth in 1970–85; this is, in fact, symbolised by the fact that Tokyo became one of the financial centres of the world in the 1980s. Finally, parts of sections IV and VII review why the successful advance of Japan in the 1970s and the early 80s ultimately brought about financial scandals and collapses in the late 1980s and after.

II

In September 1931 the Manchurian Incident took place, initially having favourable effects upon the economy which was in the midst of the great depression, but later becoming Japan's heavy burden as it expanded into her prolonged war with China and finally gave rise to the world war. During this period, the government geared the economy to the needs of circumstance; it was rapidly transformed into a controlled economy according to the totalitarian political principle, by abandoning the free-enterprise system modelled on Britain which had been established around 1885 and maintained since then until 1930. Japan was moving away from Britain towards the Nazi Third Reich.

It was Korekiyo Takahashi, Minister of Finance, who carried out Keynes-like policies before the publication of *The General Theory*. As a result of these policies Japan was able to recover from the depression very rapidly. But unfortunately these expansionist spending policies greatly helped the army circles which were preparing to spread the war into wider areas. It is not surprising that the spending policies were carried out to a larger degree than Takahashi had intended for the purpose of economic recovery from the depression. They naturally created excessive inflation, as war-time inflation was added to the one due to proper Keynesian policies. Having realised this, he changed his attitude in later years so as to minimise the increase in military expenses. Because of this, in the uprising of 26 February 1936 he was chosen as one of the targets of the *coup d'état* and killed.

As for issuing government securities, there are two ways of distributing them. One is for the government to sell them to private individuals or to institutions directly (through, say, post offices) or indirectly (through city banks), while the other is for it to sell them to the central bank which, in turn, sells them to the city banks, according to demand. In the second method, all the government securities issued are immediately bought by the central bank, so that the government will at once receive the amount it wants to raise, though the securities are eventually held by private individuals or institutions if the central bank and then the city banks succeed in selling them on. It is obvious that in the first method it takes time to sell all the securities the government wants to, so the spending policies have to be carried out gradually, whereas the second method produces an immediate result.

From this point, we may say that the second is more preferable and effective than the first. However, because the central bank becomes an administrative office of the Ministry of Finance, there is no authority which could control the amount of money, independent of the government's political aims. Takahashi adopted the second method, and thus subjugated the Bank of Japan under the Treasury. It was the start of the march of the Japanese economy towards all-out nationalisation.

In the first method, the money is transferred from the private sector to the government in exchange for the government securities sold, so that there is no creation of money, though some of the idle money held in the private sector is activated by the hand of the government which uses it to carry out its fiscal policies. In the second method, however, an amount of money equivalent to the securities issued is created immediately, although part of it will later be absorbed by the central bank when it sells the securities to the private sector. This method, therefore, will bring about a substantial decline in the value of the country's money and thus in its exchange rate against foreign currencies. Also it results in a reduction of the interest rate. Of course, the government can use the money raised in this way to achieve its aims. At the time of Takahashi, civilian departments of the government were much weaker than the army and navy departments, so the money was used to finance the Manchurian war. After the 1936 incident in which Takahashi perished, this abuse of the 'Keynesian policy' was continued by successive ministers of finance. For example, Eiji Baba who succeeded Takahashi gave in to the increasing financial demand of the military forces and his policy was similar to, or more generous than, the 'Keynesian' one originally adopted by Takahashi. Because the military forces now had the means to serve the imperialist expansion, Japan's invasion of China became unstoppable.

Japanese politicians in these years were in a dilemma: either prevent the militarists from accomplishing their purpose, or collaborate with them and minimise evils which their imperialist expansionism would bring about. It implied, as the case of Takahashi proved, death (or a political death at least) for a politician to take the anti-militarist stance; thus many of the statesmen or the politicians in pre-war Japan became collaborators of the politicised factions of the military authorities. It is then natural that Japan became isolated in international affairs; international trade treaties were scrapped one after the other. A number of Japanese exporters were accused of dumping because the cheap yen enabled them to reduce the prices of their exports greatly. But in this way Japan's trade surplus deteriorated.

In December 1931 the Japanese government placed an embargo on the export of gold, but it had to ship gold to those countries with which Japan had a big trade deficit in order to make payment. As gold holdings in Japan would be exhausted sooner or later, all the available gold mines, however poor they might be, had to be mobilised for production. As the production had to be carried out against the law of marginal productivity, some special encouragement had to be given to the gold mining industry, so an artificial incentive scheme had to be devised. The international isolation created a bigger demand for weapons and munitions; in order to satisfy it the economy had to be converted to a planned economy as quickly as possible.

Japan was already an over-populated country, so that land was one of the most scarce commodities. The entire non-residential and cultivatable land had to be shared between industry and agriculture. The former should be developed for winning the war, while the latter was equally important because, for a country like Japan which was isolated from others in international trade, self-sufficiency in producing food was a necessary condition for carrying on the war to victory. The government embarked on the introduction into the economy of planning, rationing and controls by some means or other, and intervened in spontaneous economic activities. As the theory of economic planning was very poor in those days, there was no orthodox answer, and the government could not be afraid of its idiosyncrasy.

Big companies were combined or amalgamated into even larger ones by order of the government as part of its industrial rationalisation policy. Smaller companies were annexed to larger companies to form a subcontractual factory system. In these vertical relationships between companies, the high-ranking companies had to control their own subordinates, so that the government need be concerned with handling the top companies only. The relationships were not freely competitive in the sense that these firms could behave on an equal basis, but 'obligatory'. Each company had to fulfil its own duty assigned by the government; it should, first of all, be loyal and obedient to its immediate superior. The firms were transformed from being profit-pursuing organisations into entities which were entrusted with providing everlasting national services. This period of the war or quasi-war structure (1931–45) was a return to the Tokugawa feudalism that had prevailed until 1867. We can still see its reflection in the contemporary Japanese subsidiary (*keiretsu*) system.

Also the banks, Japan Hypothec Bank and the Industrial Bank of Japan, which Japan had established in 1896 and 1900, for the purpose of supplying sufficient long-term funds to industrial companies were strengthened and reorganised so that they could give priority to the heavy and chemical industrialisation urgently needed. Banks for agriculture and industry had existed in various prefectures since 1896. After 1921 many of them were merged with Japan Hypothec Bank; they totally disappeared when the remaining five were amalgamated into JHB in 1944. To fulfil the responsibility of supplying industrial funds these banks were allowed to make long-term loans, provided that banks were granted reliable debentures and shares by way of security. The Bank of Japan issued bank notes, if necessary, without limit, i.e. without cash reserves corresponding to them.

In 1943 the government finally started to arrange 'marriages' between munitions companies and city banks. One bank, or a few banks, assigned to a munitions company took responsibility for supplying the funds it needed. Then an intimate, continuing collaboration began between them. This marriage system soon spread itself widely through the whole industry, because the definition of munitions companies was extended to include railways, warehouses, construction and building companies, etc. The system may, of course, be criticised as favourable treatment of munitions companies, discriminating against others. There is no doubt about it, but it is also true that from the point of view of industrial efficiency it is a very good organisation if consideration is confined to a medium term. The coupling of banks with manufacturing companies continued to exist in the post-war world in a modified form. The contemporary 'main-bank' system discussed later emerged in this way.

Thus Japanese industrial companies came to be well taken care of financially by their respective custodial banks. As far as this aspect of the war-time economy of Japan is concerned, it is very close to Hilferding's 'organised capitalism'.[1] The banking system is no longer merely an organisation for intermediation of payments but also the one for financing industry; industrial capital is combined with banking capital to form financial capital. This is exactly what happened in war-time Japan. There was little possibility of competition between banks. Various kinds of capital accumulated within banks were becoming money capital; it was controlled by the government and allocated to industrial companies in accordance with their perceived contributions to carrying on the war to a successful finish. The role of the central bank was dramatically changed. It was no longer responsible for maintaining the internal and external value of the currency; its main function was to utilise the available amount of money capital in order to realise the aim of the government in the most efficient way. Of course, the aim was switched from 'victory over the enemy' to 'economic growth' after the war, but the relationships between companies and banks still remain more or less intact, businessmen and bankers serving for the same aim with the same ethos.

The marriages between banks and companies brought about not only favourable effects, as stated above, but also bad outcomes, and some of the bankers and economists were critical of this change in the banking system. As the companies were assured of obtaining enough funds for their production activities, there was no incentive for them to save money. Unless they were subject to banks' strict superintendence, there was always a possibility that the funds provided by the banks were spent wastefully. Furthermore, banks themselves were also inclined to lose the sense of self-responsibility because the money they lent to the companies was provided by the Bank of Japan, which in turn enabled it to create as much money as was wanted. The post-war habits of the city banks of over-lending to the manufacturing companies and over-borrowing from the central bank originated in the tight collaboration of banks and companies during the period of the controlled economy. In any case the rate of the company's own capital to its total capital declined sharply. It was 90 per cent in 1934, whilst only 30 per cent in 1944.

The Bank of Japan lost its independence from the government. After it became the underwriter for national bonds which the government issued, the amount of currency expanded rapidly. Of course, the Bank of Japan could have sold the national bonds in the open market. If it had done so on a substantial scale, the price of the national bonds would have declined and money would have been tight – a contradiction of its principal duty of channelling a sufficient amount of money to industry. Moreover, the real output of all commodities declined enormously due to shortages of materials, war damages, etc. When Japan was allowed to join the IMF, in August 1952, the exchange rates were set at ¥360 per dollar and ¥1,008 per pound sterling, whilst in October 1934 they were ¥3.43 per dollar and ¥17.14 per pound sterling. Though this great decline in the value of yen occurred under very unfavourable conditions, it is certain that it was partly due to the continued 'Keynesian' policies during the war or quasi-war time, but also partly due to the destruction of production facilities by bombing, etc., as well as to their maladjustment to the new circumstances after the war.

Following the prohibition of gold exports in 1931, when the conversion of bank notes into gold was stopped in 1932, it was felt that Japan had given up the gold standard only temporarily. History shows, however, that she got deeper and deeper into a managed currency system as time went on. The fiduciary-reserve limit set by the Bank of Japan became elastic and more and more generous. On the basis of government bonds and other securities, gold and silver, foreign currencies and bills of foreign exchange submitted to the bank, it was allowed to lend money to manufacturing companies. Obviously, the supply of industrial funds became the prime objective of the central bank and the money was created with no consideration of how its value would be affected by its creation.

Japan became a country without a central bank in the traditional sense. Nevertheless, yen should have played the role of the standard money in the area Japan occupied. As she imported materials from the countries in the area, her trade balances against them became unfavourable. Naturally the price of yen tended to diminish in the yen bloc. If it declined, Japan would have been put in a more difficult position in collecting materials from the countries in the area. In order to maintain the price of yen, she should have sent gold to them to pay the deficits. This gold-standard dilemma in the non-gold-standard country was solved by actually sending gold, which meant that Japan had virtually no gold reserves by the end of the war. This was an obvious bankruptcy of the militarists' idea to free countries of Asia from Western colonisation. The Bank of Japan anticipated it as early as 1938; in the same year the Governor of the bank sent a document to the Minister of Finance, in which the Governor distinctly stated that the government should have a clear idea of how to reach a political settlement of the war against China, particularly in taking the capacity and feasibility of the Japanese economy into account.[2] Unfortunately, it was too late; the age of mass hysteria had already begun. The war had its own momentum; nothing favourable to stopping the war resulted from this warning of the Governor.

III

In August 1945 Japan surrendered to the Allied Powers; she had, until the conclusion of the San Francisco peace treaty in 1951, two governments, one being her own government and the other the Allied Powers General Headquarters (GHQ), the former being under the control of the latter. Of course, whilst high-ranking officials from the war time were barred from holding public office, ordinary officials remained in office. Their way of thinking or mentality was not very different from the one in war-time and often conflicted with the liberalist view of the GHQ. They still lived in the control economy, while the GHQ wanted to establish a free-enterprise system in Japan as quickly as possible. When the views conflicted greatly, the GHQ rightly and properly gave orders which the Japanese government had to carry out, but even in such cases it was possible for the government to put planning elements into the policies when they were implemented. Thus the planning-oriented way of thinking still survived when Japan got independence and naturally revived itself afterwards.

It was fortunate for the Japanese that Joseph M. Dodge, the President of the Bank of Detroit, was appointed as a financial adviser to the Supreme Commander for the Allied Powers (the SCAP) in 1948. He was a classical, orthodox banker: ascetic, diligent and thrifty and he believed in the price mechanism of the free market economy. He was a staunch supporter of the theory which said that government should be kept small and welfare spending had to be minimised. He was a person who could claim to be called a genuine Thatcherite. He insisted that government spending should be confined to its current income, i.e. tax revenues, revenues from state enterprises and others; the central bank should not pay the deficits of the government. The finance corporation established for reconstruction and redevelopment in 1946 was allowed to issue reconstruction savings debentures, provided that they were sold in the open market; its aim was to lend money to the basic industries which had difficulty in obtaining funds for equipment. However, because the corporation had not been strict enough in withdrawing loans, the GHQ ordered in 1949 that the corporation be closed. Whereas the government considered the official prices either had to be raised or abolished, Mr Dodge's line was to push down the black-market prices to the official ones by rationalising enterprises so that they could bear international competition under the given foreign exchange rates. The enterprises were allowed to rely on the price control compensation only as a temporary means. Naturally a compromise was reached between the two. Although the Japanese government respected the Dodge line, the official prices gradually rose and met the black-market prices which were declining. The equilibrium prices established in this way were perfectly consistent with the exchange rate on which Mr Dodge finally agreed with the US government.

We may say that economic controls were removed from most areas except food supplies, international trade, foreign exchange, and finance. This was, however, not strictly true. For a fairly long period afterwards, administrative directions were given to private enterprises;

the government was able to lead the economy to the desired position by treating some enterprises favourably and some others unfavourably, especially in the allocation of money capital.

In such a stage of reconstruction we could not say that competition was more essential and preponderant than planning. Enterprises, even though they were equally profitable, had to be distinguished and discriminated among from the government's policy point of view. At the very beginning of recovery, agriculture and the food industry were very important; these were later replaced in the ranking of importance by material importing traders which in turn were replaced by industries for export markets. Although the order of significance of industries was changing over time, the government had to discriminate among enterprises appropriately according to their moving significance in its national economic plan for reconstruction. As far as such a time is concerned, it cannot be said that fair competition should necessarily be more respected than discrimination.

The problem was how to use the given amount of money capital efficiently. In order to make finance to key industries smooth, the Bank of Japan bought the government securities from the city banks which held them and let the banks lend the money thus obtained to selected enterprises of the key industries. Moreover it exempted the banks from the progressive interest-rate scheme which was applied to a large loan exceeding some minimum amount. Such an operation of buying securities and bonds for the purpose of smoothing or facilitating the supply of loans to some particular enterprises was called a *himotsuki* (tied) operation. By this means the Bank of Japan took the responsibility for financing industry even in the Dodge-line period. Clearly, a *himotsuki* operation should not be confused with the open market operation for the monetary policy purpose.

In 1950 the Korean war broke out when the inflation caused by the Second World War was about to cease. There was no doubt that this new war was also a cause of another bout of inflation, because it stimulated exports greatly, so that Japan benefitted from an enormous trade surplus. The dollars earned in this way were changed into yen; therefore, the prices of commodities tended to increase as larger amounts of money circulated in the economy. To avoid such inflation, imports had to be increased in order to keep the trade surplus as low as possible. To stimulate imports some beneficial treatment had to be extended to importers. Loans were given to them on very favourable terms. This created an over-loan of the central bank to city banks which in turn made an over-loan to the importers. In this way materials for a further expansion of the economy were accumulated and even a speculative inventory investment was made with respect to imported materials.

Whereas great emphasis was laid on the stabilisation of the value of money, the Japanese government stuck to its war-time policy. This was supported by businessmen. In fact, in a letter addressed to Mr Dodge, the Federation of Economic Organisations (Keidanren) asserted that the main objective of monetary policy should be to provide necessary funds for development of such basic industries as coal, electricity, steel and shipbuilding, and to help those industries which had the potential to export their products, by furnishing them with funds for making their equipment adequate and modern. In order to secure industrial funds it was important to reform the tax system so as to promote capital accumulation, in addition to enhancement of national savings. According to the view of the Bank of Japan at the time, those funds which could be used as capital for a long period, such as the funds for collating with the US aid to Japan and the deposits to the Treasury's deposit department, should be allowed to be regarded as long-term funds for industry. The Export Bank of Japan and the Japan Development ment Bank were both established in 1951 along this line of thought. The economic and scientific section of GHQ was reluctant to make this move. It cautioned the Japanese government against allowing enterprises to use their profits, which were very big due to the Korean war, for an expansion of production facilities and inventory holdings, without returning the loans they had borrowed. As Japan became independent, she diverged from the GHQ line considerably and the Bank of Japan continued to be involved in the finance of industrial investment, as it had been so during the war, so that the official rate was kept low over a long period of time after the San Francisco treaty.

After the peace treaty, the Japanese government more loosely interpreted Dodge's philosophy of finance in such a manner that the scale of public finance could be expanded. Nevertheless, we may say that the essential spirit of the Dodge line was respected in the sense that the government gave a high priority to the stability of the value of yen; the funds needed for expanding basic sectors, electricity, shipbuilding, etc. as well as the funds for rationalising heavy-chemical industries, had to be supplied mainly by increased savings. The finance of the remaining part was left to efforts of the banking and financial organisations as it had been during war-time.

At that time, however, Japan was in a gravely difficult situation; the price level was higher than her international competitors', so that she had to tighten credit in order to secure an equilibrium of international trade balance. On the other hand, in order to reconstruct her industry an expansion of imports was inevitable, which had to be accompanied by an expansion of exports, to restore the trade balance. To stimulate imports and exports some scheme for subsidising import and export enterprises was required, for the purpose of which a credit expansion was needed. Economic reconstruction meant an easy-money policy. Nevertheless, it is true that the government had to increase the effectiveness of the available amount of money. To do so, therefore, it strengthened the progressive interest-rate scheme, rationalised the scheme for favourable treatment of the loans for imports and intensified the government's control (guidance and regulation) on borrowing for the purposes of industrial investment.

As a result, money poured into the circle of big firms; small and medium sized firms were segregated and hardly obtained funds for investment. Because of the increase in the productivity of the whole nation due to this tight financial policy, the wholesale prices of commodities declined and approached the international level. The international trade balance was considerably improved, although the production of mining and manufacturing industries became lower. In an economy like the Japanese one in this period of time, in which everything was in shortage, it was very important to select those enterprises which had the ability to perform better, and to distinguish them from others, so that in deciding on an economic policy the government's quality assessment of the enterprises was taken into account. It might be criticised as an unfair system because it was not operating according to an impersonal principle of equal opportunity. In 1953–4, however, the money market was tightened in order to improve the trade balance, and a consideration was clearly paid to the restraint of total demand. In this sense, a return to orthodox financial policy was observed to some degree. Moreover, concerning financial matters, during the occupation period, the GHQ gave directions to the Bank of Japan directly rather than indirectly via the Japanese government. Thus it contributed to making monetary policy more independent of other industrial policies.

In 1955 Japan succeeded in expanding exports greatly, so that her real GNP grew at a very high rate of 8.8 per cent. Prices were stable, trade balance was improved, and the lending–borrowing positions of commercial banks were improved. For a short period at least, the central bank was set free from the fear of acceleration of over-loan. Unemployment decreased, though the economy still had many disguised unemployed workers. In 1959 the circumstances of the labour market changed dramatically; labour at last became scarce. Competition for hiring new school leavers was getting severe. Furthermore, during the ten years from 1955 to 1965 foreign capital was introduced into the economy; this, together with the improvement in international trade, liberated Japan from the international trade balance constraint which had been very restrictive in the past.

However, an over-loan of the central bank reappeared as soon as business conditions recovered because commercial banks relied on the central bank and borrowed excessively from it in order to lend as much as possible to the firms. Such a situation should be considered as unhealthy, but it was, nevertheless, a case in which the central bank could, rather easily, manipulate monetary policies in order to encourage or discourage investment activities of the firms.

In 1955–6 when over-loan almost disappeared the government tried to establish an open market for government short-term securities, but its open market operations did not work, because it issued them excessively and insisted on the original conditions of the issue. Consequently the Bank of Japan had to buy all the securities remaining in the market. This shows how difficult it was to reintroduce free markets into the economy once citizens and administrators had forgotten how to behave in the market and how to operate it. Even though the economy was provided with a market, the price mechanism did not work there. The interest rate was not adjusted flexibly, and Japan had nothing other than an economy that would be characterised as a fixed price (or fixed interest rate) economy, in spite of the fact that the Bank of Japan wanted to have an open market where the rate of interest was flexibly changed by virtue of its open market operations. In fact, the official rate changed only three times during the post-war period of inflation and only once in the six years from 1949 to 1955. Occasionally, either rationing was carried out in the market, or a progressive interest-rate scheme was applied to large loans. Otherwise, Wicksell's fixed-interest-rate models of cumulative process was perfectly adequate for describing the Japanese economy in this period.

Why had such a financial structure continued to prevail after the war too? During the war period the interest rate was kept low in order to support enterprises. Commercial banks lost the principle of self-responsibility and played the role of tunnels connecting the central bank and the industrial firms. They lost their own individuality and they uniformly just informed the central bank of the fact that they were unable to support the firms' industrial investment by such and such an amount. All the excess demand for industrial funds were cleared by the central bank at the given, current rate of interest. There was no need for the firms to issue new shares. All stock exchanges were closed during the war-time and were only reopened again in 1949. The firms were thus financed by borrowing from commercial banks which in turn borrowed from the central bank, and this last merely printed as much paper money as requested. This easy-going 'over-loan' regime continued to prevail, in spite of Dodge's effort, after the war and even after the independence of Japan.

This occurred where the city banks lent to the firms that money which they had borrowed from the central bank, because their lending was too large in comparison with the deposits they received. The total liabilities of the city banks, except the part that was lent to the firms, were held either in the form of cash or deposits, or in the form of stocks or securities. Where the holdings in this last form were small, lending would be large, provided that holdings in cash or deposits were limited. While the stock exchanges were closed, the tradition of over-loan came to stay in the post-war economy.

Obviously the stock exchanges had to be reopened and stimulated in their activities. As will be discussed later, however, there was a reason for the fact that the business world in that period did not much welcome a very active circulation of shares but wanted to have stable share-holding. Then the Bank of Japan investigated an alternative way to overcome the over-loan phenomena. Its plan, as will be seen later, was not carried out.

In any case, to the eyes of foreigners it looked very unstable and vulnerable that commercial banks had lost the spirit of independence and self-responsibility and easily over-borrowed from the central bank. It was extremely important and urgent to restore the free financial market of the pre-war period because the role of international trade became more and more significant for the recovery and new development of the Japanese economy. On the other hand, in spite of the recognition of over-loan as being undesirable and in spite of every effort of the Bank of Japan to get rid of it, it survived. It is true that over-loan almost disappeared for a short while in 1955, but as soon as this was realised by the firms and the commercial banks, the former requested the latter to lend them more money, while the central bank had to support the commercial banks by satisfying their demand for borrowing from it. In those days where there was a limitless demand for industrial investment for recovery and the government committed itself to providing the industry with enough funds for recovery at a low interest rate; an elastic supply of money and, therefore, an inelastic interest rate were natural consequences to a certain extent, although the supply of money was restricted by introducing rationing in the event of the demand being too large.

In such emergency circumstances like those after the war, various sectors of the economy should be treated differently according to their roles expected in the whole process of recovery and development. A special and distinct treatment was, in fact, made to each of them in such a way that the economy would work most effectively. The economic principle supported in post-war Japan was planning and rationing on a priority basis but it was neither rationing on equality basis nor free competition. The following sectors were favourably treated: (1) those non-munitions industries which had been badly damaged by air raids, (2) the agricultural sectors, including the fertiliser and other agribusiness, which had to play a crucial role in rescuing the people from the serious difficulty of obtaining food in a period just after the war, (3) the international trade sector importing the materials for domestic industries, and finally, (4) promising export industries.

As for (3), the loan for establishing the funds needed for settling import bills was granted on a favourable condition in the first ten years after the war. Such a consideration was almost terminated in 1955 and completely abolished in 1966. Secondly, regarding (4), a similar consideration was made concerning the funds for settling export bills; it survived until 1973. In order to strengthen the nation's export capability the government treated selected industries favourably by providing them with a loan for investment at a low rate of interest. This scheme was criticised by international competitors as unfair, but the post-war Japanese experience shows that planning carried on the priority principle was more effective than free competition. There was, of course, a trade-off between the rate of growth of production and the depreciation of the value of the currency. Whereas generous finance in favour of industrial investment would have created excessive inflation, it would also have raised economic growth greatly. Clearly gain dominated forfeit.

Finally, it may be said that the financial policy taken by the Japanese government was 'Keynesian', while the one insisted on by Mr Dodge was 'monetarist'. According to the former, it is most important to establish nationally agreed economic policies systematically, so that it is necessary that the central bank is subordinate to the government and gives support only to those proposals which are consistent with the government's plan. On the other hand, according to the latter, the main task of the central bank is to make the value of the currency stable; the monetary policy should, therefore, be neutral and independent of the political aims of the government. Like the two-party political system, the central bank should perform a part of the Opposition to the government. Such a structure obviously slows down the speed of development, though it secures the economy against inflation and other monetary difficulties. The Japanese were 'Keynesian' after, as well as during, the war. They always run at full speed, collapse, and then rouse themselves to action again.

It is true that throughout the post-war economic history of Japan until 1970 the following Keynesian characteristics were evidently observed. First, the official interest rate was kept low so as to enhance industrial investment. Secondly, the quantity adjustment, rather than the price mechanism, prevailed in the money market, in order to pour money into industry as much as possible. Fortunately, in spite of this kind of monetary policy no serious inflation of prices was noticed in the 1960s, whereas some necessary monetary measures, including tightening of the central bank's lending regulations, were taken when the situation became serious. The financial capital of industry was supplied by banks, while equity finance deteriorated. Therefore, bankers, rather than shareholders, ruled the enterprises. Nevertheless, it is also true that the Bank of Japan tried, several times, to restore its classic sovereignty from the government; its efforts, however, may be said to have been generally unsuccessful, though it tended to be independent at a very slow tempo.

IV

Japan's surrender to Allied Powers brought her a revolution. Although the Emperor survived the war, he had to transfer most of his property to the state. The major *zaibatsu* Konzerns, the kernel of the pre-war Japanese economy, were all ordered to disband. Holding companies of *zaibatsu* groups were dissolved and *zaibatsu* families had to dispose of shares they held. Not only they themselves were not allowed to be appointed to the position of director or executive of any company which had belonged to a *zaibatsu* group previously, but also many war-time directors and executives of big companies were purged from the business world because they had been in collaboration with militarists during the war. Moreover, big companies were split up. In the case of the Mitsui Trading Company (Mitsui Bussan) and Mitsubishi Trading Corporation (Mitsubishi Shoji), for example, a new company was prohibited from forming if it employed more than two high-class members (directors of the departments or above) or more than 100 staff members and clerks of either of the two companies. Big city banks, however, were not sub-divided. In all these companies, after directors and executives had been forced to resign, the vacancies created were filled by younger people. But among them there were people who had little experience of running a company in the age of free competition. In fact, although some had experienced company management under the direction or control of the government, others did not have much experience because they had spent many years at the front as soldiers. The new presidents and executives of these companies were powerless because they had no powerful shareholder who would support them but were just promoted to the places their predecessors had evacuated. The shares they themselves held, if any, were negligible.

In Japan, it was already obvious as early as the First World War that the management of the big modern enterprises was left to professional managers who had graduated from university. Nevertheless, it cannot be said that ownership and management was separated in Japan for the reason pointed out by A. A. Berle, Jr. and G. C. Means.[3] Behind the managers of the pre-war *zaibatsu* companies, there were shareholders, i.e. *zaibatsu* families, who supported them. In the post-war economy, they were separated, however, not for the economic reason as asserted by Berle and Means that where a joint-stock company becomes large, dominant shareholders disappear as the holding of shares tends to be dispersed among many small shareholders, but for the political reason that big owners of the company were forced to give up ownership, so as to take the so-called 'responsibility for the war'. It is true, none the less, that newly appointed managers had to fill this vacuum of ownership to make the company firm and safe as well as to secure legitimacy and authority for their own positions. In fact, companies were in an extremely shaky position after the war both in ownership and management.

During the occupation period it was true for each *zaibatsu* Konzern that although it had been disbanded, chairmen of its member companies met each other and kept in contact secretly. After independence, the meeting of chairmen of ex-member companies of a *zaibatsu* Konzern became more open and regular. In the case of the Mutsubishi group, for example, the meeting was called the Friday meeting, which began to play a significant role as an informal decision-making, body around 1954, though it had existed since 1946, rather secretly, in a form of a social gathering of executives of ex-member companies of the Mitsubishi Konzern. Other Konzerns also had similar meetings, at which important matters were discussed and resolved. In this sense, it may be said that the pre-war *zaibatsu* survived and continued to be active after they had been disbanded.

However, *zaibatsu* families never came back to their own groups. This was because these families had been criticised severely from both the right and left wings – they had been, in fact, targets of terrorism in the pre-war period, so that they did not want to be reinstated in their former positions. It is also true, on the other hand, that new executives of these companies did not welcome their return. Without these former bosses, how could these companies re-establish the previous solidarity and regulation between themselves which they had enjoyed in the time of *zaibatsu* Konzern? They no longer had the holding company (or the head corporation) which had taken the role of the head-quarters; moreover, new executives were in a very weak position, because they had no powerful shareholders behind them. These were over-come in the following way.

First, each group had a big city bank and a big comprehensive trading house (*Sogoshosha*). Companies in a *zaibatsu* group were usually financed by its city bank and their purchasing of materials and selling of products were dealt with by its trading house; so the chairmen of these organisations were naturally regarded as the leader and the chief secretary of the group. Sogoshosha was not just a trading company: it had the great ability of gathering information about anything. It dealt with commodities ranging from noodles to jet planes. It is often said that Mitsui trading company is as powerful as the CIA; thus it fits perfectly in the position of the head office of the group. In order to band the companies in the group strongly together, it was devised that they mutually held a substantial portion of shares of the companies in the same group. Let A, B, C be companies in a group. If A holds shares of B so as to be able to dominate other shareholders, and B holds shares of C and C shares of A, then A is controlled by C, which is reciprocally controlled by A indirectly, because A controls B which in turn controls C. Thus A, B and C form an indecomposable group, so that they collaborate with each other in the same way as they did at the time when they formed a *zaibatsu* Konzern.[4] Thus without the holding company it was found that companies were able to form a powerful group as long as they hold shares mutually, so as to be linked with each other to make an indecomposable group.

This system of mutual holding of shares was a very powerful device, by means of which directors and executives were able to secure their positions without individual shareholders' backing. In the classical capitalist society, they themselves were either big shareholders' agents who were approved and trusted at the general meeting of shareholders, or the big shareholders themselves. Each share has an equal right to cast one vote, so that a person who has the largest number of votes behind him is most powerful in the company. This was true in the pre-war Japanese business world and it is still true in contemporary Western capitalist societies. In the exceptionally chaotic period after the war, due to an enormous vacuum created by the absence of *zaibatsu* family members from shareholding, however, it was especially true for the ex-*zaibatsu* companies that the new executives would have been powerless, unless they were supported by institutional shareholding. For this purpose the mutual shareholding system explained above worked very effectively. Because there is no person, except the chairman of company A himself, who can legitimately represent the shareholding of A, the mutual holding system may work as a mutual support system of the current chairmen of the companies in the group. On the basis of the majority shareholding of A in B, chairman a of A supports chairman b of B, who supports c of C by means of B's majority holding of shares in C. Similarly c supports a. In this way a revolutionary takeover was made by moneyless (or proletariat) managers in the ex-*zaibatsu* companies from the hands of individual owners.

In Japan, professional managers have traditionally been highly regarded since the introduction of Western technology and system of business. In almost every sphere of activity the society was already dual-structured before the end of the nineteenth century. Shoten (its literary meaning being shop) was distinguished from Kaisha (company or corporation) as the former often meant a company of the traditional Japanese style, while the latter always meant a company of the Western style. The latter needed educated professional managers and technical experts, whereas masters and gentlemen without Western education could run traditional shops and works. Moreover, where these were involved in business with government offices, they had to employ educated professionals, in order for them to be able to be a match for government officials. In this way educated persons were highly regarded in companies; the bosses or capitalists entirely relied on them. The loyalty of these employed professional managers to the boss was the most important virtue and duty in the business world. As Japan was a typical Confucianist country where education was most highly respected, this system of mutual trust worked with no trouble between boss and professional managers in the pre-war era.

Nevertheless, it is true that once the owners were purged from the companies by the GHQ, the companies were hijacked by their employed managers, who secured their own positions by inventing the system of mutual shareholding. The following case of the *Asahi* newspaper shows how firmly the standing of executives had now been established within the company. *Asahi*, originated and owned by the Murayama family, has been one of the most influential newspapers through the modern history of Japan. The family was purged by the GHQ but later wanted to restore its status as the owner of the company. The then chairman and executives of *Asahi* were, nevertheless, strong enough to resist the proposal, though they had finally to make a compromise and accepted Ms Michiko Murayama as one of the directors. From the point of view of the family this may be taken as a revolution, while from the viewpoint of the professional managers there was no revolution at all because they were lawfully appointed to the post of executive, and the company is still owned by shareholders, individual or institutional, who have decided to support them.

The device of mutual holding of shares was later found to be effective in defending the company from a takeover bid in which an outsider or a foreigner challenged its executive team. The system started, as has been seen above, to support otherwise powerless employed executive members. It was intrinsically based on an implicit assumption that the institutions involved in the scheme would never sell the shares they had bought. Such shareholders are said to be 'stable'. As unstable shareholders can never be trusted, shareholders taking part in the scheme must all be stable in order for it to work as a mutual supporting system. It is therefore very natural that the system was encouraged again and promoted in the late 1960s when Japanese companies were considered as possible targets of American takeover. It was then criticised by foreign, especially American, investors as evidence of the fact that Japan's financial markets were not open enough.[5]

In Japan, new shares used to be issued at face value and allocated to the current shareholders in proportion to the number of shares they held. In the 1970s it became popular that they were issued at their current price. It would then be of great benefit of the companies to keep their share prices high at the time of issue. Under the system of mutual holding of shares the stable holders would never sell the shares but only buy the new shares to keep their proportions. Then the prices would be kept high because a significant part of supply was inelastic and a constant proportion of demand was also inelastic; in this way, therefore, the companies issuing the new shares would acquire a huge amount of capital. Then the mutual shareholding system, originally having been successful as a means for mutually supporting powerless employed executives, was found to be also very effective as a means of raising funds cheaply and massively as well as a means for protecting the companies from possible takeover. Thus the system propagated itself to those companies which did not belong to the big enterprise groups.

On the other hand, the tendency in the opposite direction was created for the same reason. Those companies whose shares had not been listed on the stock exchange never wanted to open their ownership to the public, because they were afraid of the take-over of their companies by their own employed executives by putting them in the system of mutual shareholding. Given this mutual shareholding and given the comprehensiveness of Japanese securities firms discussed below, it is not surprising but understandable that the security market followed the full course of suicidal downfall. In Japan there is a tendency that many things tend to be comprehensive. Like the enterprise groups and the trading houses, the securities firms are not an exception. Unlike those in Britain, they are comprehensive (or universal) in the sense that each of them has within itself all the sections of securities business: underwriting, brokerage and dealing. Because there are conflicts of interest between these three, securities firms are usually specialised in only one of them to avoid unfair profits obtained by dealing with these businesses simultaneously.

For example, a securities firm S with the sections of underwriting and brokerage undertakes to buy the new shares issued by company A and sells them to those customers who want to buy them. Of course, A wants to sell them at as high a price as possible, because A will then raise the greatest amount of funds. This has no conflict with the underwriting section of S because it will then obtain the maximum amount of commission. On the other hand, the brokerage section of S will want to buy the shares as cheaply as possible, with the intention of selling them to customers. Thus there is an obvious conflict of interest between S's underwriting and brokerage sections. (Similarly, a conflict of interest is observed between brokerage and dealing businesses, i.e. brokers and jobbers.) If these were separate and belonged to different, independent companies, they would meet each other in the market, where the price would be openly and fairly determined. However, as they are sections of the same comprehensive firm, the price is decided within it; and this insider trade may, and perhaps will, produce unfair prices.[6]

Throughout the 1970s and 80s it was easy to manipulate the prices in the security market. First of all, it was (and still is) monopolised by the big four, Nomura, Daiwa, Nikko and Yamaichi, all comprehensive and uniform in the sense of behaving similarly. In addition, customers were extremely speculative in those days, so that they would not take much notice of the price level as long as they believed that prices would continue to rise in the future. By providing news and information to the effect that the price of shares of company A would be higher in the future, it is almost certain that the big four could create a speculative rush of customers to the market to obtain the shares of A. Under the mutual holding regime the institutional stable shareholders of course bought A's new shares to keep its proportion, so that the rush always created a big excess demand for the shares, producing a high price. Thus the news and information (suggested by the big four to the customers by various means) were confirmed. Repeating the same story for many cases of new issues, customers came to believe rationally and confidently that because of their economic success Japanese companies' share prices would be higher and higher in the future. The manipulation worked very well. Company A acquired a large amount of funds, huge profits accrued to securities firm S, and individual customers were satisfied because they succeeded in speculation.

So far, so good. In 1987 Nomura Securities surpassed Toyota car-manufacturing in the amount of current profits produced. And big corporations obtained huge amounts of funds by issuing new shares, so that they could pay back to the banks the money they had borrowed from them for industrial investment. The rate of the company's own capital in its total capital improved greatly, but in the 1980s there was no big, promising industrial investment opportunity; it was a period during which the financial world was much more prosperous and flourishing than the industrial world. Those companies which had raised excessive amounts of funds started to use them for financial investment and loans to their subsidiaries. They behaved like city banks and were teasingly called Toyota bank, National Panasonic bank, etc. Excessive issues of shares continued further; it then became more and more difficult for stable shareholders to remain 'stable' by buying an appropriate proportion of the new shares, because they needed huge amounts of money to do so. Thus a fear for the viability of the mutual holding system naturally emerged, and the confidence that share prices would continue to rise was shaken and faded away among individual speculators. They then started to sell the shares, and the prices actually fell, confirming their worries. Once the tide rolled back, prices declined further and further. Not only individual speculators but also institutional shareholders for the purpose of 'stability' suffered greatly.

During this process of reversion the securities firms made a serious mistake because of their internal conflict of interests. Both individual and institutional shareholders lost considerably in proportion to their holdings because of the fall in share prices. However, the securities firms treated them differently. In the case of institutional customers, the underwriting sections of the firms did (or would) benefit from those which had issued (or would issue) new shares, while individual customers were only concerned with the brokerage sections. The firms therefore compensated the losses of large companies, whereas individual customers were usually left out. This was of course a scandalous and discriminate treatment and invited criticism from various corners of the society.

Simultaneously, it was revealed that Nomura and Nikko had loaned a huge amount of money to a *yakuza* (*mafioso*). He used it for buying shares to 'take over' a company. Moreover, it was found that Nomura had manipulated the share price on his behalf. (In fact, regarding the so-called 'takeover' undertaken in Japan it is usually understood that the person who has bought the shares in a large amount has actually no intention of taking over the company but blackmails the company into believing that they will be taken over. Then the company buys back the shares at a much higher price. It is shameless indeed that leading securities firms, like Nomura and Nikko, have been involved in such dirty affairs.) Individual customers' confidence was entirely betrayed. Share prices plunged repeatedly. From this story many would agree that the mutual holding system is one of the tricky but most effective organisational innovations that the post-war Japanese business world have ever devised. It contributed enormously to promoting the strength of Japanese enterprises. It went too far, however, because of its effectiveness, and finally it resulted in a decline or at least a halt to Japan's economic growth for a considerable length of time.

V

For a university graduate, Japan is a paradise. This has been true almost from the beginning of this century. As I have emphasised elsewhere,[7] the Meiji revolution 1867–8, usually referred to as the Meiji restoration (of the direct administration of the Emperor), was an overthrow of the samurai regime carried out by samurai themselves with the purpose of transforming Japan into a modern nation-state, but it was quickly realised after the revolution that unless samurai were replaced by a new type of *samurai*, university graduates educated in the Western manner, it would be impossible to establish a country as civilised as the West. The government reformed traditional education at elementary and higher levels, just after the revolution, and conspicuous yields of the new education system were already appearing in the 1880s. Around the turn of the century, the new intellectuals had acquired a significant share of power in every corner of society. This quick propagation and great success of the new (Western) education can probably be attributed to the fact that Japan was a Confucianist country, where education was regarded as having a high intrinsic value and the classification of the people was made according to their education received into, say, literates and illiterates. Because Japan had been more Confucian before the revolution than after, education had already been widespread at a considerably high level in the feudal Tokugawa period;[8] what the new government needed to do was simply convert from the existing Chinese-style education to the Western style.

Naturally, the samurai of those clans which had led the revolution acquired high positions in various spheres of activity in the post-revolution world. As they decided not to transfer the capital from Tokyo, their clans had to shoulder the big disadvantage of all being located very far from the capital. The driving force of the clans soon expired, and this contributed greatly to an easy advancement of the university students into all kinds of circles of society. In 1926, the end of the Taisho period, five years prior to the appointment of Korekiyo Takahashi as Minister of Finance, the business world was already dominated by university graduates and was unworkable without them.

The process of historical transformation of the traditional business world to this modern type may be seen in the following. In order to quantify the movement, I have used *Nippon Zaikai Jinbutsu Retsuden*, a series of short biographies of great figures in the Japanese business world (Tokyo, Aoshio Publishers, vol. 1, 1963 and vol. 2, 1964), which contains bibliographies of 200 successful entrepreneurs and business men, to analyse how the business world changed in the Meiji–Taisho period, 1868–1926. Because 23 of them were too young to establish themselves as significant figures in this period, I have excluded them and divided the remaining 177 into eight groups according to the time of their debut. Group A consists of those who were already known as businessmen before the revolution, 1867–8; group B includes those who made their debut as established businessmen during the the first fifteen years, 1868–82; those of the vintage years 1883–90, 1891–7, 1898–1905, 1906–12, 1913–20 and 1921–6 form groups C, D, E, F, G and H, respectively. The allocations of the 177 sample members to the eight groups A–H are 11, 12, 9, 21, 18, 37, 24, 25 people, respectively. These sample sizes are very small, even if the underdevelopment of Japanese business circles in these years is taken into consideration. It must be remembered that the following analysis may be able to sketch only a rough picture of the cream of the crop of businessman.

Also, it has to be noticed that these allocations of the sample members to the eight periods represents the numbers of new entrepreneurs who were admitted as members of the business elite in the respective periods. Of course, it is difficult to determine the time when a person was recognised as a distinguished figure unless we make a detailed biographical study of each individual. Thus we must acknowledge that our allocation is more or less arbitrary, being subject to my personal judgement. We may, nevertheless, be able to conclude, from the investigation to be discussed in the following, that in the last sub-period, 1921–6, university graduates, especially those of the state university, already held the hegemony of the business world in Japan.

We classify the people according to whether they received higher education or not. In the early days after the revolution, a formal education system, particularly that of higher education, had not yet been established as a system available to ordinary young people in Japan. In order to receive higher education, boys were sent abroad. It is also very difficult, and, therefore, more or less arbitrary to decide whether an individual actually received higher education or not in a foreign country. In the biography it is usually written: 'He yugaku-su (he played and studied) in America.' But he might have mainly played and occasionally studied. Accordingly, for those persons who had visited a foreign country, a 'higher education diploma' was given by my personal, intuitive judgement. But in later years the numbers of such persons declined significantly because most of them went through the Japanese system, so that the arbitrariness resulting from my personal conferment of diplomas does not affect the general conclusion of the study.

Before the revolution, the Tokugawa central government and a number of feudal clan governments had schools for their own *samurai* boys. Most of them were transformed after the revolution into the British-type grammar school, while a few of them became schools for higher education. In particular, on the basis of the schools of the central government in the feudal age. the University of Tokyo was established in 1877; it was later (in 1886) reformed into the Imperial University, which was further reformed into the present University of Tokyo after the Second World War. In parallel with this, a few private higher education organisations were emerging in the closing days of the

Tokugawa shogunate. The most famous and influential of these was Keio Gijuku (the present Keio Gijuku University) and also Tekijuku (now the School of Medicine of Osaka University). Immediately after the revolution, private higher education gained power and led public higher education, but their relative positions were soon reversed.

Under the Imperial University a few high schools were founded and played the role of preparatory schools to the university. The Imperial University system then expanded; in 1926 there were already five imperial universities in Tokyo, Kyoto, Sendai, Fukuoka and Seoul, Korea. Also, quite a few colleges of agriculture, commerce, medicine and technology were founded and the high schools increased in number, corresponding to the expansion of the university system, especially after the First World War. At the end of 1926 there were 33 high schools in Japan and Taiwan but not in Korea. Whereas both private and state universities expanded greatly in terms of quantity, the quality of the private universities was taken as being generally much lower than that of the imperial universities throughout the last five of the eight sub-periods we are concerned with.

In the first period A, as is shown in Table 1, businessmen had no higher education. The business elite in that period consisted of traditional merchants only. In the post-revolution period B, however, new technology was introduced and educated businessmen appeared but they all studied abroad. In the third period C the business circles began to accommodate graduates of Japanese private higher education organisations, while it was in the fourth period D that they received state university graduates for the first time. As far as the entrants in successive periods are concerned, the share of those without higher education and that of those with it but in foreign countries in the total members of the sample have both declined almost monotonously. The businessmen with Japanese state university education increased more rapidly than those from private universities.

On the basis of these statistics, Table 2 is obtained on the following assumptions. (1) All the persons in group A were fully active until the end of the fifth period, 1898–1905; but only half of them worked in the sixth period, 1906–12, and they were all retired from business afterwards. Group A, therefore, appears with only half-weighting in the sixth period, whereas it has the full weight 1 before the sixth, and zero-weighting in the seventh and eighth. (2) Group B has weight 1 from its appearance to the sixth period, half-weighting in the seventh and 0 afterwards. (3) Similarly, group C keeps weight 1 from the third until it has only half-weighting in the eighth period. (4) All other groups

Table 1 The business elite of Meiji–Taisho Japan: flow table*

Period	A 1860–67	B 1868–82	C 1883–90	D 1891–97	E 1898–1905	F 1906–12	G 1913–20	H 1921–26
The number of businessmen	11	12	9	21	19	36	24	45
Classification by education:								
No higher education	11 (100)	9 (75)	7 (78)	13 (62)	9 (47)	12 (33)	7 (29)	13 (29)
Foreign higher education	0 (0)	3 (25)	0 (0)	2 (10)	1 (5)	1 (3)	1 (4)	3 (7)
State university education	0 (0)	0 (0)	0 (0)	4 (18)	6 (32)	15 (42)	9 (38)	20 (44)
Private university education	0 (0)	0 (0)	2 (22)	2 (10)	3 (16)	8 (22)	7 (29)	9 (20)

*Figures in parentheses are percentages.

Table 2 The business elite of Meiji–Taisho Japan: stock table

Period	A 1860–67	B 1868–82	C 1883–90	D 1891–97	E 1898–1905	F 1906–12	G 1913–20	H 1921–26
The number of businessmen	11	23	32	53	72	102.5	115	149.5
Classification by education (unit: %):								
No higher education	100	87	84	75	68	54	46	38
Foreign higher education	0	13	9	9	8	7	6	5
State university education	0	0	0	8	14	24	30	36
Private university education	0	0	6	8	10	15	19	20

D, E, ..., H have full-weighting in every period after they first appeared until the end (i.e. the eighth). Then the numbers of active leading businessmen for the eight periods are obtained, as we see in the second row of Table 2.

Table 2 gives statistics regarding active businessmen in the eight periods; it is clear that the percentage of those with no higher education in the business elite steadily declined throughout the Meiji–Taisho period. It started with 100 per cent and reached the low level of 38 per cent. This means that traditional merchants were constantly replaced by university graduates. The circles became more and more intellectual, and without the professional specialist knowledge concerning management and technology it became very difficult to run companies and factories. Also, from the table we may observe a clear import substitution concerning education. Japan first imported educated and capable experts though they themselves were Japanese. The share of such people quickly diminished and became one-third of its former level by the first post-revolution period, at the end of the Taisho period. The native experts with state or private higher education not only filled the new places created by the expansion of the business world but also advanced into the vacancies produced by the retirement of businessmen with foreign higher education as well as those with no education.

The table also shows that those from state universities increased more rapidly than those from private educational organisations. On the basis of these figures it may be inferred that the business world would eventually be dominated by managers and directors with state university education. The results derived from statistical analysis of the biographies of the selected great business figures in the Meiji–Taisho era are summarised in Tables 1 and 2. The section below confirms that this inference has been correct throughout the Showa period, 1926–89, at least.

VI

Dramatic changes happened in both the business and education worlds after the Second World War. As has been mentioned, the *zaibatsu* Konzerns were disbanded. Ultra-nationalistic political influences, as well as military controls and interventions, no longer existed in post-war Japan, whilst the left-wing labour movements had once been vehement and strikes had frequently occurred before Japan was transformed into a relatively easily governable country with no serious opposition group in the middle of the 1970s. The scale of the business world in 1992 has been greatly expanded. Enormous sectors of big businesses and of small and medium-sized businesses now exist in Japan. Furthermore, the big business sector as well is structured hierarchically; at the top of it, there are companies whose chairmen and presidents are regular members of the luncheon (or breakfast) meeting of an ex-*zaibatsu* enterprise group. The second stratum consists of the major companies which belong to the six enterprise groups but are not member companies of the lunch or breakfast meetings. The third would be those others whose shares are listed in Part I of the main exchanges. Of course, there are some big, powerful companies among the unlisted but they are comparatively few in number. One can compare those businessmen in the Meiji–Taisho period who were reviewed in *Nippon Zaikai Jinbutsu Retsuden*, with the directors and executives of the luncheon (breakfast) meetings of the six enterprise groups, and I shall show the result of the comparison below.

The education system also changed greatly. The system which had treated the imperial universities differently financially from ordinary state universities, and under which their autonomy in appointment of professors and in curriculum decisions had been respected by the Ministry of Education, was abolished by the GHQ as it considered that these universities had collaborated with the military forces in the invasion of the Asian countries. Imperial universities were then transformed into ordinary state universities and their special connection with high schools was dissolved. Under the new regulation the term of the usual undergraduate courses was extended from a three-year system to a four-year American system. High schools in the cities where an imperial university had existed became part of it to form a new state university in which they were concerned with education in the first two years, while all other high schools were combined with colleges of medicine, commerce, technology, etc., in the same region to form a new provincial state university. As military academies had all been closed, universities were the only means to climbing the social ladder in the secular world, so that the rat-race for obtaining a place in a state university was intense and very severe in post-war Japan. Those who were unsuccessful in the race rushed into private universities. These too, therefore, had to expand in capacity and the list of private universities became very long.

We may then classify the universities in contemporary Japan in the following groups: (1) Tokyo University, (2) Kyoto University, (3) Hitotsubashi-TIT, (4) major state universities, (5) other national and municipal universities, (6) Keio and Waseda Universities, and (7) other private universities. (1) and (2) are ex-imperial universities in Tokyo and Kyoto respectively. In (3) Hitotsubashi is the former college of commerce in Tokyo, now specializing in economics and other social sciences, while TIT (Tokyo Institute of Technology) is the former college of technology in Tokyo. These two together would perhaps make a second Tokyo University. (4) includes five former imperial universities (Tokoku, Kyushu, Hokkaido, Osaka and Nagoya) and Kobe, this last being a comprehensive university, comparable with Osaka and Nagoya, established after the war on the basis of a college of commerce in Kobe with other institutions. The universities in category (5) are influential in their respective localities but have not yet established a nationwide reputation. Among private universities most eminent are Keio and Waseda listed in (6); in terms of numbers of students, the latter is much larger, and although it is more powerful in political circles, journalism, etc., Waseda is far less influential than Keio as far as the business world is concerned. Category (7) includes huge private universities such as Nippon, Kinki and Fukuoka, as well as more moderate universities such as Meiji, Rikyo and Doshisha, etc. with some historical reputations. Also it includes small organisations, some with historical reputations but others being new enterprises.

It has already been seen that after the war employed professional managers and experts were in high positions without the back-up of powerful shareholders; they let their companies buy shares in their friends' companies and the mutual holding of shares formed in this way was used as a means of supporting their respective posts in the companies. However, this would not work unless those on the top stratum in different companies could trust each other. What would play the role of the bond of trust between them? Is it their personal friendship? Obviously not, because if so, every time the president of a company was replaced by a new person, the shareholding of the previous president had to be replaced by the one of the new, and this would create a chaotic state in the stock market which was never observed. The mutual shareholding has been stable over a long period, exceeding the span of the individual presidency. Behind this there must have been trust in the persistence of the character which the president and executives of a company have as a group. One of the elements which determine the colour or character of a company would be the composition of the universities from which its president and executives have graduated. This composition is stable over a considerably long period, so that companies which have a similar composition may trust each other. The trust is even more unshakable when they belong to the same enterprise group. In any case, the school tie is very strong in Japan.

The 1992 distribution of executives of the six enterprise groups according to the educational backgrounds may be summarised as in Table 3. Column (A) gives the percentages of those graduates from the first class state universities, while (B) gives the percentage from the first-class state or private universities. It is found from the table that there is a clear distinction between the top four ex-*zaibatsu* and the bottom two newly formed enterprise groups. Among the four, Mitsubishi and then Sumitomo are biased towards state universities, while Mitsui and the Fuyo towards private universities. In more detail, Mitsubishi is very much Tokyo-oriented, whilst Sumitomo is Kyoto-oriented. This probably reflects the history that Mitsubishi has been very much connected with the Tokyo government dominated by Tokyo graduates since the time of the Meiji revolution, whereas Sumitomo originated from the Kyoto-Osaka region. In the private university oriented groups, Mitsui's Keio faction dominated its Waseda faction by 2:1, while in the case of Fuyo, the proportions of Keio and Waseda are more or less even. On the other hand, in the case of the new enterprise groups, Daiichi-Kangyo (DK) and Sanwa, it is seen that minor national or municipal universities (5) and minor private universities (7) still have substantial shares.

The ratio $[(B)-(A)] \div (A)$, that is $(6) \div (A)$, would give a fair index for showing the relative powers of state and private universities. The lowest is the one for Sumitomo, 13 per cent, followed by the one for Mitsubishi, 25 per cent, while the highest is Mitsu's 46 per cent followed by DK's 45 per cent. Figures for Fuyo and Sanwa are 34 per cent and 31 per cent, respectively. The average of the six enterprise groups is 31 per cent, and that for all listed companies is 48 per cent in 1992. These figures may be compared with the figures obtained from the bottom two rows of Table 2. It is 56 per cent for the period 1921–6 of column H, so that we may conclude from these that the relative power of the private universities versus the state universities is much weaker in the business world in the post-war than in the pre-war years. This may contradict the intuitive view of the business world which the contemporary Japanese people would depict: but our statistics clearly support this conclusion.

Similar statistics can be obtained for the presidents and chairmen of the board of directors of various companies. Table 4 shows the distribution of presidents and chairmen according to their educational background for the six groups. The general patterns of Tables 3 and 4

Table 3 Educational backgrounds of executives of the six enterprise groups, 1992 (unit: %)

	State universities					Private universities		Others	Totals	
	(1)	(2)	(3)	(4)	(5)	(6)	(7)	(8)	(A)	(B)
Mitsubishi	36	6	15	11	6	17	6	3	68	85
Mitsui	25	7	9	15	9	26	6	3	56	82
Sumitomo	29	20	7	19	6	10	6	4	75	85
Fuyo	28	6	10	14	9	21	8	6	58	79
DK	22	6	7	13	12	22	12	7	48	70
Sanwa	15	16	5	18	16	10	12	8	54	64
Average	25	10	9	15	10	17	9	5	59	76

Note: (1) Tokyo, (2) Kyoto, (3) Hitotsubashi-TIT, (4) major state universities, (5) other national and municipal universities, (6) Keio-Waseda, (7) other private universities, (8) others.
(A) = (1) + (2) + (3) + (4); (B) = (A) + (6).

Source: *Yakuin Shiki-ho, Jojo-kaisha ban, 1992* (Executive Quarterly: Listed Company Edition, 1992) (Toyo Keizai Shimposha, 1992).

Table 4 Educational backgrounds of presidents and chairman of the six enterprise groups, 1992 (unit: %)

	State universities					Private universities		Others	Totals	
	(1)	(2)	(3)	(4)	(5)	(6)	(7)	(8)	(A)	(B)
Mitsubishi	61	10	7	5	5	10	5	2	83	93
Mitsui	43	13	10	5	0	20	0	10	71	91
Sumutomo	57	20	9	9	0	3	3	0	95	98
Fuyo	45	9	9	11	0	11	2	11	74	85
DK	46	5	6	9	3	19	3	9	66	85
Sanwa	28	17	11	8	6	8	8	15	64	72
Average	45	12	9	8	2	13	4	9	74	87

Note and Source: See Table 3.

are similar, except that the relative power ratio between private and state universities. i.e. (6)÷(A), is much lower for each enterprise group for presidents and chairmen than for executives. Even in the case of the two groups, Mitsui and DK, which are in favour of Keio and Waseda universities, the ratio falls from 46 per cent and 46 per cent, respectively, for executives, to 28 per cent and 29 per cent, respectively, for presidents and chairman. This means that the very top stratum of the business circles is still more dominated by the national universities. Mitsubishi's and Sumitomo's figures clearly reflect this general character, though the former is typically Tokyo-oriented while the latter tilts towards Kyoto.

The index of the relative power of Keio and Waseda against the major state universities (i.e. all ex-imperial universities plus Hitotsibashi, TIT and Kobe) is calculated by subdividing the enterprise groups into three sub-sectors: (I) financial companies comprising city banks, trust banks, insurance, securities and lease companies, (II) trading corporations, real estate agents, warehouse and transportation companies and recreation facilities and (III) companies belonging to other industries. These sub-groups are referred to as the financial sector, the non-financial tertiary industry sector and the secondary industry sector, respectively. Table 5 summarises the results for the executives and for the presidents and chairmen of the enterprise groups. From the table we may derive the following two conclusions: the indices for financial and non-financial tertiary sectors are generally higher than the corresponding indices for the secondary sector. This is especially true for Mitsui group. This

Table 5 The relative power of private universities to state universities, 1992: sectoral indices (unit: %)

	Executives				Presidents and chairmen			
	(I)	(II)	(III)	(T)	(I)	(II)	(III)	(T)
Mitsubishi	33	33	19	25	0	20	14	11
Mitsui	70	172	31	46	40	67	17	31
Sumitomo	17	22	10	13	14	0	0	3
Fuyo	31	36	35	35	0	100	15	16
DK	67	57	39	45	100	11	26	29
Sanwa	18	27	16	17	25	100	3	13
Average	36	46	26	30	24	39	13	17

Note: (I) The financial sector, (II) the non-financial tertiary sector, (III) the secondary industry sector, (T) the total for the group.

Source: See Table 3.

group is not very much different from the other groups as far as the secondary industry sector is concerned but has very high indices in the other two. This would not be surprising in view of the fact that Keio and Waseda are weaker and smaller than the state university in the field of science and technology, whereas they have big social science faculties, especially in economics, business, commerce and politics. Secondly, the figures for presidents and chairmen are generally lower than the corresponding ones for executives, though those for financial and non-financial tertiary sectors fluctuate greatly because samples are very small; that is, at the very top level state universities still dominate private universities more than at the executive level.

It has been pointed out that the university affiliations of the directors are different between the enterprise groups. Mitsui and Fuyo are oriented towards Keio-Waseda, while Mitsubishi and Simutomo towards Tokyo-Kyoto. From Tables 3 and 4 we may suggest that even Mitsui, Fuyo and DK do not differ from the Mitsubishi type in the sense that the ex-imperial university group; i.e. the sum of (1), (2) and (4), holds commanding power in the group; Sanwa is a mini-Sumitomo with a strong Kyoto group. Nevertheless, we may point out a remarkable similarity through these groups with respect to one other aspect of the education backgrounds of the directors, that is to say, with respect to their academic fields.

The directors are now classified into two groups: one consisting of those graduates from social science or humanity faculties and the other of those from natural science faculties, i.e. science, technology, medicine or agriculture faculties. The ratio of the number of directors of the second group to the total number of directors of both groups is calculated for various categories (for the aggregate of the financial and non-financial tertiary sectors and for the secondary industry sector) at the executive level as well as the president–chairman level. From Table 6 it is seen that the sectoral figures for executives are remarkably similar between the enterprise groups but the total figures are higher for Fuyo, DK and Sanwa than those for Mitsuibishi, Mitsui, Sumitomo, reflecting the fact that the last three have bigger (I) and (II) sectors than the first three. Comparing columns for the presidents and chairmen with the corresponding columns for the executives, it may be said that the executives from the science side are slightly less likely to be promoted to president or chairman than the executives with social science or humanity backgrounds.

It has been mentioned that each enterprise group has a city bank and a trust bank; in the case of DK, however, it has no trust bank

Table 6   The percentage of executives and presidents with a science, technology, medicine or agricultural degree (unit: %)

	Executives			Presidents and chairmen		
	(I) + (II)	(III)	(T)	(I) + (II)	(III)	(T)
Mitsubishi	6	45	30	0	42	26
Mitsui	5	49	29	0	46	26
Sumitomo	4	44	27	0	42	26
Fuyo	9	45	35	6	34	24
DK	4	46	33	0	46	32
Sanwa	10	48	38	19	45	38
Average	6	46	32	4	43	31

Note: (I) + (II) financial and non-financial tertiary sectors, (III) the secondary sector, (T) = (I) + (II) + (III).

Source: See Table 3.

Table 7   Educational backgrounds of executives and presidents of banks, 1992 (unit: %)

	Executives						Presidents and chairmen					
	(1)	(2)	(3)	(4)	(5)	(6)	(1)	(2)	(3)	(4)	(5)	(6)
Special banks	86	7	3	0	3	0	100	0	0	0	0	0
Industrial banks	54	11	16	4	2	10	100	0	0	0	0	0
City banks	41	12	10	12	3	18	64	9	18	9	0	0
Trust banks	24	8	9	12	4	21	67	17	8	0	0	8

Note: (1) Tokyo, (2) Kyoto, (3) Hitotsubashi-TIT, (4) major state universities, (5) other national and municipal universities, (6) Keio-Waseda.
Special banks: Bank of Japan, Japan Development Bank, Export-Import Bank of Japan.
Industrial Banks: Industrial Bank of Japan, Long-Term Credit Bank of Japan, Nippon Credit Bank.
City Banks: Mitsubishi, Sakura, Sumitomo, Fuji, DK, Sanwa.
Trust Banks: Mitsubishi Trust, Mitsui Trust, Sumitomo Trust, Yasuda Trust, Toyo Trust.
Source: See Table 3.

but a securities company (which is included in the category of trust banks for Table 7). It is clear that the special banks, Bank of Japan, Japan development bank, and Export-Import Bank of Japan, which play the most significant roles in the Japanese economy are almost perfectly monopolised by the three state universities, Tokyo, Kyoto and Hitotsubashi. Industrial banks (or long-term credit banks) which were created by the will of the government are heavily dominated by these three. City banks are also very important because they may be regarded as the headquarters of the respective enterprise groups, and 78 per cent of their executives come from national universities, while the corresponding figure is 57 per cent for the trust banks. Thus the dominance of the state universities increasingly great in the banking sector, corresponding to the position of the bank in the hierarchy of the banking sector (having special banks at the top and trust banks at the bottom as in the first column of Table 7). From the table we see that the same drift is more conspicuous at the president–chairman level.

VII

When the rate of interest was fixed at a low level, investment increased greatly in the 1960s; there were, of course, many investment opportunities for redevelopment and reconstruction of the production facilities damaged and destroyed during the war. This expansion in investment resulted in an increase in GNP which in turn brought about an increase in tax revenues. Thus the government had enough money to expand its expenditure. The fiscal policy worked well, which contributed to a further increase in GNP. Moreover, new facilities improved the quality of the products, so that exports increased remarkably. This produced a further increase in GNP. In the early 1960s a shortage of labour began to be felt and imports of materials for production were increased. The increase in exports was not as high as the one in imports; the trade balance deteriorated, but the rate of interest was kept low.

Naturally, then, firms borrowed greatly from city banks which in turn borrowed from the central bank. This created an atmosphere in favour of a financially centralised economy that could be regulated by rationing lending to city banks by the central bank, the rationing being called *madoguchi kisei* (the window regulation), according to which an allocation of lending to city banks is decided by the central bank on the basis of their reports of their performances in the previous periods and their prospects for the future. Of course, other measures were also proposed. One of them was that for strengthening the firms' own capital, a special fund be established within the Bank of Japan on the basis of foreign money which the government's special account for foreign exchange stabilisation held. The firms would then sell newly issued bonds and shares to the special fund of the bank and would return the money thus acquired to the city banks to pay back the money they had borrowed. The city banks would then be able to return the money they had borrowed from the central bank. Thus all of the over-lendings to the city banks would be cleared. Although the fund would lose the foreign money they had received from the government, they would have acquired the bonds and shares, on the basis of which it was thought that Japan now would be able to establish a sound and powerful securities market which would make a great contribution to increasing the firms' own capital.

It was, however, very difficult to realise this schemes, because, at the time the scheme was being considered, its most essential premises, that is the central bank's purchase of the foreign money that the government held, the issue of corporation debentures and shares and so forth, did not have a reasonable time limit for completion. Thus the over-loan remained in the economy; the interest rate was kept low, and as much money as requested was lent by the central bank to city banks. Then, as the interest rate was fixed, city banks maximised their profits by maximising the amount of their lending, so that the quantity mechanism remained prevalent in the lending market. Although the 'real' side of the economy was greatly freed and the control measures for the real economy which had been introduced before or during the war were mostly removed after the war, the monetary side was still using the method of rationing, in order to allocate the scarce resource, money, among the industrial firms. Thus, in the Japanese economy of this time price and quantity mechanisms worked in the real and monetary sub-economies, respectively, and the Japanese banking system was constructed to fit this mixed mechanism perfectly.

Under the central bank, there have been after the war two specialised banks, one for financing the activities for development and the other for promoting international trade. Japan has also established three banks for providing long-term credit to industrial investment projects. These collaborate with city banks, surrounding which industrial firms form enterprise groups. As has been shown in Table 7, the weights of the national university graduates, especially those of the graduates of the University of Tokyo, in the executives and presidents of these central and semi-central banks are very much heavier than those for city banks, whilst these banks themselves are very much dominated by the executives and presidents from the national universities. The school-tie or the academic clique in the financial sector would perhaps be the basis on which the monetary controlled system has been built; or conversely, it at least reflects the control-economy character of the post-war financial sector.

It has been pointed out that each group has one city bank and one trust bank, the only exception being the DK group with no trust bank. It is not unusual for the city bank to send its staff members to the companies in the group to which the bank belongs, as either executive or president. On the average of six groups, the city banks send 0.75 people per company, though this figure may be regarded as somewhat understating reality because the statistics book I have used does not record those executives and presidents who came from the outside to some lower posts of the companies and were then promoted within the same companies afterwards.[9] These city banks play the role of either the headquarters of the groups or the bond cementing the member companies in the groups; the staff members sent by the city bank to the companies in the same group form the arteries putting organs under its control.

Moreover, the city banks of the six enterprise groups are usually the main bank of the member companies in their respective groups – the main bank system being a legacy of the system of marriage arranged between munitions companies and city banks during the war, as has been pointed out earlier. In such a couple the city bank assumes the moral responsibility of providing the company with an amount of money that it needs for carrying out its production plan. The 'marriage' may be polygamous, especially for large companies. They may each have a consortium consisting of a few main banks. These are not on an equal basis; there are big differences in their responsibilities between the city bank which is nominated as the first main bank and others nominated as the second, third, ..., main banks. The burden of responsibility declines rapidly, where a city bank is ranked at a lower place in the consortium of the main banks. When a company wants, for example, to raise some money for introducing a new method of production, it has first to propose the idea to the first main bank which will draw its conclusion after consulting with other member banks. Therefore, the power of the first main bank is distinctly higher than that of the second main bank, and so forth. The distribution of power among them is very similar to the distribution of power between the first wife, the second wife, etc. in a polygamous family. It is much more sociological or anthropological than economic, in the sense that the distribution of power is not necessarily proportional to the amounts of money the banks lend to the company. Accordingly, when this law of distribution of power is violated, a way for 'humanity and justice' starts between the main banks of the company without any 'humanity and justice',[10] in the same way as wives of the same family fight with each other in similar circumstances. The first main bank's rights are enormous, as will be seen below, in exchange for which they are burdened with a duty to behave paternalistically. Any bank which violated the rule would be ostracised in the banking world.

Consequently, in the banking business, the competition for obtaining the position of the *first* main bank is most severe and fierce. Of course, in the case of the company being in serious financial trouble, its first main bank would be wounded severely because it would have to pour an additional substantial amount of money into the company which is in a critical condition. However, the bank will, in exchange, get the power to control not just the money of the company which the bank has loaned to it, but its entire money, otherwise the bank cannot bear the responsibility of keeping the company financially sound. Therefore, when it expands or improves its production facilities, the first main bank will be granted a right to loan a substantial portion of the necessary money to the company. This is a big attraction for banks to raise their activity levels in such an economy as Japan's where the quantity adjustment mechanism works in the lending market. The bank must have the greatest possible group of firms to which it can loan money for investment.

Thus it is very important for a city bank to become the first main bank of the greatest possible number of companies. Moreover, the first main bank has a great opportunity of sending its staff members as executives to the companies that it takes care of. This entry into companies for the purpose of control is very much appreciated by the bank because it has to find satisfactory positions for high-class staff members, to which they are willing to be transferred. Otherwise, under the notorious permanent employment system, the bank will go bankrupt because of the over-employment of high-salaried managers.

The powerfulness of the main bank differs considerably between enterprise groups. In the case of the Mitsubishi group, Mitsubishi Bank is in the position of the first main bank for 95 per cent of those twenty member companies of the Friday meeting of the group, which exclude Mitsubishi Bank, Mitsubishi Trust Bank and Meiji Insurance Company. Similar figures which show the percentages of Mitsubishi Bank to be the second and the third main bank of the same twenty companies are 5 per cent and 0 per cent, respectively. To get the overall index from those three figures we aggregate them with weights, 1, 1/2, 1/3, respectively. Of course, these numerical values for weighting are arbitrary but may be considered to be not very far from those reckoned to be reasonable. Thus the index obtained according to this formula would not be entirely out of tune for the purpose of showing the bank's power of commanding the companies in the group. The index is calculated at 97.5 per cent for Mitsubishi. Similarly, it is at 87.5, 100, 92, 92.5 and 92, respectively, for Mitsui, Sumitomo, Fuyo, DK and Sanwa. See Table 8.

From these it is seen that the most powerful bank *vis-à-vis* the companies in its own group is Sumitomo which is followed by Mitsubishi, at least in 1984. The banks of Fuji (for Fuyo), DK and Sanwa form the next group and are almost equal in powerfulness. The Mitsui group is weakest in its bank's power of commanding the companies in the group, though this situation is expected to improve for Mitsui since its bank has recently been merged with Taiyo-Kobe bank, a large city bank, to form a new Sakura Bank. In addition to these city (or commercial) banks, each group (except DK) has its second bank, a trust bank. Their main bank indices are calculated on the assumption of the same weighting system. Sumitomo's score is again at the top with an index of 44, which is followed by Mitsubishi (40) and Mitsui (31). Fuyo and Sanwa are weak, scoring 16 and 12 points, respectively.

From these observations we may conclude that the Mitsubishi and Sumitomo groups are a typical, or ideal, enterprise group whose member companies are united by means of the financial commanding power of its city and trust banks. However, Mitsui is seen to be clearly weaker than these two, confirming the usual view that Mitsui which had been the most powerful and successful *zaibatsu* before the war was overtaken by Mitsubishi after the war. DK and Sanwa are the new

Table 8 The percentages of the member companies of the six enterprise groups having their own city banks and trust banks as the 1st, 2nd, 3rd main banks, 1984 (unit: %)

Enterprise group	City bank			Trust bank		
	1st	2nd	3rd	1st	2nd	3rd
Mitsubishi	95	5	0	0	70	15
Mitsui	80	15	0	5	35	25
Sumitomo	100	0	0	0	76	18
Fuyo	84	16	0	0	16	24
DK	85	13	3	0	0	0
Sanwa	86	6	9	0	14	14

Source: *Nikkei Kaisha Joho (Nikkei Information on Companies) 1984* (Nippon Keizai Shimposha).

groups formed around a big city bank; there is still an obvious distance between them and the old Mitsubishi and Sumitomo.

Having been provided with enough money for investment by their main banks, the companies in the six enterprise groups played the role of engines bringing the Japanese economy to a place from where it could launch a fresh mission for chasing developed Western countries. Thanks to the new production facilities made available by the loans for investment, the economy was enabled to produce more products of higher quality. Also, in the 1960s Japan enjoyed a huge increase in demand from the US whose economy was booming and whose involvement in the Vietnam War became deeper and deeper, so that the procurement by the US forces from Japan became hectic. Japan's capacity of production had expanded greatly, and her cost of production diminished remarkably. Exports expanded at an enormous speed and yielded a large trade surplus. A high rate of economic growth was sustained and in spite of the boom remaining in the economy from year to year, wholesale prices were stable. Eventually a drastic appreciation of the value of yen became unavoidable. The old IMF regime at last collapsed in 1971. Obviously, the advancement of Japan was one of the factors responsible for the collapse.

The luncheon/dinner meetings of presidents and chairmen of the enterprise groups naturally produced new ideas of entrepreneurial activities, many of which were later realised by a number of member companies collaborating with each other. To establish a new business, necessary factors of production have to be brought together; they are money, knowledge about the money market, knowledge about the necessary technology, ability to construct the factory, etc., and all these are available within the group. In particular, money is provided by the city bank of the group, while the necessary market research is made by its trading house. We may therefore say that conversations in the luncheon meeting result in a major industrial innovation relatively easily.

According to Schumpeter, innovations are decided individually and secretly. However, although the meetings of presidents and chairmen are secret, what is discussed there is very difficult to be kept in absolute secrecy because the meetings are attended by many people. Once a good idea is examined in one group, more or less similar ideas would soon appear on the agenda of some other group. Thus, in Japan, innovations are observed in quick succession or gregariously. For example, a committee for atomic energy was formed in the Mitsubishi group in 1955 and then in both the Mitsui and the Sumitomo group in 1956. On the basis of these committees, companies named Mitsubishi

Atomic Power Industry and Japan Atomic Power Enterprise were established in 1958 by Mitsubishi and Mitsui, respectively, followed by
Sumitomo atomic power industry in 1959. The same story was repeated
soon after this with reference to the petrochemical industry.

In the 1970s, the (first) oil crisis immediately followed the collapse of
the international money market. Businessmen and politicians had a
presentiment of an age of uncertainty and Japan groped for industries
for the future. Then the Prime Minister, Kakuei Tanaka, the author of
'A Plan for Remodelling the Japanese Archipelago', had a very ambitious outlook concerning the future Japan. Although his premiership
was terminated after only two and a half years because of his involvement in the Lockheed scandal, the relationships of the government
with the business world were kept tight. The businessmen surrounding
the Prime Minister became very powerful; the 'national consensus' produced by them often became a topic of the presidents–chairmen meeting of the enterprise groups. Then a number of innovations were
carried out by the groups. Japan developed greatly in the field of electronics, information, computers, business machines and medical
instrument industries. Robotisation was carried out rapidly in the small
and medium-sized factories, more than in the large factories. Because
smaller factories feel labour shortage more acutely than large factories,
they had a big incentive to equip themselves with robots, and the quality of the products of robotised small firms improved greatly. It is no
doubt that all these contributed to expanding the export market and
increasing employment in Japan.

In Japan too, the problem of Keynesian theory versus monetarism
attracted the interest of academic economists in the late 1970s and the
early 1980s. It was, however, no more than a problem of academic
interest. No Japanese economist seriously believed that these theories
were able to remove imminent difficulties in that period. Japanese
politicians and businessmen, thanks to Kakuei Tanaka, were neither
Keynesian nor Milton Friedmanian but Schumpeterian as far as this
period of time was concerned. They believed that wherever a number
of innovations were successively carried out, almost always employment
would be kept high; there would be no need for a reduction of real
wages as well as no need for expanding the government's expenditure to keep employment of labour high. In addition the economy's
position in international trade was to be very favourable because
exports were kept high, thanks to the quality and novelty of the products. Thus the Japanese industries remained very aggressive. Besides
those industries mentioned above, Japan started, in the beginning of the

1980s, to extend her interest in the fields of biotechnology and oceanics. Naturally, then, ambitious institutes of research for development and think-tanks were built by many private corporations; and the government authorised in the 1970s the expansion of the technology faculties of national and private universities in order to prepare the economy for innovations.

By watching Japan in this period another important issue of academic interest will be revealed. From the textbook of international trade we know that the sum of current account, capital account and cash account is identically zero. Then, providing that cash account and non-trade balance in the current account are both in equilibrium, a positive trade balance implies a negative capital account. Therefore, during the long period of the trade balance being black, Japan's holding of capital assets in foreign countries was increasing more rapidly than foreigners' assets in Japan.

These experiences revealed the clear inadequacy of the conventional neoclassical growth theory. It usually studies the phenomena of economic growth on the assumption of the economy being closed, despite experience telling that there is no significant real economic growth under such an assumption.[11] In fact, in the actual world, only those countries which are successful in the business of international trade have shown a perceptible growth of industry which is, in turn, accompanied by an advance of their financial organisations and property businesses abroad. This repercussion of growth from the secondary to the tertiary industries has been clearly observed with respect to Japan in the 1970s and 1980s. Thus we may conclude that exports and imports are indispensable elements linking the theory of economic growth on the real side with that on the monetary side; without these the theory only traces out a continuous expansion of the industrial sector with no effect upon stock markets and foreign exchange rates. Thus the conventional neoclassical theory of growth based on the assumption of the closed economy has only made a dull caricature of the dynamic actual world.

After the war Japan had to obey the GHQ's order of land reform; big landowners had to sell their land for farming to peasants and tenant farmers. During the period of high industrial expansion and the following period of 'remodelling the archipelago', big business bought land from petty landowners for its future development or simply for speculation. Therefore, the price of land was already extremely high in the late 1970s and early 1980s. Moreover, because of the worldwide oil crises (first and second), Japan's tempo of industrial expansion became slower than the rate at which the economy had expected to grow. Consequently, the price of land was at last halted in the late 1980s. This created very damaging effects, because in Japan, in the period after 1970, land has been closely linked with stocks; in fact, small landowners bought shares with the money they borrowed by putting a portion of land as security. When the stock market plunged in the 1990s, as has been discussed above, those petty landowners not only lost their land offered as a security for borrowing money but also had to sell shares or some portion of their remaining land, in order to return the money they had borrowed to the bank. Thus the land price started to decline in parallel with the fall of share prices. These affect the value of yen adversely. To foreigners' eyes, Japan may appear to be faltering, but Japanese economists and businessmen seem to remain rather optimistic because the fundamentals of the economy are still not too bad. They may yet be right in expecting yields from the innovations which they decided on in the early 1980s for the 1990s and which are still continuing. But the depression that has started in this way is serious and deep-rooted, so that it may create grave and persistent effects upon the economy.[12]

Notes

1 Rudolf Hilferding, *Das Finanzkapital, Eine Studie über die jüngste Entwicklung des Kapitalismus* (Wien, 1910).
2 *Nihon Ginko 100 Nen Shi* (The Centenary History of the Bank of Japan), Vol. 4 (The Bank of Japan, 1984) p. 377.
3 A. A. Berle, Jr. and G. C. Means, *The Modern Corporation and Private Property* (New York, Macmillan 1st edn, 1932; revised edn, New York, Harcourt, Brace & World, 1965).
4 Hiroshi Okumura, *Shin-pan Nippon no Rokudai Kigyo Shudan* (Six Biggest Enterprise Groups of Japan, New Edition) (Tokyo, Diamond Press, 1983) p. 106ff.
5 H. Okumura, *Hojin Shihon Shugi* (Corporate Capitalism) (1984, Tokyo, Ochanonizu Shobo) p. 100 ff. R. Dore, *Flexible Rigidities, Industrial Policy and Adjustment in the Japanese Economy, 1970–80* (London, The Athlone Press, 1986) p. 70.
6 I greatly owe this analysis and the following to H. Okumura, *Kaitai suru 'Keiretsu' to Hojin Shihon Shugi* (Dismantling 'Enterprise Groups' and the Corporation Capitalism) (Tokyo, Shakai Shiso Sha, 1992).
7 *Why has Japan 'Succeeded'?* (Cambridge University Press, 1982); 'A Historical Transformation from Feudalism to Capitalism', a discussion paper, STICERD, LSE, 1986.
8 R. Dore, *Education in Tokugawa Japan* (London, The Athlone Press, 1965).
9 *Yakuin Shikiho, Jojo-kaisha ban, 1992* (Toyo Keizai Shimposha, 1992).

10 This has been clearly explained, with interesting examples, by H. Okumara in his *Ginko to Kigyo, sono Kiken na Kankei* (Banks and Firms, their Jeopardising Relationships) (Toyo Keizai Shimposha, 1978).

11 R. Harrod, *Towards a Dynamic Economics* (London, Macmillan, 1952) is a notable exception.

12 This has been confirmed, afterwards, throughout the 1990s.

Author's Preface (1983, First Edition)

Since I have been born into this world I must do something with myself, but I have very little idea of what it is I should do. I stand transfixed like a solitary person enveloped in a mist. With these apprehensions I graduated from the university. I took similar anxieties with me when I moved from Matsuyama to Kumamoto, and I went to England as a foreign student with the same unease in my heart. At length, I came down with nervous prostration and spent one unhappy day after another holed up in my lodgings. Then at the end of this desperate struggle and after more than a year in London, at last I got hold of the word 'egoism'.

I have become very strong since I got my hands on this word 'egoism'. I recovered my self-respect by saying to myself: who are these people anyway? It really was the word 'egoism' that gave me, who had been lost and in a daze, my directions, telling me: here you are, and from here on this is what you have to do.

It was in 1914 at Gakushuin University that the novelist Natsume Soseki lectured to this effect. Soseki had grasped in the Britain that we know of as the birthplace of modern capitalism what the men of letters and the thinkers of modern Japan had not been able to discover, though they had sought desperately. But the struggle involved had been such that it was said of him: 'Natsume Kinnosuke has finally gone mad.' However, Soseki himself had finally arrived at the mental state known as: 'Following the law of heaven, remove egoism', and in the end Soseki, too, was unable to penetrate right through to 'egoism'.

In the Japan seventy years on from the aforementioned lecture that Soseki called 'My Individualism', 'egoism' still has not become established. Instead, what has captured many Japanese is the word 'companism' (*kaisha hon'i*). If the spirit of modern capitalism is individualism and 'egoism', then the spirit of contemporary corporate capitalism is corporatism and 'companism'. And if we accept that Britain was the birthplace of modern capitalism, then it is surely Japan where corporate capitalism has made its greatest strides.

Nowadays, whilst voices are loud in praise of 'Japanese-style management' and we hear, 'Japan is wonderful, let's learn from her', on the other hand Japan is criticised over problems of trade friction and as an exporter of unemployment. Whether Japan is being praised or criticised, in both cases it is Japanese companies and not the Japanese in general that are involved. It is said that the Japanese work hard, but it is for the company that they work and not for their region or for their union. If we forget this and seek the principles of Japanese-style management in groupism or familism or even in community life, then in each case we will come up with a superficial theory for 'explaining' the Japanese. I have long had doubts and dissatisfactions with these sorts of theories about Japanese-style management. Despite the fact that there are many and various kinds of social organisations such as political parties, trade unions, schools, churches and the like, why is it nevertheless that from amongst all these only firms have seized and absorbed such large numbers of Japanese. This in itself is a fundamental question that has to be asked. This book was written in order to answer that question, but the principles that I have presented to you here as 'companism' are the source of a variety of contradictions in Japanese society while, at the same time, they are the secret of its strength.

It is round about ten years ago that I wrote *Hojin Shihon-Shugi no Kozo* (The Structure of Corporate Capitalism). In that book, as its subtitle 'Shareownership in Japan' indicates, I chiefly discussed the ownership of shares. However, corporate capitalism is not something that can be treated as relating merely to the concentration of shares in the hands of corporations. Therefore, I discussed in the book questions ranging from company domination to the structure of power in the business world. However, the arguments were not sufficiently developed. The term 'corporate capitalism' came little by little to be more popularly used after the publication of *The Structure of Corporate Capitalism* and a variety of discussions took place. There were among them some that distorted and somewhat diminished the importance of the debate on corporate capitalism.

Therefore it is my duty as its primary advocate to systematise it and to explain it in its entirety. Aware of this, I have already developed the debate in a variety of areas, and the present book uses previous books and articles as stepping-stones. I had originally intended to work up the articles I had already published in to a book, but in the end it transpired that everything was written anew. Thus, in the course of the narrative there are areas that overlap with what I have previously written, but I pride myself that they are only there to help systematise the whole.

Systematisation also means the attempt to see Japanese companies as complete entities and in their totality. Previous treatments of 'Japanese-style management' have only discussed the relationship between companies and their employees, but companies do not derive only from the relationship with employees. Not only are most companies joint-stock companies, but the relationship between shareholders and companies is an important one. Discussions of 'Japanese-style management' have never taken this fact into account. On the other hand, previous discussions of the joint-stock company have dealt only with the relationship between companies and shareholders, and in these discussions employees do not exist. In addition to this, it is proper that we should take into account the relationship between companies and managers and between company and company. It is the aim of this book to look at these in their totality and to attempt to explain them on the basis of a single principle.

The overall structure of the book is as follows. In Part I I shall outline the theory of corporate capitalism using the above approach, while at the same time I shall discuss the relationship between companies and their employees in the form of a critical appraisal of the theory of 'Japanese-style management'. In Part II I shall discuss the relationship between companies and their shareholders, and I shall present a concrete analysis of Japanese firms in terms of the problems of dividends and increases in capital, share prices, takeovers and so forth. I believe this will constitute a theory of the Japanese-style of joint-stock company whose content will be fairly different from hitherto existing theories of the joint-stock firm. In Part III I shall discuss the relationship between companies and their managers, and whilst criticising earlier theories of 'managerial control', I shall also present a counter-argument to the theory of control by the individual capitalist. A theory of management is an important core of the theory of corporate capitalism, which makes it all the more necessary to analyse it on the basis of concrete facts. It is likely to be fundamentally different in content from the hitherto imported 'theoretical' ideas of managerial control. In Part IV, I shall discuss the relationships among firms. Despite the fact that these relationships are important in an analysis of the firm, it has so far tended to be a neglected area in theories of the firm. It is all the more an important pillar of my own theory of the firm because the starting point of my research was the theory of company groups (*kigyo shudan-ron*).

One must also discuss the relationship between companies and the state and that between companies and society in order to have a complete theory of corporate capitalism, but I shall put these aside as topics for future research. For that reason, my theory of corporate capitalism will be an incomplete one.

HIROSHI OKUMURA

Part I
What is Corporate Capitalism?

1
The 'Companised' Society

> 'Japan is chock-full of companies; the talk in every bar is company-man talk.'
>
> Nakagiri Masao, *Kaisha no Jinji* (*People in Companies*)

'The company state'

There are approximately two million companies in Japan employing some thirty million salaried workers. When young people leave school, college or university, in almost all cases it is a question of joining a company. When a child is asked 'what does daddy do?', as if predetermined the answer comes back, 'daddy works for a company'. It is just as the poet Nakagiri Masao wrote: 'Japan is chock-full of companies.' Whether you are on a train or walking down the street, what meets the eye are company-men (*kaisha-in*). It is just as if not to be a company-man is not to be a person at all. Indeed, non-company-people are merely those preparing to become company-people, or else members of families who are supported by company-people. Everyone depends on the company and lives with the company. Thus is Japan a 'company state' and a society where 'companism' (*kaisha hon'i*) rules. When we speak of corporate capitalism, it is to this kind of state and this kind of society to which we refer.

Under the law, companies are given the status of *hojin* ('juridical' or 'legal' person – that is, incorporated), and it is in contrast to a natural person (*shizenjin*). I shall discuss the questions of what a 'juridical person' is and what a company is later on, but an especially notable phenomenon in post-war Japan is the fact that the power of companies that are juridical persons has grown greatly in comparison to that of natural persons. According to the Survey of National Wealth (SNW) conducted by the Economic Planning Agency, the breakdown of wealth by sector in the fifteen years between 1955 and 1970 – the years that constitute Japan's period of very rapid economic growth – shows that the wealth of the personal sector, which is the sum of that belonging to the household sector and to the one-man-business sector, fell from 42.6 per cent to 34.6 per cent. The share of the public sector, together with the sector containing government-owned enterprises, grew by only a small amount from 22.4 per cent to 23.3 per cent, while in contrast the wealth of the sector made up from private incorporated firms rose by a substantial amount from 31.0 per cent to 37.3 per cent.

Thus wealth became more concentrated in the hands of private incorporated firms – that is to say, companies – a fact fully realised from everyday, commonsense observation. The buildings going up in towns and cities belonged to companies, and really big buildings were the work of big companies. Land that had formerly been in the hands of private landlords became the property of companies, and the 'incorporation' of land proceeded apace. The ownership by 'juridical persons' of financial assets such as stocks and bonds also increased, and in marked contrast private individuals were kept at arm's length from them.

One of the distinctive features of post-war Japan that one is able to point to is the progress made in the equalisation of incomes. Indeed it is true that the old *zaibatsu* empires and the large landowners have gone and that differences in incomes between individuals have narrowed. However, what is of greater significance is the concentration of wealth in the corporate sector as opposed to the private sector.

When wealth comes in this way to be concentrated in the hands of companies in their capacity as 'juridical persons', it means that it is companies that now run the world. What better proof of this is there than the matter of political contributions? The overwhelmingly greater proportion of these are made either by companies or by the industry associations that are formed by companies. Nearly all of the contributions to the Liberal Democratic Party come from these two sources; whoever buys the party tickets to the 'support meetings' that politicians hold, in fact it is the company that pays for them. It is said that, besides these, other large-scale political contributions arrive through the back door, and nearly all of these also originate with companies.

It is true that before the Second World War the heads of *zaibatsu* families and wealthy landlords gave money to politicians from their own pockets, but since the war it is almost unheard of for private individuals to make political contributions.

In the United States, political contributions by companies are prohibited. It goes without saying that the making of a political contribution is a form of political activity, and the prohibition is by reason of the fact that it is only electors – that is, 'natural persons' – who can participate in political activity. If companies were to be allowed to indulge in political activities, then the rights of electors would also have to be given to 'juridical persons'. But however one thinks of it, giving the right to vote to a 'juridical person' is contrary to all reason. Americans understand this very well.

However, the Japanese Supreme Court has handed down the strange judgement that there are reasons for companies to participate in political activities. The ruling handed down by the court in 1970 in respect of the affair of the political contributions of the Yawata Steel Company stated the following: 'Companies, like the human beings who make up the nation, have the freedom to conduct political activities such as supporting and promoting specific policies of the country or a political party, or else opposing them. The making of political contributions is certainly a part of that freedom, and where a company makes such contributions, there is no requirement in the Constitution that they be treated differently from those of the ordinary citizen, even though they may influence the direction of politics.'

This affair was the result of an action brought by a private shareholder in Yawata Steel (Nippon Steel Corporation) alleging that political contributions from Yawata to the Liberal Democratic Party were an infringement of shareholders' rights. The Tokyo District Court found in favour of the shareholder, but the Supreme Court overturned this judgement: contributions by firms have been lawful in Japan. However, looked at logically and from the point of view of legal theory, this judgement was truly a declaration of victory for 'companism', by which is meant corporate capitalism. It recognised that now companies are omnipotent even in politics.

Thereafter, companies have not just made political contributions: they have also embarked directly upon electoral campaigning. These are what are known as 'company elections', where the company actively campaigns in support of certain candidates, even to the point of compelling the families of its employees to join in. Not just in elections for members of the Diet have these 'company elections' come to take place. They occur, too, in the case of elections to prefectural and local assemblies, and in the extreme case, even to the Chairmanship of the Liberal Democratic Party. This is not a case of wealthy people or managers engaging in political activities as private individuals. These are 'company elections' – that is, campaigning and voting as the company wishes – and it is political activity being conducted by companies. Having come to this point, it is illogical not to give companies in their capacity as juridical persons the right to vote.

Companies and culture

Not just politics but cultural activities, too, are being engaged in by companies. The book *The People and Language of Japan* put out by the public relations section of Mitsubishi Trading Company became a best-seller, and books authored by Nippon Steel Corporation, Nissho Iwai Trading Corporation and so on have been published one after another. Publishing activities by companies, such as those of the PHP Research Institute of the Matsushita group and CBS Sony, as well as that of TBS Britannica which was bought up for five billion yen by Suntory, have become very popular and have put a good deal of pressure on older established publishing houses.

The cultural activities of companies are permeating not just publishing but all other cultural areas: concerts, public lectures, symposia, art galleries, the theatre, literary prizes. It may appear that literature is on the decline in 'Japan the economic super-power' and that art is dying; the only flourishing cultural activities are those of companies. Thus Japanese culture is being taken possession of by large companies. Most artists and writers are employed as the luminaries of the public relations departments of great firms and the process of incorporating culture into the great Japanese company groupings goes on.

Perhaps as a reflection of this state of affairs, the *Asahi* newspaper ran a series of articles in twenty-five successive issues, from 13 September 1982, entitled *Culture and the Firm*. In these articles, there was a detailed treatment of the cultural activities of such companies as Toyota Automobiles, Suntory, Seibu Department Stores, Aji no Moto Foods, Dentsu Advertising and so on. These bore no relationship whatever to the main activities of these firms, and were many and various, ranging from cultural activities conducted according to policies dedicated to 'restoring to Japan a benefit society' to those carried on as a part of the public relations activities of companies and those cultural enterprises which were in themselves attempts to secure a profit. Large companies with limitless reserves of cash poured huge amounts of money into areas that were hitherto the province of small publishing companies and impoverished cultural bodies, so that the takeover of culture by firms was easily accomplished.

Especially noteworthy in the cultural activities of companies are the foundations. According to the series of articles in the *Asahi* newspaper referred to above, incorporated foundations in Japan numbered 10,209 as of April 1981. It was stated that foundations, set up by companies, whose permanent assets were more than one hundred million yen numbered 133. Of these, it was the Toyota Foundation that boasted the largest size with assets of eleven billion yen. It was set up in 1974 to mark the fortieth anniversary of the establishment of the Toyota Motor Corporation, and its chairman is Eiji Toyoda, who doubles as the President of the Toyota Motor Corporation. The futurologist Yujiro Hayashi, formerly a professor at Tokyo University of Technology, was headhunted to become its Representative Director. The core of its activities is to provide financial assistance for scholarly research, and it dispenses annually five hundred million yen. Oddly enough, it also provided financial assistance to Professor Hajime Nishimura who had earlier severely criticised pollution created by automobiles in his book *The Automobile Judged* (*Sabakareru Jidosha*),[1] and the group including Professor Daikichi Irokawa of the Tokyo University of Economics that carried out a comprehensive survey into the effects of Minamata disease. Hayashi stated that 'modern Foundations must constitute a pure third sector that is independent of companies too'.[2] The Toyota Foundation has its offices in a separate building from those of the automobile company, and it is said that its staff, too, are all different, with the exception of the managing executive who alone is on secondment from Toyota Automobiles. However, there is, for example, amongst the activities of the Foundation a programme called 'Let's get to know our neighbours' which is devised for the purpose of cultural exchange with the countries of South-East Asia. The *Asahi* newspaper wrote of this: 'When you take into account the fact that South-East Asia is a big export market for Japanese cars, and especially the fact that ten years ago the Thai movement to boycott Japanese products was extremely powerful, it (the programme) would also appear to suit the purposes of the sales strategy of the parent company (*Asahi*, 21 September 1982).

Other famous foundations are the Suntory foundation which invites famous overseas scholars to Japan and puts on symposia; the Mitsubishi Foundation formed jointly by the Mitsubishi group of firms; and also the Nihon Seimei (Japan Life Insurance) Foundation whose assets total 4.3 billion yen but which outstrips the Toyota Foundation with annual disbursements of six hundred million yen. All of these great foundations ought properly to be known as 'company foundations' and all had their assets supplied by companies. An 'anti-company' mood was strong in the country after the oil crisis of 1973 and there was a boom in the setting up of foundations as a measure to counteract this feeling. From this arose the large number of company foundations. But at the present time when the anti-company storm has receded, these foundations are active in a positive sense by shouldering the burden of companies' cultural strategies.

In the United States, which is the home of the foundation, there are 22,300 of them. With assets of 41.4 billion dollars and an annual disbursement in financial assistance of 2.8 billion dollars, they are incomparably larger than their Japanese equivalents. The Ford Foundation is the largest of them. The Rockefeller Foundation that vies with the Ford Foundation loses out to it when judged merely by size, but there are besides the Rockefeller Brothers Foundation, the Rockefeller Family Foundation and the J.D.R. 3rd Foundation, each respectively founded by the family. It is well known that, when it comes to funding, American cultural activities are maintained by these foundations. However, both were established as the gift of very rich individuals, the Ford Foundation by Henry Ford the First and the Rockefeller Foundation by J.D. Rockefeller the First, who as individual capitalists established them by gifting them with shares that they owned. It is said that, on the face of it, this is an espousal of philanthropy, and in carrying out the deed the individual capitalist is able to satisfy his philanthropic instinct; but in fact, it also simultaneously serves the same purpose as do holding companies and is used as a tax-avoidance strategy by the individual concerned. In practice, foundations that have become large share-owning enterprises are many, and data from the American Securities Exchange Commission shows that in 1981 foundations owned 32.9 billion dollars worth of shares, which came to 2 per cent of the total of all quoted shares in the United States.

In contrast to the fact that in the United States foundations are the result of gifts from individuals, in Japan most is the outcome of donations from companies. Herein lies a great difference. Individuals give to satisfy their philanthropic instincts; companies have no philanthropic instincts. The scholar of comparative culture Tohru Shiga says the following:

> When cultures passed through their pioneering stage and enlarged themselves quantitatively, from the earliest times there were always patrons. The aristocracy in the post renaissance west was such; and in Japan, the *daimyo* (feudal overlords) put money into art and took

artists under their wing so contributing to the development of culture. Rich companies are the aristocracy and the *daimyo* of the present day.[3]

Certainly it was always said that from ancient times what sustained culture and art was that it was the pleasure and the diversion of the rich and it cannot be gainsaid that whether it be the east or the west culture has been sustained by money of this sort. However, there is an essential difference between an individual giving money to provide for his amusement or to satisfy his philanthropic instinct, and a company becoming a sponsor of something. A company has no body and no mind, and it possesses no real philanthropic feelings. For a company as a 'juridical person' to sponsor cultural events implies that it will treat those events as something to manage and manipulate. On this point it differs from wealthy individuals and the aristocracy.

The 'companisation' of education

The 'companisation' of education is also proceeding at a rapid pace. A few years ago it was business organisations like the Japan Foreign Trade Council (Nippon Boeki Kyo-kai) and the Federation of Economic Organisations (Keizai Dantai Rengo-kai) that created the opportunity to exacerbate the school textbook problem. They raised the issue of accounts in middle school textbooks of social studies that were critical of companies, and went as far as to get them expunged from the textbooks. Afterwards, company intervention in education proceeded to the point where junior schoolteachers were invited to visit companies to receive instruction in their activities. Business organisations even came to intervene in the content of school education, and recently the Special Education Committee of the Japan Federation of Employers' Associations (Nihon Keieisha Dantai Rengokai) has taken up the problem of violence on school campuses. The report of the committee, on the Problem of Recent Violence on School Campuses (July 1983), states the following:

The Special Education Committee of the Association has, for some time, been studying current problems in school education and in company education and so forth, and has published the results in the form of proposals as the occasion demanded. On this occasion, over the course of the year or so since last March, it has been listening to the ideas of many sections of the intelligentsia, and in addition, conducting an examination of the actual facts of campus violence. The reason why we businessmen have taken up this problem is that the recent frequent occurrence of violent incidents, chiefly on the campuses of middle schools, is an exceedingly serious matter. Consequently, we are concerned that it will have considerable influence upon the social outlook and the outlook upon work of the pupils who will, in the future, bear the responsibility for our national industries, and therefore inevitably even upon the future destiny of our country.

On the question of the effects on the management of companies, the report had the following to say:

> From the point of view of company managers, too, we are anxious about the effects of campus violence and the misconduct of young people. One aim of school education is to teach people about the relationship between society and the individual, and a state of affairs where rules are ignored because of campus violence and where strength predominates must strike at the very roots of education of this kind. Nowadays when we are compelled to take notice of minute changes in the attitudes to work of new company recruits and the morale of current employees, for that very reason we would wish to treasure and uphold the diligence and group consciousness that has raised the Japanese economy to its present position. In this sense, too, it is important in school education that pupils be led to be able to form a correct view of society and of work.

In short, if nothing is done about campus violence amongst middle school pupils, it will eventually have an effect upon the attitudes to work of new company recruits and will work to the disadvantage of companies. Therefore, the business world has to remedy this, and by virtue of this it takes up the problem of the middle school students who are to be its future recruits.

The penetration of 'companism' has been even more intense in the case of the universities than with middle and high schools. It has been said for some time that the careers offices of universities are subcontracting organs of the personnel departments of companies, and that the universities themselves produce an education which is readily acceptable to large companies in order to improve their graduate placement record. In addition, there is open and large-scale cooperation between the universities and industry involving not only academics in the natural sciences but those in other fields too. We can say that the universities in their entirety are truly becoming sub-contractors to companies.

The abnormal growth of company consciousness

'Companism' permeates the whole of Japanese society, and everyone is inundated with knowledge and information to do with companies. In a bar, there is nothing but talk about what is happening to people in the company, and in bookshops there are mountains of books on 'company information' and 'company affairs'. The *Quarterly Company Reports* (*Kaisha Shiki-ho*) put out by the publishers Toyo Keizai Shinpo-sha sells in its hundreds of thousands and is said to be a goldmine for the company, and its close imitation, *Nikkei's Company Information* (*Nikkei Kaisha Joho*), first put out a few years ago by the Nihon Keizai Shimbun-sha company (Nikkei), is also a quarterly that sells in its hundreds of thousands. This is a phenomenon which is probably peculiar to Japan. In the United States there is also a company handbook, namely *Moody's* handbook published by the Moody company, but this is a publication aimed at specialists such as securities companies, institutional investors and analysts. It is expensive and one has never caught sight of it piled on the shelves of ordinary bookshops as its nearest equivalents are in Japan.

One after another a variety of books about companies are published in Japan in addition to the two mentioned above. For example, monographs on Toyota Automobiles or Matsushita Electric alone number in their dozens, and there are also on the market such instant 'Complete Company Collections' as *The Company Series* published by the Asahi Sonorama company. As well as introducing one to the company and its workings, they all tell how wonderful the company is, and they all make tedious reading. But, in times when books on economics are not selling, why are these companying potboilers alone pouring on to the market?

Still more thoroughgoing are the company guides put out as career guidebooks for university students. *Recruit Book* put out by the Japan Recruit Centre was first published in 1963 under the title *An Invitation to Companies* (*Kigyo e no Shotai*), and later amended to its present name. It is distributed free of charge to university students seeking employment, has regional editions for Tokyo, Osaka, Nagoya and Fukuoka, and it is said that the number printed each year is four million.

Depending on the target audience and the publishing company, there may be nineteen versions of the *Recruit* book, such as *Big*

Businesses in Japan, Research into Industry, Careers Information, Expanding Companies to Watch, and so on. Each volume is around one thousand pages in length, and they are delivered in rapid succession by special delivery to families who have in them university or high school students coming up to graduation. UPU, which was set up to rival the Japan Recruit Centre, also produces in large numbers a 'Company Guide' and distributes it to university students; furthermore a number of publishing companies have entered the field recently, so that career guides have swelled into a deluge.

As a result of all this, the knowledge that university students have about companies has become greater and greater. Even students who have no interest in the movement of the Japanese or the world economy, whose knowledge of such matters is trifling and who do not even read newspapers or journals, have an extraordinarily well-developed knowledge of the way companies rank against each other and of their capital value. Not just students but their families, and even housewives with no connection with students, know in detail such things as which companies are first-class and which are third-class, even though they may know little about anything else. To be of the section 'chief class' in a quoted company is to be made eligible for housing loans and to receive membership status with credit-card companies, so that a person's worth comes to be judged by the status of the company to which he belongs. Thus nothing but knowledge of companies is disseminated amongst those who will join the ranks of companies as well as those already employed by them, and even amongst those unconnected with companies, and information about professional baseball and about firms are the two subjects which enable the evening papers and the weekly magazines to prosper. This is the state of affairs in Japan, a state envisaged by Orwell in his novel *Nineteen Eighty-Four*.

2
The Logic of Corporate Capitalism

Organisations and people

> Those unseen monsters that we call organisations insert themselves in amongst human beings that are their slaves. They unjustly magnify the things that are useful to them, disgorge those things that are of no use to them and grow stronger and stronger as they trample things down around them.[4]

Sei Ito wrote this in 1953 in an essay called 'Organisations and People'. The organisations he had in mind at the time were states, political parties and the family, but at the same time he discussed along with them, as one form of organisation, the publishing companies that maintained the literary world. But it is unlikely that even the splendid Ito would have imagined at that time the present extent to which those organisations we know as companies have grown obese and have engulfed human beings. At the time Sei Ito was writing this essay Japan had not yet entered its period of rapid economic growth, and even at their zeniths, firms only ranked alongside various other organisations and by no means were they able to envelop the majority of Japanese. It was a few years after Ito wrote 'Organisations and People' that the system of 'companism' began to operate.

After Ito's essay, the subject was much discussed by writers and philosophers. However, if we discuss only the relationship between people and organisations in general, then the debate will necessarily remain at the conceptual level and will prove sterile. With the rapid growth of the Japanese economy after 1955, from amongst a great variety of organisations it was those we know as companies which alone grew enormous and enveloped the majority of people. Japanese writers were unable to grasp that fact. Despite Ito's pioneering work, the subject itself ended up as a barren one because of the failure of Japanese writers to come to grips with the organisation known as the company. It came at best to persist in the form of the 'company novel', far removed from the world of literature. These 'company novels' were unable either to deal with the great theme of 'organisations and people' or to explore the deeper aspects of the company itself.

What, then, is the organisation we know as the company or the firm? There are a variety of different organisations in the world, so why is it that the firm as an organisation has thus seized and engulfed so many people?

The first things that enter our minds when we think of organisations are the family, the village and then the country. Those who write about 'Japanese-style management' are apt to interpret the firm as an extension of the family and talk of 'managerial familism'. Or else they take the firm to be an extension of the village community. Regardless of the rights and wrongs of this approach, the fact is that those born into a family or a village or a country have no choice in the matter. This is fundamentally different from the case of the company. We cannot choose of our own volition to be born into a given family. We are born into a family or village or country irrespective of our wishes. To understand how difficult it is to try and escape from those roots, we have only to think of the works of the naturalist school of writers from the Meiji period onwards. They were truly tales of revolt against the family and the oppression it exerted. The situation was even more desperate when it came to breaking away from one's country, especially in a country like Japan from which to exile oneself was scarcely a possibility.

If we borrow the theory contained in Masao Maruyama's book[5] and look at it from the two perspectives of 'nature' and 'artifice', then the family, the village and the country are all 'natural' organisations and not 'artifices' constructed by the people born into them. By contrast, the school, the sports team, the trade union and the political party are 'artificial' organisations. We humans are not born company workers; still less are we born as workers in a particular company. Like the sports team and the political party, the company is an organisation that is constructed through the wishes of we human beings; or else we choose to enter a given company.

This being so, anyone at anytime can choose to go into a company, which is an 'artificial' as opposed to a 'natural' construct, and to that extent we would suppose it to be a 'soft' organisation (*yawarakai soshiki*). Like the sports team or the political party, if we come to dislike it we can leave it at will. Despite all this, why is it that the 'soft' organisation, which is the company, so completely envelops we humans? This is really the core subject of a theory of corporate capitalism.

Loyalty to the company

> Is it not true that, in all times and in all places, we can think of no organisation other than the limited liability company whose objective is the pure, self-interested pursuit of gain, and which has this aim endorsed both by society and its institutions?[6]

It was Moriaki Tsuchiya who wrote thus. It is certainly the case that we can think of no other organisation amongst the great variety that exist where the pursuit of profit is both the declared and the actual aim of that organisation. Assuming for the moment that universities and hospitals were well advanced towards becoming money-making organisations, they would still go to any lengths to deny this as their declared aim. However, the pursuit of private profit is, throughout, both the ostensible and the real aim of the company. So what does it mean when such profit-making organisations come so completely to dominate the lives of humans? This is where the fundamental question of Japanese corporate capitalism is to be found. It is not a question that can be dealt with by saying that the entire Japanese race is hell-bent on making money:

> The company has an existence of its own which is antagonistic towards the conscience and the freedom of thought of those who work for it. I believe that the broad tendency from now on will be for the prime movers within companies to be monster-like figures whose natural disposition in terms both of character and intellect will accord with the lifestyle of the company.[7]

Sei Ito wrote this in the essay that we referred to earlier. It has to be said that his prediction was splendidly accurate. The company-man is a person whose natural disposition melds with the lifestyle of the firm, and indeed this is required of him in order to live in a company society. People who are not of this kind will be excluded. The company as a mere 'juridical person' has no corporal existence and hence no emotions and no will. Thus there will be born within it no consciousness of sin or wrongdoing, nor any feeling of shame. However bad the things a company has done may be, since it knows no sin it cannot mete out punishment. In fact, under Japanese criminal law a juridical person does not possess the capacity to commit a crime. Even though it is clear that the 'juridical persons' that are companies sent people to their deaths as a result of their activities, as happened in the case of Minamata disease and other events involving chemical pollution, yet they incurred no punishment under the criminal law. The juridical person has no corporal existence, and if none, then it has no will and therefore no capacity to act. The failure to penalise companies was based on the interpretation that something with no capacity to act could not be supposed to have behaved criminally.

Thus no matter how badly a company behaves, it cannot be punished because it has no notion of wrongdoing. Of course, the company must take the responsibility defined by the commercial law and pay fines imposed, but any company-man involved in wrongdoing tends to lose his understanding of what constitutes it, if it is approved by the company. If an ordinary person were to cause another person to ingest agricultural chemicals, not only would this be a crime but that person would probably be tormented throughout his life by the knowledge of his crime. However, he will have no consciousness of having committed a crime if he had done it on behalf of his company. This is where the company-man differs from the ordinary person:

> The people who caused the incident did not do so out of self-interest or the prospect of gain. It was all done on behalf of the company, and it can be said that zeal in the performance of their duties was the cause of the incidents. Far from it bringing obloquy upon them from others in the company it aroused sympathy.[8]

These words were spoken in the final proceedings of the Lockheed – All Nippon Airways route case by the lawyer for the defendant Tokuji Wakasa. In the hearing that dealt with the six principals from ANA, besides the lawyers fees there were also the costs of the people included as part of the company presence who were there as bodyguards. Six days before the concluding remarks from the prosecution on the investigation, the defendant Wakasa said the following at a meeting of the managing directors of All Nippon Airways:

> With regard to the fact that I shall hear the summing-up of the prosecutor as the incumbent chairman of the board of this company, I confess I am utterly at a loss. Although I talked it over any number

of times with the president, the chief executives of the company, gathered together in this very room, exhorted us to go on, telling us not to resign and to stick it out. On that occasion, I said that I would sacrifice my very life for ANA. By sacrificing my life I mean that I am prepared to do anything for the sake of this company.[9]

The logic behind saying 'I am prepared to do anything for the sake of the company' implies a sense of values whereby everything done for the sake of the company is virtuous whilst things done not for the sake of the company are bad. Consequently, however severe the punishment received for doing something on behalf of the company, no consciousness of wrongdoing arises.

Such a notion can arise because the 'juridical person' that is the company is non-corporal and therefore an entity with no consciousness of wrongdoing; and persons who are natural human beings who unite themselves with the company become its personification. It is because they are indeed the 'human representation of the company'. It is because the logic of the 'juridical person' (the company) which is an abstract and non-human entity has enveloped natural human beings.

The notion that a 'juridical person' is a non-corporal entity further gives birth to the logic that 'the company is immortal'. Sankei Shimada, the executive director of Nissho Iwai Trading Company who committed suicide as a result of the Douglas-Graman affair by leaping from a building, wrote the following famous words in the note he left behind: 'The life of the company goes on forever. For that immortality we must sacrifice ourselves.' We refer to the joint stock company as a 'going concern'. The shareholders may change but it persists. Of course, in reality, companies do go bankrupt and break up; but logically, the company cannot die. As long as it is a non-corporal 'juridical person' only, a company cannot know death. Here it is different from a natural human being for whom death is unavoidable. To give up one's life for the company as an immortal entity that cannot know death and to pledge one's loyalty to it is to make that loyalty absolute and unconditional.

When one human being pledges loyalty to another, sentiment comes into the matter since it is inevitably a relationship between two flesh-and-blood people, and it often happens that loyalty turns into betrayal. As long as we are dealing with natural human beings with real bodies, this is unavoidable. However, when it comes to the loyalty of a natural human being towards a company, which is not flesh and blood and which logically cannot therefore know death, the relationship differs from that between flesh-and-blood people and eternal loyalty becomes a possibility. Betrayal may be inevitable between human beings, but there is no such thing as a 'Juridical person' betraying a real person. Thus, as long as the company man as a human being swears his fealty, this fealty will continue in perpetuity.

The logic of this loyalty towards the company gives rise, at the same time, to an aggressive attitude towards rival companies. Instigating feelings of hostility towards rival companies in order to cultivate loyalty towards one's own company is something that can be widely observed amongst Japanese firms. In the past, it was said that Yutaka Haniya's 'Kill or be killed: he is your enemy so kill him' was the guiding principle of all organisations. Amongst all organisations, it is the military which embodies this principle in its most extreme form:

> As each of us knows, the military is made up of three skillfully-combined elements: the guiding principle that there is your enemy so kill him; the absolute nature of the orders through which this principle is made capable of achievement; and the tightly-knit structure of rank instituted to maintain the absolute nature of these orders.[10]

Along with the military, it is the company that possesses these three elements. The principle of leadership, the absolute nature of commands, the tightly knit structure of rank, these are all indispensable in the modern company. The enemy for the company is its rival companies. To survive, the company must do battle with its rivals. Therefore the company employee unites with the company and fights to overcome its rivals, and this itself gradually increases his loyalty to the company. It is thanks to these principles of organisation that the company as *Gesellschaft* (an association pursuing benefit) which originally could not have anticipated becoming a community, has become a body that is fictitiously regarded as a community (*Gemeinshaft*). I shall deal in some detail in Part IV of this book with the question of the fierce inter-firm competition in Japan, and with how, on the other hand, firms combine and co-exist. The logic of this inter-firm competition is not that of the competition described in textbooks of economics. It is of a kind which, put strongly, would seem best described by the word 'combat' (*toso*).

'The status of the company' and 'the status of the human being'

When companies are battling one with another, then, naturally enough, differences arise amongst them. Then the 'rank' or 'status' of the company eventually determines the 'status' of the human beings associated with it. In no other country is the standing or the status of a company given as much emphasis as in Japan, and the rank-ordering of companies is a constant topic of discussion – whether a company is first, second or third class, whether or not it is quoted in the first rank of the stock exchange or unquoted, and so on. Moreover, this is not merely a matter of people's perceptions. There are real differences among companies. Wages are higher in first-class companies than in those of the second or third class. They also have more comprehensive and better company welfare systems. Productivity is higher in first-class companies, and there is a tendency for their labour forces to be more stable and less mobile. The interest rates on their bank borrowings are lower than they are for second- or third-class companies. When such is the case, it is unsurprising that people in general choose first-class companies before those in the second or third rank.

Rodney Clark in his book *The Japanese Company* has something interesting to say about this propensity in Japan to rank companies. He cites banks and the universities as strengthening the tendency to rank companies in this way. The higher the class of the company, the more ready are the banks to grant them favourable borrowing conditions and to lend them larger amounts. By contrast, firms of lower rank are charged higher rates and the amounts loaned are reduced in size. Having said that, there is also a clear rank-ordering in the case of banks, too, with the city banks at the top, then the regional banks and then the mutual banks and so forth:

> The effect of this hierarchy of banks on the gradation of industry is to reinforce a universal tendency of banks to favour big borrowers over small ones – other things being equal. The larger, national banks borrow money cheaply and lend it cheaply to large companies. The smaller banks pay more for their deposits and borrowings, and charge more to the small companies to which they lend. Even more important, the smaller the bank the less able it is to provide large loans to individual small customers; so that small enterprises have difficulty in raising money to buy new and expensive capital equipment in order to become big and more efficient.[11]

Furthermore, Clark has the following to say about the importance of the role of the universities in reinforcing the differences in rank amongst firms:

> Another set of institutions which contribute to industrial gradation in the same way as banks, by imposing on the mass of companies

their own hierarchical tendencies, are the universities, of which there are about four hundred. Just as bigger banks lend cheaply to bigger companies, 'better' universities send their graduates to 'better', and therefore usually bigger, companies. The Japanese education system is dominated by a handful of major universities, particularly the great state universities of Tokyo, Kyoto, Osaka, and Hokkaido. Entrance to these is by competitive examination, and is aspired to by large numbers of high school leavers. High schools which are notably successful at getting their pupils into these universities in turn attract many applicants from middle schools. Thus children are selected for and channelled towards the 'best' universities from an early age. It follows from this that a big firm, which is able to recruit from the University of Tokyo, is likely to get graduate entrants of a higher intellectual quality than a small firm which can only recruit from a little-known local university.[12]

It is a matter of judgement whether or not the employees of a firm that employs graduates from Tokyo University are of a better quality, but there is no doubting the fact that universities do play a role in reinforcing the stratification of companies.

Corporate capitalism is thus a society of hierarchy, and it is not organised in a form that will simply rank individuals in a hierarchy of higher and lower. The 'rank' of his company will also determine the 'rank' of the individual. On this point it differs from the status society (*mibun shakai*) of former times. In a status society, differences in the rank into which a person is born will determine what income he will command and what property he will possess. By contrast, in a society where corporate capitalism prevails, the 'rank' of the company will decide the 'rank' of the individual, and the value of a person will stem from whether within the company he holds the position of divisional chief or head of department or section head. This is what a hierarchical society is, but the nuclei of the hierarchy are its companies. At the same time, in such a society, function is 'status-ised' and the 'rank' of a person is not determined simply according to how capably that individual performs his function. Unlike in what we know as meritocracies, irrespective of whatever merits he or she may possess as an individual, the worth of a person must be measured according to his status given within the company. Or else that individual's capabilities are always and only measured in relation to his rank within the company.

3
The 'Companism' System

Japanese-style management

In the second half of the 1970s, a tendency to sing the praises of 'Japanese-style' management grew stronger both inside Japan and abroad. Everywhere one came to hear the assertions: 'Japan is powerful. The Japanese are superior.' Before that time, it had been the premodern aspects of Japanese-style management that had been the issue, and the thrust of the argument had been that it was because of this that Japan was 'a hopeless case'. At about that point came a complete turn-around, and the assertion began to be made that it was 'because of Japanese-style management that Japan excels'. There are peculiar circumstances which account for this great turn-about. After the oil crisis of 1973, the world economy was beset by 'stagflation' and all the advanced capitalist countries of Europe and North America suffered from both rapid inflation and high rates of unemployment. While this was occurring, Japan, too, was buffeted for a while by wild increases in prices. However, it soon overcame this problem, and was able to come through the second oil crisis with little adverse effect. Manufactured goods made by Japanese firms conquered world markets, and from this point on the image of Japan summed up in the words '*dame na Nihon*' ('hopeless Japan') gave way to an image summed up in the words *subarashii Nihon* ('wonderful Japan').

But this was not the whole of it. In one sense, it may be natural that, in the eyes of those looking at her from abroad, Japan's stock should rise, as she remained relatively stable while the rest of the world economy was beset by the problems of stagflation. However, the way the Japanese looked upon 'Japanese-style' management changed more dramatically than the way foreigners looked at Japan. In the earlier period

21

of rapid economic growth, Japanese-style management was referred to as backward and management required modernisation in order to catch up with the advanced countries of the world. Now, by contrast, after the oil crisis and in a period of slow economic growth, one became accustomed to hearing this same 'Japanese style' management being referred to as 'splendid'.

Influential in this was probably the effects of national revivalist and anti-foreign currents. These were of precisely the same character as the 'Japanism' and 'Japanist' ideology which were current during the militarist period in the early years of the Showa period which began in 1926. We should not forget the fact that these sorts of ideological factors were at work behind the great vogue for 'Japanese-style' management. However, most of the scholars of management and the commentators who were loud in praise of Japanese-style management were not conscious of these ideological factors, nor were they awake to their own role in the matter.

Theories of 'Japanese-style' management have their merits of course. Earlier management theory and economic theory concentrated on introduction of imported theories or on interpretations of classical theory. By contrast, the fact that the theory of Japanese-style management was forged on the basis of the actual facts concerning management in Japan was of considerable significance. As we all know, the three pillars of Japanese management are lifetime employment, seniority-based wages and company-based trade unions. It was a great achievement to have examined the evidence and studied how this system and these practices were formed and what role they played.

However, as the debate as to whether the organisational principles of 'Japanese-style' management were those of the family (*ie*) or the village (*mura*) became ever louder, research based on evidence gave way to the mere citing of illustrations. Eventually it developed into cultural anthropology, and in the final analysis it became part of the debate on Japanese 'uniqueness' (*Nihonjin-ron*). Thus it became popular to argue that the familistic notions of the Japanese, or else their village consciousness, were carried over into the company and became Japanese-style management. But if so, why was it only concerned with the company and why did it neglect other organisations – labour unions, political parties, or schools? There are many types of organisations in a society; nevertheless, they were not all based on the organisational principles of the Japanese-type family or village. So why was only the company discussed in that way? There is no consciousness amongst proponents of Japanese-style management. What we now need above all is not to discover the organisational principles of Japanese organisations in general, but how to find a way of handling the Japanese company.

The second point to make is that, originally, the theory of a 'Japanese style' of management emerged out of studies of Japanese types of labour and management practices and that these studies were more evidence-based than the sociology- or cultural anthropology-based theories of 'Japanese-type' management that laid stress on the family or the village. For that reason alone there is much that we can learn from them. However, since the bulk of these evidence-based studies was carried out by the Labour Problems Research Group of Tokyo University's Institute of Social Science, interest centred on the labour side alone. Although what they did was termed as being in the area of labour–management relations or labour–capital relations, no work at all was done on management or capital. In these studies, whether the 'management' in labour–management or the 'capital' in labour–capital relations referred to capitalists or to managers or even to the firm was left extremely vague. Therefore, research into labour–management relations was a very one-sided affair. The reality of the present cannot be explained by means of the classical concept of the capitalist. Then without clear notice, the term labour–capital relations was confused with and changed into labour–management relations. If so, who were the employers? In practice, it was with managers that the labour unions carried out their negotiations, and these managers were no more than the representatives of their companies. Thus when trying to grasp the idea of the employer, we have to take it as referring to managers and to the firms that form the background to their activities. Such a realisation is lacking amongst the researchers who gave us theories of 'Japanese-style' labour–management practices. The *sine qua non* for being able to deal with the concept of 'Japanese-style' management is to understand how to deal with the Japanese company.

Thirdly, although theories of Japanese-style management discussed relationships between employees and firms or relationships among employees within firms, firms are not merely constituted out of the relationships as such. Because most of the companies are joint-stock companies, we would naturally expect their relationships with their shareholders to be the first and foremost issue. As I shall describe in some detail later on, there are some exceedingly 'Japanese' features to be seen in these relationships that went completely unnoted and undealt with by the theorists of 'Japanese-style' management. Relationships between firms and their managers is another important subject, but none of the exponents of theories of 'Japanese-style' management deals with these directly. Furthermore, relationships with other companies are an important element in the day-to-day activities of firms. These, too, are not dealt with. Besides all these, research into the relationships between companies and society and between companies and the state is important for an understanding of firms. These viewpoints are completely absent in theories of 'Japanese-style' management.

Thus we have to conclude that theories of 'Japanese-style' management isolate only one facet of the Japanese company from a really narrow and limited point of view, and then propagate it in exaggerated fashion. What we now need to do is to discuss the relationships between firms and their shareholders, firms and their managers and those between firm and firm, and not just the relationships between firms and their employees. And then by also looking at the relationships between firms and society and firms and the state, we shall be able to grasp the company in its totality. That is to say, what we are really seeking is a complete theory of the Japanese-style firm or company; and in addition it is the attempt of this book to try and supply this need from the viewpoint of a theory of corporate capitalism.

Internalising into the company

As I have already stated, lifetime employment, seniority-based wage payments and company-based unions are the three pillars that support theories of 'Japanese-style' management. Formerly these were the accepted facts – the common sense – of these theories, but now a scholar of labour problems has appeared to challenge them. He is Professor Kazuo Koike, and he has challenged them by means of factual international comparisons published in his books.

Turning first to lifetime employment and looking at figures for the length of continuous service, we see that in Japan there is a smaller class of workers who are employed only for short periods in comparison with the countries of the European Community (EC). However, there is in the EC countries a rather larger class of workers employed continuously for long periods. Further, when we compare Japan and America, there is in the latter a larger category of workers who are employed for less than one year, but at the same time the category of workers employed continuously for fifteen years or more is larger in America than in Japan. Thus, in terms of comparisons of lengths of continuous service with one firm, Japan has fewer workers in the short-term category; but Europe and America have more workers in the category of those employed continuously for long periods of time, so that we cannot conclude that Japan is the country of 'lifetime' employment.

Why is this the case? There has been established in the United States a seniority system whereby workers who have only been employed for a short period of time are first in line when it comes to laying people off. In Western Europe too, although not to the extent of the United States, workers with long periods of continuous service are given protection. Therefore, in these countries, there are on the one hand many workers who are employed only for short periods, but there are also many with long periods of continuous service. In Japan, by contrast, since older workers are first in line even when 'voluntary' retirement is sought, it is this class of worker who bears the burden. Thus we are unable to say that Japan is the country of lifetime employment.

When we look at the second of the 'accepted facts' of Japanese-style management – seniority-based wage payments – we see that it is the case with Japanese blue-collar workers, but that this is not so in Western Europe. However, wages in Japan decline severely for blue-collar workers who have reached the later stages of their careers, and the fall is especially marked in large companies. On the other hand, both Japan and the countries of Western Europe operate systems of seniority wage payments for white-collar workers, but in Japan, white-collar workers, like blue-collar, experience a marked reduction in wages from their mid-fifties.

Thus, although systems of seniority wage payments are said to operate in Japan, they operate also for white-collar workers in Europe and America, so that all this means is that blue-collar workers in Japan are treated like their white-collar counterparts. On top of this, wages decline severely for older workers. The fact that blue-collar workers are treated like white-collar workers merely reveals that the differentials between manual and other kinds of labour have diminished – a marked feature of post-war Japanese experience. We should emphasise that this is a markedly Japanese characteristic that comes out in comparisons with Western Europe and the United States.

When we turn, thirdly, to company-based unions, we find that in the United States, too, it is the local unions that play the important role in actual negotiations with management, so that the power of union organisations based on the place of work is great. Furthermore, organisations of factory employees in West Germany (*Betriebsrat*) perform an important function, so that we cannot say that the company-based union is a feature of Japan alone.

Professor Koike asserted the above on the basis of factual surveys conducted in America, Europe and Japan, and so proved that what the exponents of theories of 'Japanese-style' management had hitherto insisted were peculiarly 'Japanese' could not necessarily be said to be so at all.

So, then, do management–labour relations in Japan have any distinctive feature? If the answer is yes, then what remains is the on-the-job training (OJT) that Professor Koike drew attention to. In Japan, workers are trained within the firm and it is there that their skills are formed. In Europe, vocational skills are acquired at the worker's own expense at technical schools and the like, but in Japan they are encompassed within the firm. Furthermore, Japan has labour markets that are internal to firms, and the relocation of labour takes place within the company. This is something which differs from the 'lay-offs' that firms in America resort to, and the distinctive feature that Japan exhibits is to be found in the internalising of labour markets within companies. What is meant here by internal labour markets are 'arrangements whereby there is a tendency for workers to stay in the company and obtain skill by taking OJT and to move to work within the company that pays higher wages'.[13]

When workers are incorporated or internalised into the firm in this fashion, the vicissitudes of the firm come to govern the destinies of the individual worker, and so it inevitably comes about that there is an increase in the worker's consciousness of (belonging to) the firm. In order to establish a system of internal promotion of this sort where the worker is incorporated into the firm, trained and enabled to succeed within it, first of all the firm has to be in a situation where it can offer long periods of continuous employment; and in addition to that, it has to develop stability in the markets for its products. Furthermore, the firm has to proceed with the internal division of labour for it to maintain its system of internal promotion, and on top of this the factory and the company has to increase in scale. Professor Koike tells us that the precondition for all these things to come about is that there must be an increase in the strength and ubiquity of monopoly capital.[14]

Thus the merit of Professor Koike's theory is not simply that he has challenged the orthodoxies of theories of 'Japanese-style' management, but that he has located the 'internalising of labour into the firm' at the heart of Japanese-style labour–management relations. In other words, is this not the onset of 'companism' in the relationship between companies and their employees?

As Professor Koike has said in respect of lifetime employment, whilst American firms have established the principle of 'last in first out' for their workers, Japanese firms are exceedingly fortunate in that they can require their older workers to opt for 'voluntary' severance. Younger workers are both low-waged and necessary for the firm, and the fact that there is a system in the United States for protecting older workers when lay-offs are imminent is the outcome of the victories achieved by workers through long years of union activity. Even though this may have brought about unemployment amongst younger workers and the increase in crime that this causes, it still has to be assessed as the product of the labour movement. In Japan, the labour movement has achieved no such result, a fact which has been extremely fortunate for its companies. In addition, the system that operates in Japan where workers take a sharp cut in wages from their middle fifties onward also places companies in a fortunate position. The reduction in the differentials between blue-collar and white-collar workers as the former become more like the latter is also useful in inculcating the notion of 'companism'. The reason for this is that where differentials are great there arise no feelings of oneness or unity amongst employees. The fact that under the electrical industry wage system and the 'market basket' formula for wages of the early post-war period wage differentials between white- and blue-collar workers markedly narrowed, and that this gave birth to 'company familism' in Japan, is a noteworthy feature of post-war history. Thus the system that was extremely favourable for companies was brought about by the 'internalising' of labour into firms and was, in other words, the system of 'companism'. We can, at the very least, say that a system of 'companism' became established in respect of the relationship between employees and their firms.

The utility of the fiction of the corporate person

Looking at the relationships between companies and their employees in the way we have done above, we are able to say that what was called 'Japanese-style' management is in fact a system of 'companism'. Therefore, what happens when we scrutinise the relationships between companies and their shareholders? This is a subject we shall look at more closely in Part II of this book, but to state the conclusion in advance, this too turns out to be a case of 'companism'. One often hears of 'management that is negligent of shareholders', mostly in the context of company entertainment expense accounts that are larger than the dividends companies pay. Phenomena such as these all stem from the fact that the relationship between companies and their shareholders has become one where 'companism' prevails. We shall look at relationships between companies and their managers in Part III, but since managers are the representatives of their companies and operate on the basis of 'companism', they are representatives neither of shareholders nor of employees. They represent 'the company and it alone' and managers are persons who are expressive of this fact. We shall look at relationships between firms in Part IV, and we shall conclude there that it is these relationships that make possible the system of 'companism' described above.

Relationships between companies and society also need to be studied, and especially those between companies and the state, but these are subjects in my future works. By way of a preparatory consideration, I shall here touch briefly on the question of the corporate tax system.

Ever since the Shoup recommendations of 1950, the Japanese corporate tax system has been built on the legal fiction of the corporation as a (juridical) person. By this is meant that 'a corporation is an assemblage of individuals got together to pursue a given undertaking'. It is based on the principle that the company as a 'juridical person' belongs to its shareholders and therefore it is appropriate to levy taxes on the profits that accrue to the company at the stage when they are received by shareholders in the form of dividends. Thus the company is not recognised as an independent object of taxation, and is no more than a convenience for purposes of collecting taxes due. That is to say, it is the same as a tax that is withheld at source, and ultimately all adjustments are made at the time when tax is assessed on the dividends shareholders receive. By very reason of this way of thinking, corporation tax has become a proportional tax levied at a uniform rate of 42 per cent (30 per cent for firms with a capital of eight million yen or less). Needless to say, the tax on the incomes of private individuals is a progressive tax and the rate of taxation increases along with increases in income. The reason why, in contrast to this, corporation tax was from the first not progressive was because of the presupposition that corporations had no need to pay taxes and that tax would be assessed only on the dividends shareholders would receive.

From the point of view of the corporation as a legal fiction, the dividends companies receive are non-taxable. The reason for this is that companies that receive dividends are assessed for taxation when they themselves pay dividends to their shareholders, so that to pay before that on the dividends they receive would amount to double taxation. Thus, as a rule, dividends paid to companies in Japan are non-taxable.

The idea of the corporation as a legal fiction which is the foundation of such a tax system, is based on the belief that the entire company is owned by its shareholders, and that there is nothing belonging to the company itself separate from its shareholders. However, the major premise upon which this notion is based is that shareholders are each and every one natural living persons. In theory, there is no such thing as the corporate shareholder; and even assuming there were, if we were to retrace our steps from the corporate shareholder to its shareholders, we would ultimately arrive at a shareholder who is a natural living person, and it is there that taxes are to be levied on dividends received. If this were not to be the case, the notion of the corporation as a legal fiction would not stand. But in Japan something occurs which is in complete contradiction to this. Private shareholders of Japan's top quoted companies own less than 30 per cent of the total of shares in these companies. Therefore, from the standpoint of the notion of the corporation as a legal fiction, these private shareholders who own less than 30 per cent of shares must be liable for the whole of the taxes payable on the profits made by Japan's listed companies. Can one conceive of such an irrational state of affairs! But if one follows the notion of the corporation as a legal fiction to its logical conclusion, it is there that we must arrive.

Next, a curious thing happens because of the idea that dividends received by companies are non-taxable. Let us assume that there is 100 per cent mutual shareholding; that is, the total shares issued by all companies together are owned by companies. In such an eventuality, all dividends received are non-taxable, so the result is that no one pays any tax on the profits that companies make. In reality, corporation tax is to be paid at source; but since there are no natural living persons around who would ultimately be expected to conclude the process by paying progressive taxes, the base for the corporation tax disappears.

Of course, there is no basis in reality for the assumption that all shares are owned by companies. However, the idea of the corporation as a legal fiction where all shares are owned by living persons is even further removed from reality. Above all else, the assumption that the profits of companies accrue only to the private shareholders who own less than 30 per cent of the shares means that, however much tax private shareholders pay, they cannot pay all that is due. The contradictions that bedevil Japan's corporate tax system as a result of the position it adopts on the corporation, as a legal fiction, has been investigated by the 1968 Report of the Tax Commission. It said:

> Taking into account the realities of contemporary society and the economy where the ownership of companies and their management have become separated; and on the basis of the notion that it is

appropriate to recognise corporation tax not as advance payment of the income tax levied on private shareholders but as a burden on companies themselves, we should adopt what might be called a profits tax formula and adjust the tax burden between corporation tax on dividends and income tax.

It then proposed the so-called profit tax formula. However, this idea was not implemented; and above all, in the debate on the notion of 'managerial control' where ownership and management are separate, no notice at all was taken of the problem of the decline of the private shareholder that I explained above.

Thereafter, the phenomenon of 'corporatisation' grew apace in regard to ownership of shares and there was a great decline in the proportion of shares held by private shareholders, so that now the irrationality of the idea of the company as a legal fiction that I have just described is abundantly clear to everyone. But the surprising thing is that, as it has become clear that it contradicts reality, so, conversely, has the proposition formerly made by the Tax Commission ceased to command attention. At the time when restructuring the public finances became an important issue, the Tax Commission set up a Sub-Committee on Company Taxation in order to examine corporate taxation. Its conclusions were gathered together in a report published in 1979. One of its conclusions was that: 'It is appropriate for the present to maintain the existing basic framework of the corporate tax system.' It avoided taking issue with the essential problem of what does constitute a corporation tax by stating that 'we can ill-afford mischievously to add to this sterile debate'.

It goes without saying that the fundamental problem with corporate taxation to which we here allude is whether the corporation actually exists, or whether it is a legal fiction only. The Report of the Sub-Committee on Company Taxation referred to this question as follows:

If we look at the reality of the activities that corporations perform in society, there can be no doubting the fact that they carry on economic activities and achieve results as entities quite separate and independent from their shareholders. However, at the same time we have the feature that the income from the economic activities of the corporation is distributed among their shareholders in the form of dividends and so on. Furthermore, we have to admit that this is the raison d'être of the company form of the corporation. It may be imagined that it will always be difficult to give a single, clear-cut proposition which says that the corporation is either real or a legal fiction in the case of an entity which has dual aspects.

Thus was the question of the basis of corporation tax avoided. But we should not be prepared to carry on with the idea of the corporation as a legal fiction merely because the idea of the corporation as a real entity is also a little strange. In short, the report disposes of the problem by stating that although its compilers do not understand the fundamentals of the problem it would make no sense to discuss it further. On top of that, they take the defiant stance that the present corporation tax system is the proper one. Thereafter, the big political problem became the increase in personal income tax and the introduction of a consumption tax, and no one paid any further attention to corporation taxation.

Now it goes without saying that the present system of corporation taxation that the Sub-Committee on Company Taxation of the Tax Commission takes to be fundamentally correct, based as it is on the notion of the corporation as a legal fiction, is extremely favourable towards companies. There is no end to the advantages that we can cite: the slight proportional rate at which it is levied; the system whereby various categories of undistributed reserves are exempt from tax; the light taxation of dividends; the system of non-inclusion of profits on dividends received. In Japan, even very tiny firms are classified as 'juridical persons' and because of their inclusion as company organisations, the number of companies amounts to some two million. Since the tax system advantages companies, this means that they are flooded with special privileges. The origin of this, as scholars of commercial law point out, is not that there is a problem over tiny firms organising themselves like limited liability companies even though they do not have the form of the joint stock company. The reason is to be found in the corporation tax system itself which is so 'company-centred'.

Notes to Part I (Chapters 1–3)

1   H. Nishimura, *The automobile Judged* (Sabakareru Jidosha) (in Japanese), Chuokoron-sha, 1976.
2   *Asahi Janaru* (*Asahi Journal*), 6 January 1981, pp. 12–13.
3   *Asahi Shimbun* (*The Asahi Newspaper*), 6 October 1982.
4   Sei Ito, *Understanding the Novel* (in Japanese), Kawade Shobo, 1955, p. 202.
5   M. Maruyama, *Study of the History of Political Thought in Japan* (in Japanese), Tokyo Daigaku Shuppan-kai, 1952.

6   M. Tsuchiya, *The Social Responsibilities of Firms* (in Japanese), Zeimu Keiri Kyokai, 1980, p. 13.
7   Ito, *Understanding the Novel*, p. 197.
8   *Asahi Shimbun-sha*, economic section, 'Japan Inc: A Diagnosis' (in Japanese), 1981, p. 10 ff.
9   Ibid, pp. 10–11.
10 Yutaka Haniya, *Politics in the Midst of an Hallucination* (in Japanese), Miraisha, 1963, p. 132.
11 Rodney Clark, *The Japanese Company*, Yale University Press, 1979, p. 71.
12 Ibid, p. 34.
13 Kazuo Koike, *Workers' Participation in Management* (in Japanese), Nihon Hyoronsha, 1977, p. 13.
14 Kazuo Koike, *Factory-Based Trade Unions and Participation* (in Japanese), Toyo Keizai Shimpo-sha, 1978.

Part II
The Japanese Company

4
The 'Corporatisation' of Shareownership

The dispersal of the private shareholder

After the Second World War, in the 1950s and 1960s, it become fashionable to discuss whether or not capitalism had changed, calling the debate 'the theory of contemporary capitalism'. What was said was that capitalism had now conquered its crises, that the theme had changed from the business cycle to that of economic growth, that incomes had been equalised and that the 'affluent society' had arrived. This argument was popular in Western Europe and Japan as well as in the United States, and what was cited as a major underpinning for the idea that capitalism had changed was the arrival of what was known as 'people's capitalism'. In concrete terms, this referred to the fact that shares were widely dispersed and that large numbers of ordinary people had become shareowners and thus capitalists. In Japan, too, through the dissolution of the *zaibatsu*, a large number of shares had been confiscated from *zaibatsu* families and from holding companies and released and dispersed into the hands of the masses. The idea was that through the dispersal of shares and the mass of people becoming capitalists, capitalism itself had changed.

However, the situation changed greatly from about the middle of the 1960s. The Survey of Shareownership by the Stock Exchange shows this more clearly than anything else. The proportion of all shares owned by private individuals, which had formerly stood at more than 60 per cent, now began to fall rapidly towards the 20 per cent mark. This is nothing other than a denial of the fact of 'people's capitalism'. Now no longer can anyone say that the mass of ordinary folk are capitalists.

Nor did this simply signify the failure of the 'theory of contemporary capitalism' or the denial of the idea of 'people's capitalism'. At a more basic level, it signified a crisis in the joint stock company system itself, which we should recognise as the very foundations of capitalism. Or else it signified a heightened recognition that the Japanese joint stock company was a defective product. It is customary for the Prime Minister to address the annual Securities Congress (*Shoken Taikai*), where it is also customary for him to say that 'the decline of the private shareholder is a grave problem, and it is the duty of those in the securities industry to foster the private shareholder'. The chief subject of debate in the Securities Bureau of the Ministry of Finance is the problem of the private shareholder, and it is the one problem over which they have absolutely no control. Thus, whilst on the one hand it is extremely fashionable to argue that 'the "Japanese-style" of management is magnificent, and Japanese firms are superior – summe cum laude as it were', we also hear in direct contradistinction to this that 'the Japanese joint stock company is a deficient product, and Japanese companies are the despair of the private shareholder'.

In one way, the decline in the proportion of shares owned by private shareholders is a worldwide trend. In that sense, we can say that it is a retrogression from the erstwhile idea of 'contemporary' or 'people's capitalism'. However, it is not a retrogression in the sense that the ownership of shares by the mass of ordinary people that came about after a time when the bulk of shares were owned by a few, large private shareholders has, in turn, been replaced by a state of affairs where shares have reconcentrated in the hands of a small number of large private shareholders. We can say what has happened represents a reversal of the trend away from the dispersal of shareownership towards its concentration, but the nature of the reconcentration is different from before. Here there is a difference between the reconcentration of shareownership in Japan on the one hand and the United States and Britain on the other. In Japan, it is a concentration of shares in the hands of corporations. In the United States and Britain and elsewhere, it is concentration in the hands of certain institutions. As we shall see in detail later, institutional ownership is a kind of indirect investment by private individuals, and not something entirely divorced from the private ownership of shares. Against this, corporate ownership is quite separate from private ownership, and is ownership by banks and other companies by and for themselves.

Thus, in Japan the decline in the proportion of shares owned by private individuals has occurred because the proportion owned by corporations has increased. This is the origin of the problem. Up to the present, a number of reasons have been adduced as the cause of the dispersal of the private shareholder: for example, a falling-off in the attraction of investing in shares, problems with the tax system, the business stance of the securities companies, and so on. However, the basic cause lies in the increase in the corporate ownership of shares. Originally, the objective criterion for investing in shares for the private investor was the dividend yield. Shares were bought because, in comparison with the interest rate on deposits or the yield on bonds, the yield on shares was believed likely to prove better. In such a case, the criteria for judging came to be not only the present yield, but also the anticipated future yield which took into account the likelihood of a firm to grow. Thus was born the idea of the growth share, and in respect of that, too, there was the objective criterion of yield that is calculable. However, as I shall explain later, corporations do not acquire shares on the basis of a calculation of their yields. They acquire them as a means of control in their linkages with various other firms. There is a fundamental difference between the value of shares acquired for profit and those acquired for purposes of control. In concrete terms, corporations eschew the calculation of yields when acquiring shares for the purpose of strengthening their *keiretsu* relationships with other firms or their relationships with other firms within their group. As a result, share prices rise through 'corporate buying' and go outside the range indicated by the yield calculations made by private investors. Thereupon the private investor divests himself of shares that are no longer a profitable means of saving and finds himself other more advantageous outlets for his invest-worthy funds. At the same time, those private investors who remain come to deal in the shares they hold for reasons other than what the yield criterion tells them, only with the aim of profiting from the increase in their prices. Thus on the one hand, the private investor is squeezed out, while on the other, those who remain become pure speculators and turn over their shares very rapidly. As a result the market for shares in Japan has become a speculative market, reduced to a gambling joint rather than a bastion of 'people's capitalism'.

The phenomenon of 'corporatisation'

The Survey of Shareownership shows the changes in the proportions held by different categories of owners of the shares of all first-rank quoted companies in Japan. In 1989, the combined total of shares owned by financial institutions and ordinary businesses reached 67.1 per cent of the whole. This concentration of the ownership of shares in the hands of financial institutions and ordinary firms – manufacturing and others – is what is meant by the phrase the 'phenomenon of the corporatisation of shareownership'. However, life insurance companies are included amongst financial institutions whereas, strictly speaking, they should be excluded. Life insurance companies make use of the assets deposited with them by policyholders to buy shares and bonds, and the profits made by using these assets in this way must revert to the policyholders. In this respect, life insurance companies merely make use of their assets as proxies for policyholders. Thus within these limits, life insurance companies should be regarded as institutional investors like investment trusts, and indeed in the United States it is so stipulated. However, in the case of institutional investors, the aim above all else is to produce the best results possible from the use of their assets in order to make profits for their beneficiaries, and the fruits of their efforts must revert to these beneficiaries. However, when one examines the makeup of shareownership by Japanese life insurance companies, it appears that most shares are owned with the objective of securing profitable loans made by the insurance companies; or they are bought with the aim of securing pension funds or group insurances rather than with the aim of producing the best returns through the purchase of shares. There is also the related objective of strengthening the ties that bind the *keiretsu* or group to which they belong, and thus the pattern of ownership (the mix of shares in their portfolios) is rigid. Furthermore, they do not often return the fruits of their shareholding operations to their policyholders. Since they own shares with the same aims as the banks and other institutions, we should not refer to them as institutional investors but as 'pseudo-institutional investors'. Therefore the fact of the matter is that life insurance companies in Japan are best thought of as corporate shareholders rather than as institutional investors. The situation is the same with regard to non-life insurance companies that deal with fire, damage, theft and so on. About the only institutional investors in Japan that behave as institutional investors are supposed to, are the investment trusts.

Next, in those organisations classified as ordinary, that is to say, non-financial corporations, it is said that there are a good many individual managers of small or medium-size firms and others who, while really owning shares themselves, have them nominally held in the name of their company for purposes of tax avoidance and so on. Strictly speaking, these cases ought to be treated as shareownership by private individuals; but since we cannot know the true state of affairs regarding such cases, we have no recourse but to classify them here as a part of corporate shareownership.

If we look at the figures for shareownership by corporations, we see that the number of shares so owned was small shortly after the end of the war, as was the proportion of the total of shares. The reasons for this were that the shares held by holding companies were dispersed into private ownership in the process of dissolving the *zaibatsu*, and holding companies were made illegal with the passage of the Anti-Monopoly Law in 1947. Shareownership by ordinary non-financial corporations was also, in principle, forbidden, whilst financial institutions were permitted to own only up to 5 per cent of the shares issued by any given company. Thus the restrictions on corporate shareowning were severe. However, the shares released in the process of *zaibatsu* dissolution did not pass directly into the hands of private investors. Although the shares of the issuing companies were nominally passed over to the officials and employees of those companies, we may suppose that in actual fact a good many of them were owned by the firms themselves as own shares (*jisha kabu*).

It was in the first half of the 1950s that the concentration of shares in the hands of corporations first increased noticeably, when the opportunity to acquire was presented to corporations through the relaxation of the restrictions on shareownership by financial institutions and by ordinary non-financial firms as a result of the amendment of the Anti-Monopoly Law. This stage saw, on the one hand, the reconstitution of the *zaibatsu* in the form of company groupings (*kigyo shudan*). On the other hand, it was the period when the setting up of *keiretsu* linkages by large firms was taking place, so that overall it was a time when the monopolisation of Japanese capitalism was proceeding apace. In conformity with this trend, the concentration of shareownership in corporate hands was also happening, and as a result there was a strengthening in the linkages amongst corporations.

The second stage of reconcentration took place between the middle of the 1960s and the 1970s. In response to the liberalisation of capital that was proceeding at that time, the strategy of the 'stable shareholder' was adopted (that is, having a substantial proportion of the issued shares of a company held on a long-term basis by corporate shareholders who were 'friendly' towards that company). This was the stage when there occurred a further strengthening in the ties that bound groups of firms which had been part of the former *zaibatsu* and when the three large new company groupings based on the Fuji Bank (Fuyo group), the Dai-ichi Kangyo Bank and the Sanwa Bank were growing stronger, which together brought about a further concentration of shareownership in corporate hands. Thereafter, with the oil 'crisis' of 1973, overall 'corporatisation' marked time and did not proceed ahead. But nor was there any retreat. During this time, there was a change in the composition of corporate shareownership in that the proportion of shares held by ordinary, non-financial companies fell, whilst the decline was counterbalanced by a similar increase in the proportion held by financial institutions. But taken overall, the 'phenomenon of corporatisation' has been built into the structure of the economy, and one sees no indication at all that it will be eradicated.

The significance of companies owning shares in companies

At the time when Japan imported American-style anti-trust legislation and passed its Anti-Monopoly Law, the drafter of the Bill, Ryogo Hashimoto (then Chief of the Corporations Section of the Fiscal and Money Bureau of the Economic Stabilisation Office), said the following:

> The stipulations of Clause 10 (those which forbade in principle the owning by ordinary, non-financial corporations of equity shares in other corporations) are the most important and influential of all those in the Bill. Since we are so accustomed to the system of company law we have had since the Meiji period, we think of the acquisition of shares in a company by another company as entirely natural. However, this is a system that has significant advantages and disadvantages, and we must first of all fully comprehend the purport of the enactment of this legislation. The Report of the Edwards Special Study Group referred to earlier touches on the subject of Japanese company law; but I believe that the probable heart of the problem is the system whereby companies acquire shares in other companies.[1]

As Hashimoto commented, it has been regarded as perfectly natural in Japan since pre-war times that companies should hold shares in other companies. But from the point of view of the principles of the limited liability company, it is proper to consider the holding of shares in a company by another company as irrational. In the United States it was originally prohibited. However, the acquisition and retention of shares in a company by another company was first recognised in the company law enacted by the state of New Jersey in 1888, and similar regulations were introduced thereafter in state law in Delaware and elsewhere. As is well known, this created a boom in the setting-up of holding companies in the United States, and made possible the first merger movement. The ownership of shares in a company by another company renders possible what is known as securities subrogation (*shoken dai-i*). Suppose there is a company A with a capital of one hundred million yen. If we also suppose that company B owns 51 per cent of the equity capital of company A and further suppose that company C owns 51 per cent of the equity of company B, the majority shareholder of the equity shares of company C can, by virtue of this fact, control both company A and company B. The rights as shareholders of those who own shares in companies A and B are thus impaired. Through the owning of the shares of a company by another company, the rights of the shareholders who were the original investors in – that is, suppliers of capital to – the company are invaded.

I have already discussed the fact that since taxation law in Japan is based on the fiction of the corporate person, and since the fiction of the corporate person was originally based on the premise that all shareholders are natural living persons, the result is irrational outcomes when shareholders are in fact corporations. On the one hand to accept the fiction of the corporate person on the premise that all shareholders are natural living persons, and then to approve the ownership of shares by corporations in contradiction to this, in fact accelerates the onset of 'companism'. Herein lies a fundamental problem.

The reason why corporations own shares is as a means of control with respect to the linkages among firms. Of course there are also cases where the incidental objective is to profit from selling off the shares at a higher price, but the fundamental purpose of ownership is to have them as an instrument of control. Let us assume that, in general, the fundamental characteristic of shareownership has two aspects to it: namely, securities held for purposes of profit and securities held for purposes of control. There are in addition the speculative and the material aspects, but these are incidental or else of a secondary order of importance. But what is generally said of the ownership of shares by corporations is that it is done in order to intensify relations with organisations with whom the owning firm already has a transaction relationship; or else owning shares in another company becomes a way of establishing an association with it, as it plays the same role as the normal exchange of name cards! However, it is important to ask why it is necessary to own shares in a company in order to conduct transactions with it or to establish a connection with it, and to address this question at the theoretical level. Shares have no aspects that can be described as 'transactions' characteristics or 'getting to know you' characteristics. Holding shares in another company in order to have commercial dealings with it amounts to owning shares in that company in order to exert over it a certain influence by that means. That is to say, it owns shares in a company for purposes of control (to be referred to hereinafter as control securities – *shihai shoken*). I would prefer here to think of control in the broad sense as meaning 'through one's wishes or commands to regulate or restrain the conduct or arrangements of another organisation'.

Thus, owning shares as control securities creates stronger linkages among firms and strengthens monopoly type arrangements among them. For these very reasons, the ownership of shares by corporations is closely restricted in the United States by the anti-trust laws, and regulation of corporate shareownership was included in the Japanese anti-monopoly law. There are scholars who insist that the ownership of shares by Japanese corporations is unrelated to the desire for control over companies. These are people who do not see the true state of affairs, and who have no understanding whatever of why it is that anti-trust and anti-monopoly laws regulate such conduct.

Mutual shareownership

Ownership of shares by corporations takes two forms: unilateral or one-way ownership, and mutual ownership. Where a parent company owns shares in a subsidiary or affiliated company, unilateral ownership is the norm, and in general this corresponds with a *keiretsu* (chain form) relationship among firms. By contrast, there are also cases where large firms mutually own each other's shares. This we know as mutual shareownership (*sogo mochiai*), and it is noteworthy as a form of ownership which is characteristic of Japan. A simple case of mutual ownership is one where company A owns shares in company B whilst company B likewise owns shares in company A. In addition, there is mutual ownership of the pattern A B C…A, and the matrix pattern characterises the company groupings where firms within the grouping hold shares in each other. And then there is the radial pattern of mutual ownership that occurs with firms independent of *keiretsu* or groupings.

If we take the Mitsubishi Group as an example of a company grouping, as we see from Mitsubishi Heavy Industry's holding of 3.46 per cent of the shares of Mitsubishi Bank, its 1.91 per cent holding of the shares of Tokyo Marine and Fire Insurance Company, its 3.85 holding of those of Mitsubishi Trading Corporation and its 1.99 holding of those of Mitsubishi Electrical Machinery Corporation, firms own only a few per cent at most of the shares of each of the other firms in the group. We cannot say that Mitsubishi Heavy Industry controlled each of these companies with only that proportion of their shares in its hands. But like Mitsubishi Heavy Industry, other companies in the group are major shareholders in the firms named, and if one totals up the shares in these companies owned by all Mitsubishi Group members, the proportion of the shares in one particular member company owned within the group would come to several tens of per cent. Thus Mitsubishi Group companies own an average of 29 per cent of the shares of each member of the Mitsubishi Group, and we can say that all of them together easily exert a controlling interest as the major shareholder. Therefore the meeting of the presidents of the companies in the Mitsubishi Group, known as the Friday Club, *de facto* performs the function of a meeting of their major shareholders in respect of each of the firms in the group.

Individual companies acting on their own cannot exert a decisive right of control. However, when they are assembled together as a group of firms, they are able to exert such power of control by virtue of their status as major shareholder. Moreover, an important point is that the companies who are holding these shares simultaneously have their own shares held by the same set of companies, so that amongst the group members who are exercising control there are also included some that have control exercised over them. In that sense, mutual control is being exercised.

If we look at the major shareholders in Japan's large companies, we find that corporate shareholders do not, individually, own all that large a proportion of the shares of any given company. The general pattern is that large corporate shareholders vie one with another, so that when totalled, the proportion of a company's shares held by the largest ten or twenty corporate shareholders is indeed great. The outcome is that, if these large corporate shareholders were to oppose one another, no single one would be able to exercise control. But if they were to contend amongst themselves, there would be no point in these major shareholders owning shares as instruments of control (control securities). Therefore, a sort of tacit arrangement is reached among the major shareholders by means of which they protect their controlling authority as a collective. Scott refers to this state of affairs as 'control through a constellation of interests',[2] and when we further invoke this logic in the case of mutual shareholding, it is applicable to the case of the independent large firm with no group ties where there is no coordination among its major shareholders. In the case of a group of companies, coordination takes place at the level of the meeting of company presidents, but the cases are the same in that they both involve mutual shareholding by corporations.

In concrete terms, the annual shareholders' meetings of large Japanese companies are set up by power of proxy of the major corporate shareholders, and there are scarcely any instances of them opposing the measures introduced by the company. But there does exist a tacit arrangement amongst the major corporate shareholders, so that if the company's results were to slump, or if the managers were to provoke a scandal, then the major corporate shareholders acting in concert would get rid of them.

In contrast to the company grouping where mutual ownership is in the form of a circular loop, the independent large firm goes in for the radial type of mutual ownership where company A owns and is owned by companies B, C, D, ... but where it is generally the case that no relationship of mutual ownership exists between B, C and D. To that extent the individual firms involved are strongly independent, but looked at from the point of view that tacit arrangements can be made among the major shareholders, the logic of the case is no different from that explained above. In the majority of cases, the companies that have a relationship of mutual shareownership with the independent firm are themselves members of company groupings. Furthermore, there are also instances where companies who are 'independent' of company groupings own shares in each other. In this manner, large firms in Japan are able to link directly or indirectly one with another by means of the ownership of each other's shares. It is on top of this structure that the world of finance and business representing total capital is formed.

Institutional ownership and corporate ownership

In the United States after the Second World War, ownership of shares by institutional investors increased, so that a state of affairs arose where 70 per cent of the sales turnover in shares on the New York Stock Exchange was accounted for by trading by institutional investors. According to a survey by the United States Securities and Exchange Commission, in 1980 the proportion of all shares owned by institutional investors came to 33.05 per cent. Institutional investor here refers to pension funds, life insurance funds and investment trusts, etc., while in addition to these the trust departments of banks are also included as institutional investors. The trust departments of banks are entrusted with the management of the assets of pension funds and private individuals, and they do so through share operations. Pension funds, life insurance funds and investment trusts as well as the trust departments of banks all work on behalf of the real owners (beneficiaries), and conduct their share operations with the assets of the beneficiaries; they themselves have no shares as assets of their own. Therefore, they have to manipulate these assets with the interests of the beneficiaries foremost in their minds. So, when we look at the circumstances of shareownership by institutional investors, we see that they constantly shift between the shares of different companies and there are few instances where they continue to hold the same shares for five or ten years. Looking at the turnover rate for shares, we see that it is higher for institutional investors than for private individuals.

By contrast, Japanese corporations do not manipulate assets as a proxy for and for the profit of beneficiaries. They own shares simply as assets of their own. Moreover, the objective is not to earn dividends or to reap capital gains; it is to own shares in their role as control securities in order to strengthen linkages among firms. Even in the United States ordinary non-financial companies own shares for their potential as control shares, and if the calculation is made in the same way as it is in Japan, they make up about 15 per cent as a proportion of all outstanding shares in the United States. Naturally in America, too, we cannot say that the owners of these shares are institutional investors. They are frequently the recipient of anti-merger regulation under the Clayton Act, and the ownership of shares by corporations is regarded as partial merger and, as such, controlled. This is because it is clearly ownership for the sake of the control of a company. Furthermore, commercial banks in the United States are forbidden to own shares, a situation very different from that which pertains in Japan. American commercial banks are only allowed to own shares as trust property (*shintaku zaisan*).

It was in these circumstances that the relationship between the ownership of shares by institutional investors – chiefly the trust departments of banks – and the control of companies became an important issue. The problem was taken up in 1960s by the Patman Committee of Congress, and a massive report was published. In addition, there was also published the later report of the Metcalf Committee. From these reports it was clear that the trust departments of banks, and in particular those of the great New York banks, owned large quantities of shares in large companies. At the same time, it was apparent that directors of these banks also held directorships with the companies whose shares they owned (overlapping directorates).

Thus, it was asserted either that the trust departments of the banks were exercising control over companies by holding shares in them; or else they were exercising a certain influence over them. Besides the arguments in repudiation from the American Bankers' Association, even among scholars the debate centres on the problems associated with the control over companies by banks. It is asserted by those who oppose the view that banks exercise control that a 'Great Wall of China' stands between the trust departments of banks and the banks proper, and that neither information nor personnel pass between them; and also that, due to the existence of a trust agreement, trust departments deal in shares in such a way that the interests of the consignor always take precedence.

There is no way of knowing whether or not the trust departments of banks do exercise control over firms by owning shares in them other than by appealing to the factual evidence on the matter; but one may well imagine that they do exert an influence in their capacity as major shareholders. At the same time, however, we have to remember that they are unable to hold an unchanged mix of shares over a long period of time. For shares to become 'control securities' – that is, instruments of control – it is necessary that they should remain in the portfolio unchanged over long periods of time, and there are limits on the ability of institutional investors in the United States to behave in this way.

By contrast, from the very outset Japanese companies hold a little-changing mix of shares for long periods of time for purposes of control, and the rate of turnover on these shares is extremely low. This clearly confirms the fact that the object of corporate ownership of shares is control over companies. However, on this point the case against institutional shareholders is not conclusive and we must make a clear distinction between corporate ownership and institutional ownership in this respect.

However, when the trust departments of American banks exert a controlling influence over companies by means of owning shares in those companies, in concrete terms the managers of the banks are not doing so with shares that they themselves own, but through the use of shares owned by other people. By the same token, when Japanese corporations own shares, it is the managers who represent these corporations that exert control over other companies. Here, too, control is exerted not by means of the shares they themselves own but by the use of shares owned by another party. Thus, corporate shareownership and institutional shareownership are the same in that both involve control by managers on the basis of shares owned by another party. It may be that we should refer to this as 'the usurpation of ownership'. However, there is the distinction that, in the case of corporate ownership, the other party is the corporation, whilst in the case of institutional ownership, the other parties are private individuals. Such is the thoroughgoing nature of shareownership by corporations, and in this respect institutional ownership is, by comparison, less far-reaching and comprehensive. Put differently, in the case of institutional shareownership, there is a kind of dualism in that shares held for the purpose of profit also perform the function of instruments of control securities. In contrast to this, we can say that corporate shareownership is more thoroughgoing and conclusive in that, from the very outset, shares are held only as instruments of control.

5
Dividends and Share Prices

The erosion of dividends

The joint stock company is part of a system where companies gather together the invested monies of their shareholders, set them to work as capital and return the profits thus obtained to the shareholders. This being so, it is a fundamental right of the shareholder to be able to claim that profits be distributed. No one will deny this fact. If a company belongs to its shareholders, then more importance must be attached to dividends than to anything else. Managers, to whom the running of the company is entrusted by the shareholders, must endeavour to ensure that dividends are as large as possible. However, it is fair to say that there are in Japan scarcely any private individuals of the sort who invest in shares for the sake of the dividends they might earn, and there are hardly any managers of the kind whose first consideration is dividends. According to a survey by the National Tax Administration Agency, Japanese companies paid out 3688.3 billion yen in dividends in 1988. As against this, they paid out in the same period some 4550.3 billion yen on their expense (for entertainment, etc.) accounts. Do Japanese companies exist to make profits and to return them to their shareholders as dividends; or do they exist in order that their managers and employees can eat out and drink in style? At any rate, it would not be strange to say that in Japanese companies expenses are thought of as having priority over dividends.

In general, in textbooks on the theory of the joint stock company, we are told to think of dividends as a rate of interest. The reason for this is that shareholders think of the dividends they receive on the money they use to purchase their shares in the same way as they do interest. That is to say, investors have a variety of outlets for their investible funds besides shares, and so they compare the interest rate on bank deposits with dividends. Companies then do not return as dividends the whole of the profits they have earned, but pass on dividends at a level that accords with the interest on loans. Thus, conceiving of dividends as a rate of interest proceeds by means of a two-stage process, and the shareholder is taken as having become a sort of rentier whose income is derived from investments. However, large private shareholders that are investors do not merely become rentiers but own shares as instruments of control (control securities). Nevertheless, even though they may be large private shareholders, they can only obtain on their shares dividends paid at the same rate as the rate paid on shares owned by rentiers. Thus profits accumulate within the company, which makes internal financing possible and eventually leads to 'managerial control'. This is how the theory of the joint stock company unfolds.

However, when we look at the facts of the Japanese case, the dividend yield on shares listed in the first rank of the Tokyo Stock Exchange is less than one per cent. This is clearly less than the interest on bank deposit accounts (time deposits), and less, too, than that on current accounts. If we examine the situation case by case, we find no shares that give yields of the 6 per cent level obtainable on deposit accounts. Far from dividends becoming like interest, they have sunk to a level that is far below them. If, in this connection, we look at yields on shares in other countries, we find that in North America and Europe there is not one where yields are as low as in Japan. Therefore we cannot say that in Japan the shareholder has become a 'rentier'; he has achieved a status below that of a rentier. The theory of the joint stock company whose premise is that dividends have come to function like interest has ceased to hold good, at least in the Japanese case.

The fact that yields on shares are low is due either to the fact that dividends are so low, or else to the fact that share prices are high. But this was not something characteristic of Japan in the past. Until this situation arose no later than in the last few decades, the average yield on shares not only exceeded that on current accounts in banks, but also the rate on deposit accounts. Things changed greatly from the 1970s, and the cause was the phenomenon of the 'corporatisation of shareownership' that I described earlier. As I shall describe later, share prices rose rapidly due to this process of 'corporatisation'. Not merely did it raise share prices, but it also severed the connection between dividends and share prices. It dashed to pieces the notion prevailing up to that time that yields were the standard for judging the profitability of investing in shares. It banished the attitude amongst investors that dividends were the objective, or that they should be the criterion used when buying shares. As a result, the significance of dividends lessened, and the senses of both shareholders and company managers with respect to dividends were numbed. Needless to say, this was a very favourable development as far as firms were concerned. Since dividends paid needed only to be small even though firms were profitable, the retaining of profits and building of internal reserves became possible, so that the funds that companies were free to dispose of as they wished became very great. This itself was truly a part of the system of 'companism'.

Dividend policy in Japan

On the basis of figures for dividends for all stock exchange listed companies in Japan (excluding those whose results are published irregularly) we may point out that, for some twenty years or so, the trend in dividends as a proportion of owned capital – that is, equity capital – has been downwards. Although the value of dividends in absolute terms has been rising, so too has the total of equity capital, so that the former as a percentage of the latter has fallen.

If we turn next to the ratio of dividends to earnings or pay-out ratio (money passed on as dividends as a proportion of after-tax profits), we see that it has declined more or less consistently from 59.32 per cent in 1975 to a low in 1988 of 28.13 per cent.

When we look further at the relationship between profit rates and the ratio of dividends to earnings for individual companies, what clearly emerges is that the higher is the ratio of dividends to earnings the lower is the profit rate of the company, and the higher the profit rate of the company the lower the ratio of dividends to earnings.

Why has this come about? It is because of the policy of 'stable dividends' that has been adopted whereby companies do not lower dividends when profits fall, but neither do they raise them when profits rise. The form this policy takes is to try to hold at a fixed rate the dividend paid per share.

If we look at the year 1988, we see that 444 companies paid a dividend per share of five yen, and that these companies made up 27.4 per cent of the total of companies that paid dividends in that year. If we also include those companies paying between five and seven yen per share, we find they make up 60.9 per cent of the total. Thus, when we say that individual companies are committed to 'stable' dividends, it is not merely that they try to maintain dividend rates at a given level despite fluctuations in profit rates; we mean that the overwhelming majority of companies pay dividends of between five and seven yen fifty sen (7.5 yen) per share – that is to say, a ratio per share of between 10 and 15 per cent. Of course, there is no objective basis for paying a dividend per share of five yen. It is merely that somehow or other a ratio of 10 per cent on the face value of a share has come to be accepted as common sense, so that even companies with poor profits strive desperately to pay dividends at that rate. Conversely, companies with high rates of profit do not pay dividends at a very much higher rate than this. Although a figure of five or seven yen has no real objective basis, because it has come to be accepted as only common sense, this itself has come to be the basis for sticking to it.

Companies in the United States resemble those in Japan in that those with low rates of profit have high dividend payout ratios. However, the difference is that companies with high profit rates at once increase dividends and thus try to keep the payout ratio constant at a high level.

In Japan, too, it is often asserted that companies ought to adopt a policy of keeping the dividend payout ratio constant. In its report published in 1976 entitled *Changes in the Structure of Shareholders and the State of the Capital Market* (*Kabunushi Kosei no Henka to Shihon Shijo no Arikata ni tsuite*), the Securities Exchange Council (Shoken Torihiki Shingikai), which is an advisory body to the Minister of Finance, included an item called the 'Importance of the Dividend Pay-out Ratio' as a policy for 'restoring the attraction of investing in shares'. The report included the following passage:

It has been pointed out that, although in Japan in recent years the rate at which new shares have been issued has slowed down and the rate of profit on capital has increased, the propensity to pay dividend has declined because the rate of dividend to face value tends to be kept constant, and therefore, the attraction to the run-of-the-mill shareowner of investing in shares has diminished. … In actuality, in the decade from 1965 to 1975 when there was a marked diminution in the number of private shareholders, the trend in dividend pay-out ratios was a downward one and the ratios were low compared to other countries. In order to cope with the change in the composition of shareholders, greatly increase the number of private shareholders and increase the size of the capital market, it is important that the companies' propensity to stress internal accumulation has to be controlled to the extent that it does not diminish the attraction of investing in shares.

It also had the following to say about 'stable' dividends:

> Confronted with the friction produced by zero or falling dividends in periods of recession, companies tend to contrive to keep dividends stable by building-up internal reserves in periods when business is good. On the other hand, there may well be shareholders who wish for unchanging levels of dividends. However, it would be true to say that, in their original form, shares as instruments of profit did pay out dividends that varied with the performance of the company. Nor must 'stable' dividends come to be synonymous with rigidly low levels of dividends. We may conjecture that the reason for the tendency in Japan for dividends to be kept rigidly at low levels is that the development of a true understanding of the (appropriate) level of dividends has been hampered by the generally held idea that the rate should be fixed with respect to par values. Therefore, in the future, the rate of dividends must more seriously be regarded as a criterion for the dividend policy of the firm as well as a criterion for a decision-making of investors.

Despite this proposition, there has been no change whatever in companies' dividend policy. It is because there are good and sufficient reasons for this.

Why dividends do not increase

As can be seen from the earlier comparison with the United States, problems arise from the fact that companies in Japan with high rates of profit do not increase dividends and, as a consequence, dividend payout ratios are low. Why, in fact, do they not raise dividends? Broadly speaking, there are two reasons for this. The first is that large corporate shareholders do not demand that they do. The second is that their share prices remain high even though they do not raise dividends. Let us start with the first reason.

I have already described how the shares of Japanese firms are concentrated in the hands of companies and how nearly all shareholders of individual companies are other companies. Naturally, if these major shareholders were to put pressure on a company and demand that it increased its dividends it would be compelled to do so. If at the annual general meeting of shareholders the major shareholders were to join together, vote down the accounts presented by the company and demand that dividends be increased, the company would have to accede no matter how firmly it was under 'managerial control'. Suppose for the moment that the major shareholders do not go that far, but that they do express dissatisfaction with dividends and dispose of their shares through the market. The price of these shares would then fall and the management of the company would be in difficulties.

This sort of thing is happening in the United States at the present time. Institutional investors who are major shareholders – for example, pension fund managers or private trusts – need dividends to furnish themselves with a given increase in income. The reason for this is that pension fund managers need a gain in income as a source of revenue in order to deliver pensions to their subscribers. The same circumstances apply in the case of private trusts, life insurance companies and investment trusts. Therefore, these institutional investors constantly demand of companies that they raise dividends. Furthermore, in cases where there is dissatisfaction with dividends, shares are also sold before demands are made for them to be raised. This is known as 'the Wall Street Rule'. When shares in a company are sold off by a major shareholder, their price falls and places the company in difficulties. This provokes an increase in dividends. Precisely because there is this resort, they can in the United States construct the rule that, when profits increase, payout ratios are kept constant by increasing dividends.

However, as I shall describe later, even though in Japan life insurance companies demand an increase in dividends as a premium rebate on new shares acquired at market price, large corporate shareholders do not demand increases in dividends. Quite the contrary: banks and other organisations that are also major shareholders often demand that companies reduce their dividends. This is because they place more importance on the safety of their loans than they do on dividends. Corporations did not originally acquire these shares to profit from them through the dividends that they paid out; they acquired them as control securities, and for that reason they do not demand that dividends be raised. Furthermore, they do not sell off the shares they hold merely because they are dissatisfied with the dividend policy of companies. This represents a difference between institutional investors and corporate shareholders, and is a major reason why the dividend policy of American companies based on the wholesale acquisition of shares by institutions differs from that of Japanese companies which is based on the wholesale acquisition of shares by corporations.

Of course, even though they are corporate shareholders they receive the same rate of dividend as do institutional and private shareholders; and however many shares they hold for purposes of control, this does not mean that dividends on them will disappear. Therefore, as long as they are holding shares anyway, there is nothing better than receiving high dividends, even though they may be corporate shareholders. Why do they nevertheless refrain from demanding an increase in dividends? This is where we run up against the structure of mutual shareownership. As long as corporations are in mutual possession of one another's shares, then the demand for an increase in dividends by one company will lead to similar demands from others. The result would be that if they all raised their dividends no advantage would accrue to any single company. Or else it would prove disadvantageous to companies since they would also raise dividends to private shareholders and institutional investors who own shares but do not have their own shares owned by anyone. Mutual shareownership amongst corporations thus encourages the erosion of dividends.

When we examine companies individually, we can say that dividend rates are low for companies where mutual shareowning is advanced in the way that it is within company groupings. By contrast, they are high for companies that have a high proportion of their shares owned by large private shareholders.

The second reason for not raising dividends is that share prices will remain high even if dividends are not raised, or that even if they are raised, this does not mean that share prices will be raised thereby. In a word, this is due to the fact that the relationship between share prices and dividends has been severed, and share prices have become like 'a kite whose string has been cut'. In the past, companies like Pioneer and Sony have indulged in large increases in dividends, but share prices showed no response at all to these actions. If share prices were to rise in response to a rise in dividends, then perhaps companies would follow this course. However, even if share prices have become completely divorced from considerations of remunerative yields, and yields have fallen below those on current (ordinary) accounts in banks, then a little increase in dividends would have no effect at all on share prices. If companies were to try, by means of raising dividends, to get their shares bought on the basis of the yield calculation, they would have to increase dividends ten times above present levels. No one expects that this will happen.

The share price mechanism

What prompts the purchase of shares as instruments of profit is the return on them. When a private individual buys shares, he does so having compared the return on them with that from other investment outlets, chiefly fixed interest bonds and bank deposits. It goes without saying that the return on shares is the dividend divided by the price of the share. Since the dividend is not fixed in the case of equity shares, to that extent there is a risk involved. Therefore, it is normally the case that the return on shares will be higher than that on fixed interest bonds by an amount that is enough to compensate for the greater risk. This is classical share price theory and was the explanation given in older textbooks on the subject.

However, there occurred in the United States in the 1950s a phenomenon known as the 'yield revolution', and eventually the revolution was transmitted to Japan. It was known as the 'yield revolution' because the average return on listed shares fell below that on fixed interest bonds. This occurred first in the United States as a reflection of the structural change in capitalism after the Second World War, and the switch to growth as opposed to cyclical fluctuation. Growth in capitalist countries was due, more than anything else, to the fact that companies have grown. This being so, we ought to take, as the criterion for judging the yield on shares, not present dividends but those which take future growth of the company into account. If a company grows, so will its profits. If this is so, dividends, too, will increase; and if these are anticipated, share prices will rise further and yields will fall below those on fixed interest bonds. This was the nature of the 'yield revolution' in the United States.

A little later in the second half of the 1950s, Japan also experienced something like America's 'yield revolution'. This was because the American concept of the 'growth stock' was introduced into Japan. It was known by the name *seicho kabu* (growth share), and it became a way of buying into the future growth of a company. However, the mechanism by which the 'yield revolution' and the 'growth share' operated in Japan differed from the United States. The increase in (equity) capital achieved by Japanese companies at that juncture was almost all assigned to – that is, raised from – existing shareholders at par values. If we assume that the price of a share is one hundred yen and that the dividend is six yen per year, the yield is 6 per cent. Let us also assume that at this point the company doubles its capital, but that after the increase it still pays a dividend per share of six yen. The shareholder who bought a single share at one hundred yen would, through his share subscription at par – in other words at fifty yen per share – come to possess two shares. Therefore, the unit cost per share would become seventy-five yen, and the yield would be six yen divided by seventy-five yen, which is 8 per cent. Due to the increase in capital, the yield has risen from 6 to 8 per cent. Therefore shares will continue to be bought until the yield falls to 6 per cent, and, therefore, share prices will rise. An important consideration here is that, if dividends are nominally left unchanged, or even reduced, after the increase in capital, in practice they will have risen after the increase is made; and this becomes possible due to the growth of the company.

This is the mechanism by which Japanese-style growth shares operate, and the precondition for its operation is the system whereby increases in capital are assigned to – that is, derived from – current shareholders at par values. Under this system, if a company increases its capital the yield on its shares will increase. Then a rise of the share price will follow and the yield will fall to the extent of this rise. But if we take into account the next increase in capital and the one after that, share prices will rise even further and yields will continue to fall. Share prices will therefore increase even more.

Thus, the current yield on shares will fall to less than that on fixed interest bonds. But the important thing is to calculate what will happen to future yields after an increase in capital has taken place. One should certainly not disregard the calculation of yields altogether. However, this involves estimating future growth, and to that extent it means that the element of uncertainty increases and a speculative dimension enters the process of estimating share prices. Furthermore, the basis for forecasting the size of dividends after an increase in capital is whether or not, despite the increase, earnings will be as high as dividend is possible. Therefore, the anticipated gain per share will become an important criterion for determining the price of shares. This is the price/earnings ratio (PER), that is, the market price of an equity share in a listed company divided by that company's earnings per share, and the PER has come to be an important consideration in stock markets.

With the boom in growth shares in the period 1955–65 share prices rose by means of this mechanism and speculators from amongst the ordinary people bought shares briskly. In addition, investment trusts that should be thought of as indirect investors grew very rapidly. Soon after this, the Japanese economy began to grow according to a different pattern. Companies' earnings ceased to increase, whilst on the other hand, they began to place new issues on the market on a large scale for public subscription in order to raise funds for capital growth, rather than raising funds from existing shareholders by allotment at par values. Because of this, earnings per share diminished and share prices fell. This brought on the 'share crisis' (*shoken kyoko*) of the mid-1960s, and the 'Japanese-style' mechanism by which growth shares operated collapsed. The Japan Joint Securities Company (Nihon Kyodo Shoken) and the Japan Security Owners Association (Nihon Shoken Hoyu Kumiai) were then set up as a means of counteracting the 'share crisis'. These organisations bought up shares on a large scale using funds from the Bank of Japan in order to support prices, and by this means the crisis was overcome.

Demand, supply and share prices

Eventually, along with the recovery in share prices that took place from about 1967–8, the frozen shares in the hands of the Japan Joint Securities Company and the Japan Securities Holding Association were released on to the market. At exactly the same time the Japanese government declared that it would undertake the liberalisation of capital transaction and simultaneously there began to occur the 'stable' or 'safe shareholder' manoeuvre as a counter to capital liberalisation. This manoeuvre was adopted because of the belief that it would be a very bad thing if, as a result of liberalisation, foreign capital were to buy up the shares of Japanese companies and take them over. For this reason frozen shares were reclaimed and put into the hands of corporations, whilst in addition it frequently happened that floating stocks that were bought on the market passed into the hands of corporations deemed to be 'safe' shareholders.

Needless to say, this brought about the 'corporatisation' of share ownership. When corporations go on buying large amounts of shares like this, in time the relationship between the demand and the supply of shares on the market will come under strain and the price of shares will rise above the level determined by normal demand and supply. This tendency became marked in about 1970 as share prices rose due to corporate buying, and with the rise in prices, yields fell.

On the other hand, raising capital by issuing shares at market prices began to occur at just about this time. Under the system of raising capital by allocating shares to shareholders at par value that had operated up to this time, no matter how high the price of shares, new issues were always made at fifty yen per share, and as a result of this the price mechanism did not operate. This was inconvenient for firms raising capital and was dubbed a practice characteristic of 'backward' Japan. Therefore, the business community and the Ministry of Finance took the lead in a shift towards issuing shares at market price. The securities community who had opposed the move at first on the grounds that it would destroy the share price mechanism, were soon following suit. Starting with the issue at market price of the shares of Nihon Gakki (Yamaha) in 1969, the practice thereafter spread rapidly.

When this happened, the mechanism of the Japanese-style growth share ceased to operate. Since shareholders no longer had the right to receive their allocation of new issues at par value, they ceased to enjoy increases in yields as a result of increases in capital. Moreover since share prices went on rising because of corporate buying, yields went on falling. Private investors, who were no longer able to buy shares for the yields they gave, could either divest themselves of their shares or else become speculators whose aim was to profit from the rise in their prices. Thus the criterion according to which one formerly expected share prices to be determined – namely, their yields – was lost. Corporations had always owned shares for the purpose of control, but of course this prospect did not exist for private shareholders. The phenomenon of the 'corporatisation' of shareownership thus produced a situation where share prices are not determined according to finals' profits and dividends or ordinal market rates of interest, but instead by the relationship of demand to supply. Dividends steadily eroded and came to be unrelated to the price of shares. This is very convenient for firms. There is no need for them to increase dividends in order to raise share prices. It is sufficient to control the demand and supply relationship by means of the 'safe' shareholder device.

Growth in the practice of issuing shares at market price

Probably no country other than Japan has made such a rapid and large-scale transition from a system of raising capital by allocating shares to existing shareholders at their face value to a system of raising capital by offering shares for public subscription at market price. The earlier practice of allocating shares to current holders of shares at face value had been peculiar to Japan: but beginning in 1969 with the issue at market price of shares in Nippon Gakki (Yamaha), things changed to such an extent that in a very few years all new capital was raised by issues made at market price. This was not because of any particular revision in the law. Nor were firms coerced into it by anyone. However, this transformation did not occur merely as a result of a switch in fashion. It was consistent with the true character of corporate capitalism, and issuing shares at market price became so popular by very reason of the fact that it was the way of doing things under a regime of 'companism'.

The proportion of new capital raised by public subscription at market value which had been no more than a few per cent until 1968 had, in 1972, risen to 66 per cent of the total. Thereafter, despite a short-lived fall, it rose again from 1976 onwards and at present it is in the region of 80 per cent. The remainder is raised by allocation to existing shareholders or to third parties. However, even when new capital is raised by allocating shares to current shareholders, most issues are made at a price that is intermediate between market value and face value. Very little capital is raised by issues trade at face value.

When the method of raising capital by issuing shares at market prices flourishes like this, then naturally shareholders' equity in a firm – also known as owners' equity capital or net worth (*jiko shihon hiritsu*) – will increase. Formerly low shareholders' equity was characteristic of Japanese firms, but from the second half of the 1970s the ratio increased rapidly. The reason for this was that firms kept dividend rates down and made large share issues at market price, even though firms' revenues had increased whilst simultaneously investment in capital equipment had fallen off.

In 1981, the issue of shares at market price for public subscription reached an unprecedented value of 1.28 trillion yen. The reason for this was that due to a revision in the Commercial Code, more than one-half of new capital raised had to be counted as capital owners' equity, and there was a good deal of raising of capital 'before the revision of the Code' occurred. When raising capital by public subscription at market price came to be as widely practised as this, voices critical of the practice became louder. At this juncture, the *Asahi* newspaper which had been running a series of articles on the subject of 'securities', took up the problem of raising capital via market price share issues (25 January 1982). Under the title 'Modern-day Alchemy', it criticised and attacked the practice under such headlines as: 'Firms Thrust High Prices On Us In Their Longing For Margins On New Capital Raised'; 'A Critique From The Inside' and 'A Total Loss For The Private Shareholder'. Furthermore, the Association of Life Insurance Companies which for some time past had been the most severe critic of the practice of issuing shares at market prices, made public in September 1981 the results of its survey: 'The Outcome of Investment in Publicly Subscribed Shares'.

The survey complained about how bad had been the earnings rate on publicly subscribed shares up to that time, and how numerous had been the issues where the offering price was broken.

The question was also taken up in the Diet. On 15 March 1982 at a meeting of the Budget Committee of the House of Councillors, Ryoichi Yasutsune of the Japan Socialist Party put the question: 'Should we not consider levelling a tax of around 10 per cent on that part of the funds raised from share issues made at market price which constitutes a premium?' To this the Minister of Finance, Watanabe, responded: 'This is a contentious issue. Accepted opinion is that, even though the issue is at market price, it is the same as the capital subscribed by shareholders and therefore to tax it would not be a good thing.' But at the same time he replied that, since these funds are used and not counted as capital, 'it is a fact that whether or not to tax them is a subject for examination'.

Even the Ministry of Finance could not ignore the problem when voices critical of the practice of issuing shares at market price were raised to this level, and so in July 1982 the matter was brought for deliberation before the Commission of Inquires into Share Dealing. At the meeting, the Ministry of Finance presented the following recent criticisms of market price share issues and took the views of the Commission:

1. Even though a premium has been paid by shareholders and ought to be distributed as dividends, the share-issuing company regards it as a cost-free source of funds and uses it without paying dividends on it. 2. There are many instances where as a reaction to the raising of share prices by manipulation, new shares are put up for public subscription at a reduced price, soon after their allotment. 3. One of the causes of the recent rapid fall in share prices and the decline in the proportion of shares held by private individuals is the high-handed issuing of new shares without heed to the interests of shareholders.

(*Yomiuri Shimbun*, 19 June 1982)

The biggest criticism of the issuing of shares at current market prices relates to the issue price. As explained by the Ministry of Finance, the criticism is based on the suspicion that share prices are forced up and then a new issue is made at the higher level of share prices. As I said previously, the Ministry of Finance promoted the issuing of shares at market price under the banner of introducing the price mechanism into the new issues market. But the fact is that if the price is one that is created by the issuing company, far from having a price mechanism, we have a mechanism for manipulating prices. The greatest problem is that share prices which the company should consider to be sacrosanct and inviolable are in fact not.

Exploiting high share prices

At the end of July 1981, Toyota Motor Corporation issued seventy million shares at a paid up market price of 1415 yen per share and by so doing raised overnight funds to the tune of 99.05 billion yen. At the end of September in the same year, Toshiba issued two hundred million shares for payment by subscription at a paid up market price of 408 yen per share and so too raised overnight funds to the sum of 81.6 billion yen. Under the system where shares are issued at market price, the higher the price per share the greater the money going into the firm. For example, in Toshiba's case, had the price per share gone up by ten yen, the extra funds acquired would have totalled two billion yen. In the case of convertible debentures, too, since they are convertible into shares at market price, the more advantageous it is to the company the higher the price per share.

Normally, the only way to raise the price of its shares is for a company to improve its performance. This is not easily achieved. However, with the prevalence of the 'corporatisation phenemenon' share prices are not now determined by company performance and the size of dividends, but by the workings of supply and demand. It became common knowledge in the 1970s that share prices rose because of 'company buying'; and that if this were the case, share prices would rise if issuing firms could get other firms with whom they did business to acquire their shares through this process. If the company then issues shares at this high market price, it can obtain any amount of money for nothing and makes its fortune at one stroke. This is something that, with hindsight, seems patently obvious, but it has to be said that the person who first hit upon this form of alchemy was a very clever man.

I shall refer to this kind of alchemy as 'exploiting high share prices', but the person who first discovered it and used the term is said to have been the managing director of Sanko Shipping Company. Although not by public subscription but by the method of allocating to a third party, four times between 1971 and 1974 Sanko Shipping used high share prices in making issues at market price, so raising 91.2 billion yen in funds. Although at the time Sanko Shipping got itself in bad odour in the Ministry of Finance and in financial circles for using this method, 'high share price exploitation' spread to many large firms and is now commonly practised by the typical Japanese firm. It is now so generally resorted to and commonplace that the term is not even used.

The 'safe shareholder strategy' was originally used to prevent takeovers. Firms got financial institutions and firms with whom they regularly dealt to buy and hold their shares to prevent their shares being bought up and themselves taken over. That was what the strategy was for; but when buying occurred on a large scale and 'corporatisation' advanced, market forces tightened their grip and share prices rose as a result of 'company buying'. It was at that juncture that raising new capital by issuing shares at market prices became popular. Then at the next stage the 'safe shareholder manoeuvre' was resorted to in order to make market price issues at high share prices. Thus, the 'safe shareholder manoeuvre' changed from being a device to prevent takeovers into a method for exploiting high share prices.

Firms cannot, of course, buy their own shares and so raise their value. Under commercial law in Japan, it is forbidden in principle for firms to own their shares. Therefore, they get other firms to own their shares for them. But, even in this case it infringes the 'Law Relating to Share Dealing' (*shoken torihiki ho*), which forbids the manipulation of share prices, if the buying is done in order to secure a temporary hike in share prices. However, although it may amount to manipulation if share prices are jacked-up on a temporary basis it is not in violation of the law if a 'safe shareholding manoeuvre' has been conducted regularly for some time in the past. This may seem strange when one thinks about it, but it passes as reasonable in conditions where 'safe' shareholding has become part of the structure of things.

Problems arise if share prices fall after new capital has been raised by means of an issue at market price. Therefore, the 'safe shareholder manoeuvre' has to be persisted with after the issue has been made. Of course, if the issuing company appeals to a firm with which it customarily has dealings to become one of its 'safe' shareholders and then its share price falls, it will have caused trouble for the firm that has agreed to hold its shares. For this reason, it again attempts to keep its share prices up by resorting to the safe shareholder device. Through this circular line of reasoning, the 'safe shareholder strategy' gets built into the system.

In the early days, many of the new shares that resulted from raising capital by the market price route were taken up by other corporations, the issuing company then taking them off their hands and foisting them upon specific firms with which it had long-term dealings (this was known as *oyahike* – parents' prerogative). However, this practice came in for criticism and so the securities business instituted a self-imposed rule which kept the practice within fixed limits. However, the shares bought by private shareholders by subscribing to market price issues were rapidly sold (a process known as *uchikaeshi* or striking back), bought back by securities companies and installed into corporations. As a result, although raising capital by public subscription might have been expected to raise the proportion of shares held by private individuals immediately, this result did not happen at all.

The American way of thinking is encapsulated in the phrases: 'The price of its shares is a mirror that reflects the true state of the firm', and 'share prices are God'. For this reason, managers' instinct is to maximise the share price and to attempt, by however little, to improve the firm's results in order to raise the price of its shares. But Japanese managers are atheists, and they have found a way of tampering with the mirror whilst doing nothing to change the true state of the firm. This form of alchemy is the most certain and expeditious sway of gathering money into the firm and of raising the proportion of own capital.

6
Takeovers

The joint-stock company and takeovers

Buying up (cornering) its shares and taking over a company – this is an everyday affair in the United States and in Britain. If you go to Wall Street in New York or to the City in London, you still hear plenty of talk of takeovers. It is a major factor in the movement of share prices. In the United States, second and third rank companies such as newly-formed companies and conglomerates engage in takeovers, but in recent years many cases involved first-rank companies such as General Electric and Mobile Oil, and there are instances when the money needed to buy up shares for this purpose has been in the region of tens of billions of dollars.

In America and Britain, the takeover bid has been the most widely used method for cornering the shares needed for a takeover. The method is that whoever wishes to take over a firm places an advertisement in the newspapers and buys shares in the target firm directly from the owners of these shares. It is therefore a method of acquisition that takes place outside the market, and normally the price at which the shares are bought is somewhat higher than their market price. At the same time, the condition is imposed that whoever is proposing to conduct the takeover will decide on the time period and the number of shares needed. If in the scheduled time the scheduled number of shares are not forthcoming, those doing the taking-over can withdraw the offer to the shareholders from whom they proposed to buy the shares. The takeover bid system was instituted because in the past the buying-up of shares had given rise to certain misgivings about behind-the-scenes activity. The system represents an attempt to make the process transparent and protect the interests of the shareholders, whilst at the same time smoothing the course of the takeover.

The system was introduced into Japan, too, and passed into law in 1972 with the revision of the Law Relating to Share Dealing under the name *Kokai Kabushiki Kaitsuke Seido* (The Public Buying-up of Shares System). However, the system has only been used in three cases, and in each of them the number of shares acquired was small, whilst in none of them a takeover was the real objective.

Buying up a firm's shares and taking it over is extremely rare in Japan compared with the United States and Britain. Moreover, the cases that have occurred up to the present have been ones where shares have been bought up quietly on the market, famous incidents being the buy-ups, for example, of Yowa Fudosan (Yowa Real Estate – now Mitsubishi Property) by Kyujiro Fujitsuna; of Shiroki-ya (now the Nihonbashi branch of Tokyu Department Stores) by Hideki Yokoi; and of the Japan Line Company by Sanko Kisen (Sanko Shipping). However in the middle of the process the shares that had been acquired were subrogated to other companies and company takeovers were not the outcome. Of course, we cannot say that cases of takeover after the cornering of shares never occur, but they are extremely rare.[3] This is one of the great characteristics of the joint-stock company system in Japan. Furthermore, the takeover bid system is used in the United States and Britain as a method of achieving mergers between firms. In Japan, there are scarcely any instances of merger taking the form of the prior acquisition of shares followed by merger. Instead the method used is that both sets of managers seal a merger contract, and then afterwards one exchanges its shares for those of the other.

The principle of decision by majority at the annual shareholders' meeting is a fundamental principle of the joint-stock company. The 'decision by majority' principle differs somewhat between the joint-stock company and politics in that it is 'one share–one vote' in the former as opposed to 'one person–one vote' in the latter. Nevertheless, it is the basis for company democracy. The principle of decision by the majority was introduced into the company from the world of democratic politics, and under this principle, anyone who buys up a majority of its shares acquires the right to exercise control over a company. The directors of the company are elected at the annual general meeting of the shareholders according to the majority principle. In that sense, it is natural and in accordance with the principles of the joint-stock company that someone who buys up the majority of its shares takes over the company. This is sanctioned under the laws of all countries.

Another principle is the freedom to deal in shares. Anyone is free to purchase shares. Although there are certain restrictions imposed under the Anti-monopoly Law and the Law for the Control of Foreign Exchange (*Gaikoku Kawase Kanri Ho*), basically all are free to buy and sell shares. In which case, anyone is free to buy up a firm's shares and try and take it over. In Japan, too, commercial law accords with this principle. But in Japan, taking over a company is regarded as a crime on a par with hijacking an airplane, and the chairmen of large Japanese companies calmly say things like: 'buying shares and taking a company over is the same as murdering someone in the street for his money'. In Japan there is no concept of takeover, nor any of buying and selling firms.

The safe shareholder strategy

The first reason we can cite to explain why company takeovers by share acquisition are so exceedingly rare in Japan is the use of the 'safe shareholder' as a device for preventing them. As I previously explained, this device is one where the issuing company gets a bank and/or another firm with which it deals to acquire its shares. All of these organisations are corporations, and as long as nothing untoward happens, upon becoming a safe shareholder these firms ordinarily do not sell their shares; or if they do, they normally obtain the consent of the issuing firm in advance. In such an eventuality the issuing firm will find another 'safe' shareholder and get it to hold its shares.

It is not known when the words 'safe shareholder manoeuvre' (*antei kabunushi kosaku*) came to be used, but it was already in use in the 1950s to mean that cornered shares were taken over and put in the hands of 'safe' shareholders for them to hold. When in 1952 the shares in Yowa Real Estate were bought up, it was firms within the Mitsubishi group that took them over. We can say that this was the first instance of the manoeuvre. Next in 1954 after Mitsubishi Trading Corporation (Mitsubishi Shoji) had emerged out of a large-scale amalgamation, it undertook a large increase in capital by allocating shares to third parties, and these shares were held for it by firms within the Mitsubishi group. This, too, was said to have been done in order to create a set of safe shareholders.

Thereafter, the 'safe shareholder manoeuvre' came to be used to ensure before the event that a firm's shares would not be cornered by a hostile party. However, at that time it was firms within the same *keiretsu*, or firms that belonged to the same group; or else the bank with which it primarily dealt. Thus, the manoeuvre was at the same time a way of consolidating the *keiretsu*, or, the company group.

The safe shareholder manoeuvre came to be used on a large scale after the 'share panic' of 1965. The cause of the manoevre was capital liberalisation. The Japanese government took Japan into the Organisation for Economic Cooperation and Development (OECD) in 1964, and by the terms of the agreement had promised to undertake capital liberalisation. If liberalisation came about, then foreign capital would be free to buy up Japanese shares. It would be anathema if that happened, and so 'safe' shareholding received a tremendous boost in its capacity as a countermeasure to capital liberalisation. It was triggered off by Toyota Automobile Corporation, and because of the fear in the motor industry that firms would be taken over by the likes of General Motors and Ford as a result of liberalisation, it was carried out most vigorously in that industry. However, it spread to other industries, and eventually across the whole spectrum of industries. In the first instance the form the manoeuvre took was to buy up 'frozen' or 'dead' shares from the Japan Joint Securities Company (Nihon Kyodo Shoken) and the Japan Securities Holding Association (Nihon Shoken Hoyu Kumiai) and foist them on 'safe' shareholders; but at length it became the general practice to syphon-up shares floating on the Stock Exchange and pass them on to 'safe' shareholders. In addition, the government encouraged firms in this manoeuvre while at the same time it proceeded with capital liberalisation measures. Its conduct was contradictory in that on the surface it liberalised capital movements whilst behind the scenes it prevented it.

As I said previously, it is fundamental to the joint-stock company that anyone is free to buy up its shares and take it over. However, the 'safe shareholder manoeuvre' is designed to prevent this happening, and moreover it has to be said that should the share-issuing company do the buying up, it is rather strange, given the principles of joint-stock company law. To put it in concrete terms, the basis of the joint-stock company is that the shareholders should choose the directors by majority decision and that they should leave the management of the firm to them. The 'safe shareholder manoeuvre' means that managers choose their shareholders! This is for all the world as if a member of parliament were to choose the electors he wanted, although democracy requires that the electorate chooses the representatives it wants. We are unable to conclude that this is democratic corporation.

Of course Japanese company law prohibits companies that issue shares from holding their own shares, so that it is in breach of the law for them to buy their own shares from the market and pass them on to a 'safer' shareholder. Therefore, they always call upon another company to do the buying of their shares for them. However, it is precisely because it is done on the initiative of the company itself that it is known as the 'safe shareholder manoeuvre', and it is an unmistakeable fact that the issuing company intervenes positively in the process.

The law in many American states recognises the right of companies to own shares in themselves. Since companies acquire their own shares using company funds, they make public the conditions under which they bought them. But in Japan, although acquiring shares in one's own company is prohibited, the issuing company intervenes to see that a 'safe' shareholder gets hold of its shares. Moreover, this takes place without the terms and conditions ever being made public. Therefore, there also arises the question of insider dealing by those inside the company who know the details of the 'safe shareholder manoeuvre' before the event.

Companies in Japan protect themselves from takeovers by means of this peculiarly Japanese manoeuvre and this is an exceedingly convenient thing for companies and the managers who represent them. In such a way is the system of 'companism' assured.

Cornering shares: the Japanese way

We have seen that cornering its shares in order to take a company over is very rare in Japan, but buying up shares with no such intention in mind or without intending to go quite that far is extremely common. For example in the second half of the 1970s alone, there were dozens of cases such as those instanced below where firms had their shares cornered: the engineering company Chiyoda Corporation (Chiyoda Kako Kensetsu), Diesel Machinery and Tools, Miyaji Ironworks (Miyaji Tekko), the machinery firm Seika (Seika Sangyo), the bookseller Maruzen, Kyoto Bank, the spirits maker Takara (Takara Shuzo), the brewer Asahi Brewelies (Asahi Biiru) and the Department Store Takashimaya. These buy-ups were carried out by groups of speculators within Japan and by medical corporations like the Juzen Association. Besides these, there were the buying-ups carried out by Wang of Hong Kong. These were of Kao Soap, Oji Paper, Aji no Moto, Meiji Milk Products and the textiles and apparel firm Katakura Industries. In each case, between 10 and 30 per cent of issued shares were bought up.

Nearly all of these incidents were settled by means of the issuing company taking over the cornered shares and subrogating them to safe shareholders. What I have called 'share-cornering Japanese-style' refers to this sort of buying up of shares with the object of making the issuing company take over the shares, or at least with the expectation that it will. It goes without saying that the group who corner the shares are able to make a profit from the rise in their prices that this produces.

I have already described the case of Yowa Real Estate in the 1950s where cornered shares were taken over and passed into the keeping of safe shareholders. Thereafter, the most celebrated case was the buying up of shares in the Japan Line Shipping Company by Sanko Shipping. At the time, Sanko Shipping acquired more than 42 per cent at the outstanding shares in the Japan Line Company, and the takeover effort was on the point of success. In reaction to this, Japan Lines got the later infamous Yoshio Kodama to act as intermediary, took over the shares, handed them on to safe shareholders and thus settled the case. Later the entire story of this affair became clear in the opening attacking statement of the prosecution in the 'Kodama route' trial in the Lockheed affair. Even now it is not clear what the intention of Sanko Shipping was when it bought up the shares in Japan Line; it is only known that the cornered shares were recovered by the issuing company through the intermediation of this well-known right-wing figure Yoshio Kodama.

Thereafter, a succession of share-cornering incidents took place where the intention was to have the issuing firm recover the shares and pass them on into the hands of a safe shareholder. But what would have happened had the issuing company refused to recover its shares? The party that had cornered them did not do so with the intention of taking the company over; and had it done so, it is unlikely to have done it successfully. Therefore, at some point they would have had to get rid of the shares they had bought up, and by doing so their price would have fallen and they would have incurred a loss. This means that, had the issuing company made it clear from the outset that it would not recover its shares the buy-up would not have taken place.

So why does the issuing company buy its cornered shares? The first reason we can adduce is that, even if it was clear that the cornering parties objective was not a takeover, the issuing firm might still face problems if its shares were later subrogated to one of its competitor companies. Second, for whatever reason, the feeling amongst managers is that if speculators who do not know the concrete circumstances of the firm were to become major shareholders, they might make a great nuisance of themselves. In practice, because there often are instances of harassment of this kind, firms do try to recover shares held by troublesome shareholders. Intertwined with that, it often happens that the group of speculators is approached by some important right-wing big-wig or politician to discuss doing a deal with the issuing company. Japanese managers are not good at resisting this sort of behind-the-scenes political dealing. This was clearly shown in the case when the important right-winger Yoshio Kodama intervened over the shares in Japan Line Shipping.

These reasons are all very well as far as they go, but the biggest factor in the background to all this is the 'safe shareholder manoeuvre'. Often when shares are cornered in Japan, the criticism is that 'managers have neglected to perform the safe shareholder manoeuvre'. So much is the manoeuvre thought to be a duty incumbent upon managers, and from long ago safe shareholding to prevent buy-ups was considered to be the natural thing to be done. Or else, if a buy-up happened, one would naturally recover the shares and get them into the hands of a 'safe' shareholder. Had the 'safe shareholding manoeuvre' not existed, it is unlikely that 'Japanese-style share-cornering' would have occurred. Originally it was intended to prevent takeovers; but in fact it has caused the continual occurrence of share-cornering Japan-style.

If nothing is done about share-cornering Japanese-style, it will happen any number of times. And if groups of speculators are left to make huge profits from the practice, it is capable of eating into the large company structure in Japan like a bacillus. Therefore the government and the financial community in Japan took a firm attitude towards buy-ups such as those carried out by the Seibi Group and the Juzen Association and began to take action to destroy them. So for a time share-cornering Japanese-style subsided. However, in the 1980s new groups, intent on buying up shares, appeared one after another and cornering Japanese-style became very popular once again. Obviously the reason for this is to be found in the 'safe shareholder manoeuvre': unless the latter is eradicated, share-cornering Japanese-style will not cease.

'Companism' and the prevention of takeovers

As I have already explained, the main reason why company takeovers through share acquisition are so few in Japan is because of the 'safe shareholder manoeuvre'. But it is also necessary to point to a second factor which supplements the first, and that is the Japanese-style view of the company. For example, we often see in Japan cases where even the labour union is opposed to a company takeover. This is unthinkable in the United States or in Britain where unions will oppose takeovers if there is likely to be a deterioration in employment conditions, but otherwise will not intervene. Since the role of unions is to defend employment conditions, this is quite proper. But since in Japan the attitude is 'defend our place of work', even the unions oppose takeovers. A company is not simply something that belongs to its shareholders; it is the place where its employees work and it is their stronghold. A fortress should be defended unto death and, if it is to fall, all should die a heroic death in its defence. It is therefore a nonsense to talk of buying and selling it. This view of the company as one's castle makes takeovers difficult. Thus, if the consent of the employees is not forthcoming, the takeover will not go well even if accomplished. This habit of thinking of the firm as one's castle is really the idea behind the 'safe shareholder manoeuvre'. The then chairman of the board of directors of the Toyota Motor Company which first promoted the 'safe shareholder manoeuvre' as an antidote to capital liberalisation, Ishida, went ahead with the strategy with the words: 'It is our castle, we will defend it'. Already at that time Toyota was confident that it could take on General Motors and Ford in the realms of car performance and price. However, it felt it would be helpless in the face of the massive foreign capital available for buying up its shares that these two could command. Therefore, it was forced into the 'safe shareholder manoeuvre' in order to 'defend its castle'.

Whether one talks of the 'safe shareholder manoeuvre' or whether one expresses one's view of the company with the words 'our company is our castle', both represent the way of thinking we have called 'companism'. It has ensured that takeovers could not happen in Japan, and that the system of 'companism' was possible. The reason I say this is that, had its shares been bought up by foreign or even domestic capitalists who did not understand the character of the firm, and who appeared suddenly one day with the words 'This is my firm. From now on you will do as I say', it is unlikely that managers and workers would render devoted service to that firm and dedicate their lives to it. The prevention of takeovers is an indispensable condition for the existence of 'companism'.

However, to Tadanori Nishiyama the fact that there are no takeovers in Japan is testimony to the fact that 'Japan is not a capitalist country'.[4] I have in the past made my critique of Nishiyama's arguments.[5] Nishiyama merely asserts that there are no takeovers (although even in Japan it is not true that there are absolutely none) and does not see what has occurred in order to prevent them happening. The important thing is that over the same period that so few takeovers have occurred, the formation of *keiretsu* and firm groupings (*kigyo shudan*) has proceeded by means of the 'safe shareholder maneuvre'. This fact that *keiretsu* and groups have become stronger by this means has prevented the occurrence of takeovers. Seen from the macro-economic point of view, industrial restructuring and moves towards increased firm concentration have taken place in the United States and the United Kingdom by means of takeovers. By contrast, this means that in Japan, industrial restructuring and increased firm concentration ratios have occurred through the strengthening of groups and *keiretsu* as the result of the 'safe shareholder maneouvre'. To forget this point and to talk as if moves towards increased concentration have not occurred in Japan is to be mistaken. It is even more ridiculous to speak of Japan as not being a capitalist country.

In relation to this, we should also note that, compared with the United States and the United Kingdom, mergers between firms have not been all that popular in Japan. In particular (leaving aside cases where subsidiaries have been absorbed by the parent company), since 1970 there have been few large-scale mergers. We can say that this, too, is because in Japan the common way of combining firms is through the formation of *keiretsu* and groups, and that from the macro-economic viewpoint this fulfils the same function as does the merger in America and Britain. Thus the formation of *keiretsu* and groups of firms proceeded on the basis of the 'safe shareholder maneouvre', and this brought about the 'corporatisation' of shareownership. Links of this kind among firms established corporate capitalism as a system of 'companism'. I shall deal with this matter in some detail in Part IV. The 'safe shareholder manoeuvre' as a policy for preventing takeovers spawned, as a by-product, Japanese-style buy-outs. Since this gnawed away at Japan's large company system, leaders of finance and industry and the government launched a crusade against it. This crusade seemed temporarily to succeed, but what was awaited was an assault from outside forces whose power was incompatibly greater than the domestic perpetrators of buy-ups – that is to say, criticism from the United States and from the European Union to the effect that 'Japan is closed to penetration by foreign capital'. In concrete terms, this would be criticism of Japan's *keiretsu* and firm groupings and attacks on the way takeovers are prevented. I shall have more to say on this, too, in Part IV.

Notes to Part II (Chapters 4–6)

1   Ryugo Hashimoto, *The Anti-Monopoly Law and the Japanese National Economy* (in Japanese), Nihon Keizai Shimbun-sha, 1947, p. 78.
2   John Scott, *Corporations, Classes and Capitalism*, Hutchinson, 1979, p. 43.

3 For details, see H. Okumura, *Buy-ups, Take-overs and Take-over Bid* (in Japanese), Shakai Shiso-sha, 1973, and *Buying-up Firms* (in Japanese) Iwanami Shinsho, 1990.

4 T. Nishiyama, *Japan is not a Capitalist Country* (in Japanese), Mikasa Shobo, 1981, p. 71 ff.

5 H. Okumura, 'What is Corporate Capitalism' (in Japanese), parts 1 and 2, *Keizai Hyoron*, January and February, 1983.

Part III
Managers

7
Who Rules Japan?

An invisible structure

Who rules Japan? At one time, this was a question that Japanese social scientists used to put to each other, but now it seems that the very question has disappeared from those circles. However, it still lives on in the minds of most ordinary people, some of whom reply that it is the prime minister who rules Japan, others that it is the bureaucracy, and still others that it is the mega-rich like Konosuke Matsushita, the founder of the firm that bears his name. It is the responsibility of social scientists to resolve this question both theoretically and empirically. But in Japan, this responsibility has long since been abandoned. This is the first reason why the structure of control in Japan is invisible to the mass of the people and why each person can only answer the question from his or her own experience. This is the fault of Japanese scholars who used up their energies in importing foreign works and in explaining and interpreting them, and who did not construct an independent theory on the basis of the actual situation in Japan.

Ever since the publication in the United States of Wright Mills's book,[1] the question of who controls American society has been a very live one amongst sociologists, and though a minority concern amongst economists, research into the question has continued. In the United Kingdom and Germany, too, a fairly large number of books have been published that have produced evidence relating to this question. However, in Japan there have been no books presenting this kind of evidence. Instead, there are merely translations of books discussing in abstract terms questions such as class or ownership.

It is not that the question has never been studied in Japan. Quite the contrary, the dispute over the nature of capitalism in Japan in the first year of the Showa era (1925) really began with the question of who controls Japanese capitalism. Was it the Emperor system or was it monopoly capital; and if it was the former, what was the basis of that system? The Lecture School (Koza-ha) and the Workers and Peasants School (Rono-ha) who between them disputed these questions can be seen, with the benefit of hindsight, to have made many mistakes, and their analysis may have been crude. However, what we must not forget is that this debate dealt with the most important issues, and that many scholars risked their own personal safety in joining the debate. The debate is now largely forgotten, and if anyone does remember it, they are merely inclined to comment on how mistaken the Koza-ha were or how crude were those in the Rono-ha. No one now attempts to ask the questions posed by the scholars of old. Has the controversy over the nature of Japanese capitalism withered away; or is it that scholars have been worn down?

In the midst of this state of affairs, the argument that is still repeated is that individual, mega-rich capitalists must rule Japan. But since this contention is incapable of proof, out of it is born the argument that Japan has 'capitalism without capitalists'; or else the extraordinary assertion that 'Japan is not a capitalist country'. It is the theory of corporate capitalism that tries to correct these popular but mistaken views and to address itself to the essence of the question of who rules Japan.

The second reason for being unable to answer this question is that the rulers are difficult to detect. Here precisely is the strong feature of the theory of corporate capitalism. Before the war, whether it was the Mitsuis or the Iwasaki family of Mitsubishi, the richest people in Japan ran the largest companies as their largest shareholders and they had close connections with politicians. It was clear to everyone that they lived in the finest mansions, and that through nepotism they were tied up with their fellow capitalists or with the aristocracy and the politicians. There are no such starkly visible great capitalists in contemporary Japan. Of course there are some very rich people, and there have been some very large private shareholders like Konosuke Matsushita and the Kajima family. However, most large Japanese companies do not have large private shareholders amongst the ranks of their shareholders. The buildings and factories of big companies like Mitsubishi, Mitsui, Hitachi or Toyota are visible to everyone, but who are the people who control these companies? They are difficult to detect. The corporate body that is the firm is in full view but the real people – the human beings involved – are hidden in its shadow. When this is the state of affairs, it is difficult for ordinary people to get a solid sense of it. For this very reason we have to explain the mechanisms involved by means of theory and evidence, and make plainly apparent the invisible structures.

The power structure of the business community

The structure of control in contemporary Japan is said to consist of a composite of politicians, bureaucrats and businessmen. Which is to say that politicians, bureaucrats and businessmen make up a trinity that together rule Japan. Bureaucrats are weak *vis-à-vis* politicians but they have the ascendancy over businessmen. Politicians are feeble when confronting businessmen and the latter have the ascendancy over them. However, bureaucrats hold the ascendancy over businessmen. At all events, the three groups are in a relationship of mutual dependency and form a structure where they are mutually interlinked. Although it cannot be said that the facts relating to politicians and bureaucrats within this relationship of mutual dependency have been well researched, their existence is known to everybody. What we do not know much about is the business community, and research into it has proceeded least of all.

Before the war the words 'business community' (*zaikai*) were used more or less synonymously with the 'economic community' (*keizai-kai*) or the 'world of industry' (*jitsugyo-kai*), but since the war the words have come to be used in a more specialised sense. Here I shall adopt the following definition: By the 'business community' is meant a group who form a power elite in the economic world which consists of large firms and their managers. Through its organisations it reflects its interests in the formation of government policy, and it exerts influence over Japanese society as the core of a composite group made up of politicians, bureaucrats and businessmen.[2]

In concrete terms, the business community is often taken to refer to groups such as the Federation of Economic Organisations (Keidanren), the Japan Chamber of Commerce and Industry (Nihon Shoko Kaigi-sho), the Japan Federation of Employers' Associations (Nikkeiren) and the Japan Committee for Economic Development (Keizai Doyu-kai). However, there are instances where a businessman is referred to as a man in the 'business community' even though he may not belong to one of these groups. In any event, the collection of managers of large firms who constitute the core of these groups are the essence of what we know as *zaikai*.

It was in the post-war years that *zaikai* came to be constituted in this form, and as everyone knows, it has come to exert a powerful influence over government as the representative of the will of total capital.

It must be stressed that, above all else, the role or function of the *zaikai* is to exert its influence on politics. It participates in the formation of government policy in a variety of forms and wields its power in this process. Furthermore, it influences the political parties, and in particular the Liberal Democratic Party (Jimin-to) in the days of its hegemony. It also exercises its influence over local and regional government. In so doing, the interests of individual large firms as well as those of the entirety of large firms are reflected in the political process. In return for this, large sums of money in the form of 'political funds' (*seiji kenkin*) find their way from the business community into the pockets of politicians by official and unofficial routes.

At the same time, we ought not to neglect the role of the *zaikai* in coordinating and adjusting interests amongst large firms, or between large firms and small and medium-sized companies. Various conflicts of interest crop up among firms and among industries, or between large and small and medium-sized firms. They also occur when firms are seeking to represent their interests to government. In abstract terms, one might consider that these conflicts of interest among firms would be resolved through the price mechanism, but in the contemporary world this is not so. It is not possible to leave the adjustment of conflicting interests to the price mechanism at the stage when the connection between politics and firms is at its closest. Therefore it is necessary to find a resolution within the *zaikai*, and the power of the business community increases the more, if it is more successful in achieving these resolutions of conflicting interests. If the *zaikai* loses its capacity to resolve these matters, it will inevitably experience a weakening in its influence over the world at large.

Thus the fact that the *zaikai* performs the function of resolving conflicts of interest among firms signifies that the power structure of the business community reflects exactly the power relationships among firms. Strong companies and the groups to which they belong exert power as mainstream factions even within the *zaikai*. It goes without saying that it is the large firms who wield the greatest power within the contemporary company system in Japan. Amongst these large firms it is the six large groups of Mitsubishi, Mitsui, Sumitomo, Fuyo, Daiichi Kangyo and Sanwa who are in a dominant position, together with large independent firms such as the Nippon Steel Corporation (Shin Nittetsu), nine Electric Powers Corporations and Industrial Bank of Japan. Most of these companies belong to the heavy industrial and chemical sector of industry, or in the finance and trading company sectors.

The managers of the firms in these six large groups and those of a small number of large independent firms make up the mainstream factions within the *zaikai*. For example, at the time of writing, the chairman of the Federation of Economic Organisations (Keidanren) was the former chairman of the board of directors of one of these large, independent firms, Eisaburo Saito. The vice-chairmen were the heads of the Mitsubishi, Mitsui, Sumitomo and Fuyo groups, and managers from large, independent companies such as Tokyo Electrical Power Corporation (Tokyo Denryoku) and Hitachi Engineering (Hitachi Seisaku-sho).

Mainstream factions within the *zaikai* are therefore made up of managers of the dominant capital that runs Japan; that is the managers of its giant firms. Even in the Japan Chamber of Commerce and Industry where, properly speaking, the membership is overwhelmingly made up from among small and medium-sized firms, almost all presidents and vice-presidents are supplied from the ranks of managers of very large companies. What we may call the private capitalist is an outsider as far as the *zaikai* is concerned, and those who may have made it to the inside are very few in number.

Managers of large firms

Although it is only a small paperback volume of scarcely more than two hundred pages, the classic work of analysis of Japan's class structure is Takanori Ohashi's work.[3] According to this book, there were 1,756,000 capitalists in Japan in 1965. Amongst them, officials of very large corporations with capital of more than one billion yen were designated as monopoly capitalists, and these numbered seventeen thousand in all.

According to the Annual Statistical Report on Corporations for 1982 (*Hojin Kigyo Tokei Nenpo*), profit-making corporations in Japan (excluding finance and insurance companies) numbered 1,748,967. Of these, 2,195 were capitalised at one billion yen or above. As a proportion of all companies they were a mere 0.13 per cent, but they owned 41.4 per cent by value of the total assets of all Japan's corporations. Therefore, it is probably fair to say that large firms with a capital of one billion yen or more form the dominant part of the world of companies in Japan. The total number of officers in all Japan's corporations number over 4,200,000, but of these only 29,609 are officers of corporations with capital of one billion yen or more. Firms in the finance and insurance industries are missing from these figures, so we need to add them in. However, since there are those who are officers in two or more firms by virtue of holding overlapping directorships, we have to subtract these from the total. Having performed this operation, we will probably be left with a total of officers of large firms of between twenty and thirty thousand.

According to the 1984 version of Kigyo Keiretsu Soran (General Survey of Affiliated Companies) published by Toyo Keizai Shinpo-sha, at the end of 1982 there was a total of 30,192 officers (directors and auditors) in Japan's 1,773 quoted companies. However, second-rank quoted companies with capital of less than one billion yen are included in the total, while on the other hand non-quoted companies with capital of more than one billion yen are left out. Furthermore, officers of the kind referred to above who hold posts in more than one company are included, so that there is some double counting. Therefore, when we have taken all this into account, we are unlikely to be much mistaken if we estimate the number of managers in large firms with capital of one billion yen or more to be between twenty and thirty thousand. In my view, when it comes to the query 'who rules Japan?', these twenty or thirty thousand managers of large firms are the people in question. Let us divide them into two groups and examine them: those who are owners of firms (including those who belong to the same family as the owners), and those managers who are merely salaried.

The data showing what proportion of total firms are family-run is now somewhat out of date, but according to the November and December 1975 issues of Tokei Geppo (Monthly Statistics) published by Toyo Keizai, there were 158 firms with a capital of one billion yen or more where the officers held 10 per cent or more of the equity shares of the firm. Almost all the shareholding by officers in these firms was accounted for by officers who were also the founders of the companies, or else from the same family as the founders. This means that the managers of large firms who belong in the owner or owner's family category probably number at most two or three hundred. This is no more than about one per cent of the twenty or thirty thousand managers of large firms. The remaining managers belong in the category of those who are salaried.

Of course, even managers in the group of those who are salaried own shares in the company for which they work. Details of this are recorded in Yuka Shoken Hokoku-sho (company reports, containing, *inter alia*, balance sheet and profit and loss data, equity ownership in the firm). However, the number of shares in their firm that they own is small and probably does not amount to a proportion of total equity that would lead us to believe it is connected to control. So then, it is likely that there are no managers who control firms in the capacity of major shareholders. Looked at across the board, manager-owned shares in all Japan's quoted share-issuing companies come to 1.6 per cent of the total. We cannot conclude that this is a ratio that would make control of companies possible. Since there are in this number companies of the family-owned type referred to above, excluding these would enable us to judge that the proportion of shares in large non-family-run firms owned by their managers is not great enough to present a problem from the point of view of control.

Large private shareowners

Almost all of Japan's about two million firms are either privately owned or family-run businesses. However, there are very few firms among those with a capital of a billion yen or more, or among those quoted on the stock exchange, that are controlled by large shareholders who are either private individuals or a group of people from the same family. This tendency is particularly conspicuous in Japan as compared with the United States or with Europe. In the United States, there are among large firms a fair number, like Ford, Dupont or Melon, which are controlled by large shareholders who are private individuals or families and who furthermore control the foundations associated with these firms. These matters are explained by Lundberg, and Birch.[4]

There are an even greater number of family-controlled businesses in Europe. If you read those books concerning family businesses, you will be surprised by the large number of family firms there are, compared with Japan, amongst the ranks of big companies. Thus if we draw international comparisons for the present day, we see that family control of large firms is least evident in Japan. However, there is no mistaking the fact that in America and the nations of Europe the progression is from family control to 'managerial control'. Consequently, judged from the point of view of this historical tendency, Japan has gone furthest in the drift from family to managerial control of firms.

One can adduce various reasons to explain why, as the scale of firms increases, large private shareholders become fewer and family control is lost. One has to do with the question of inheritance taxation. Since in Japan inheritance tax is levied at the high rate of 75 per cent on estates valued at five hundred million yen or more, it is quite common for shares to be disposed of, or else handed over to the state as payment in kind. Also, one naturally thinks of shares being distributed amongst the remaining members of a family as their inheritance, and that among these there will be those who will sell their shares since they have no appetite for company management. Also, strife within the family may result in the segmentation of control.

However, the most common reason is invasion by powerful external capital, which results in incorporation into a *keiretsu* (*keiretsu-ka*). It is an iron rule of capitalism that large corporations swallow up small and medium-sized companies. Firms that started out as one-man businesses or family firms eventually become prey to powerful capital interests and are incorporated into *keiretsu*. It goes without saying that these powerful capital interests are either groups of firms or else giant independent companies. A good example is Toyo Industries (Toyo Kogyo), now known as Mazda. It was founded by Jujiro Matsuda, grew very rapidly under the presidency of Tsuneji Matsuda of the next generation, ran into operating difficulties in the era of Kohei Matsuda of the third generation and effectively came under the control of Sumitomo Banking corporation so that the control hitherto exercised by the Matsuda (Mazda) family was broken. Because at the time of Tsuneji Matsuda's presidency of the firm it had repeatedly raised new capital on a large scale, the proportion of total equity owned by the Matsuda family had fallen. In contrast, the proportion held by Sumitomo Bank, Sumitomo Life Insurance and others in the group, and thus that by the group as a whole, had risen. But despite the fact that, seen from the point of view of shareownership, ownership and control had ceased to lie in the hands of the Matsuda family, the family still held the controlling position, as long as things were going well, by dint of filling the president's position from within the family. We may call this state of affairs fictional family control, but as soon as some kind of problem arises with the firm, the fiction is revealed, family control ceases and the firm is drawn into the *keiretsu* or the group by the powerful capital interests it is subjected to. Even at present, there are a fair number of companies where fictional control by a single family operates. A typical example is the Toyota Motor Company which would be a mistake to regard in the same light as a company that is family controlled on the basis of family ownership.

Another reason why in Japan the family-controlled type of company is particularly rare is because the large private shareholder was unable to keep up with the rapid pace at which new capital was raised. For example, if we look at the proportion of total equity in Matsushita Electrical Industries owned by the founder, Konosuke Matsushita, we find that in 1950 he was still a major shareholder with 43.25 per cent. By 1955 this proportion had fallen to 20.43 per cent; in 1975 it had become 3.8 per cent and in 1983 only 2.9 per cent. In this period, the aggregate capital of Matsushita Electrical Industries swelled from a total of 120,000,000 yen to 79.2 billion yen. A large part of Konosuke Matsushita's income came from dividends, but he was unable to subscribe, out of these dividends to the new capital issues at a fast enough pace, so that he was compelled either to sell his old stock or else not subscribe to the new issues. Broadly speaking, increases in private wealth were unable to compete with increases in corporate wealth, which, as I said in the first chapter, is an indication of the trend towards corporate capitalism.

It is a general tendency in corporate capitalism that there will be a waning of the influence of large, private shareholders in big companies, and that family control will disappear. However, it is in Japan that this tendency has been particularly marked.

From private capitalism to corporate capitalism

As we have seen above, as companies got bigger in the post-war period continuation of family control over them became unsustainable. Even assuming people from the founder's family became managers in their company, eventually family control was bound to become of the fictitious kind. However, this had not been the case with firms before the war. No matter how large firms were to become, if they were *zaibatsu* affiliates, control over them would ultimately remain in the hands of a *zaibatsu* family; for example, the Mitsui, the Iwasaki or the Sumitomo families. The primary reason why this state of affairs changed so greatly in the post-war period was because of the dissolution of the *zaibatsu*. Through this process, the core company (the holding company) of each *zaibatsu* such as Mitsui or Mitsubishi was dissolved, the family had their shares in the organisation confiscated, and thus the basis for their control over the companies in it was taken from them. Although after *zaibatsu* dissolution the various affiliated firms reconstituted themselves into groups, the bonds between the firms in these groups were of the interlocking kind due to the practice of fractional mutual shareownership. Pitted against the groups of firms that restarted from the old 'big three' *zaibatsu* there were the new groups, concentrated chiefly around each of the great banks and made up of firms who had belonged to second or third-rank *zaibatsu* or else, those belonging to the new *konzern*. The post-war structure of large firms was constructed out of the dominating capital interests that these groups together came to represent. These large firms then incorporated into their *keiretsu* or groups the new firms that had started-up post-war as family businesses, as well as other independent companies; this is also a process that simultaneously eliminated family control of these firms. Controlling agglomerations of capital will reassemble other capital in imitation of their own form. Through the historical circumstances such as these that surround agglomerations of dominating capital, the road was opened from private capitalism or family capitalism to corporate capitalism.

Next, in the period of rapid growth of the Japanese economy after 1955, the country's politics, its monetary and fiscal policies and all other policies were conducted for the sake of 'companism', and therefore firms grew larger but private assets did not keep pace. As we saw with the earlier example of Konosuke Matsushita, the proportion of all shares held by private shareholders fell during the process of rapid economic growth.

Although the switch from private capitalism to corporate capitalism took place in the way described above, the primary factor above all else responsible for it, namely *zaibatsu* dissolution, was a phenomenon peculiar to Japan and not replicated elsewhere. But deeper down still, a great global current was flowing. As stated above, compared with Japan the countries of Europe and North America had many more family companies controlled by large private shareholders. However, after the Second World War, even in Europe and America the institutionalisation of shareownership proceeded apace and there was a marked tendency for institutional investors such as the trust departments of banks and life insurance companies, who supervised and operated pension funds and the assets of private individuals, to become major shareholders in companies. The fact that institutional investors as major shareholders were exercising control over firms was made clear in the Reports of the Patman and Metcalf Committees. As previously stated, institutional investors take the assets of their true owners and put them to work to earn money by converting them into shares. Therefore, in this respect they clearly differ from Japanese banks and commercial and manufacturing companies who own shares as part of their own asset structure. However, they share a common characteristic in that both corporations and institutions have become major shareholders in firms in place of private individuals, and both have come to exercise control over companies. Although we can say that since institutional ownership is not as thoroughgoing as shareownership by corporations, and its relationship with private shareownership has not yet been severed, the former lags behind the latter; nevertheless it is still fair to say that the world-wide trend from private capitalism to corporate or institutional capitalism is evident in each, differing only in circumstance and degree.

So in the place of capitalists who were the major shareholders, managers of large corporations have come to control companies, and they have come to control the capitalist nations in which they each respectively operate. This is not 'control without ownership' as adumbrated by the theory of 'managerial control'; it is control premised upon the ownership of corporations or institutions. It is not an idea premised upon ownership signifying the ownership of private wealth. The way these managers of large corporations go about things differs from country to country. However, they are everywhere tied in with politicians, bureaucrats, the military and the rest, and they each control their respective countries.

8
Managers and Shareholders

The structure of top management in Japan

Up to this time various characteristics of the Japanese top-management structure have been pointed out by many writers, among whom Akihiro Okumura has found the following specific features by comparing Matsushita Electric and RCA. However, it should be noted that for Japan, 'top management' refers to the directorship only and does not include the audit committee, whilst for America, the term includes both directors and officers.

(1) The proportion of outside directorships in America is substantial, whereas in Japan it is extraordinarily rare.

(2) In America, policy-making occurs in the boardroom while operations are in the domain of the executive officers. The two roles are distinguished. In Japan, the directors frequently have management functions in addition to their policy-making positions and the two roles are indistinct.

(3) In Japan, directors hold their own positions within the company whereas in America they seldom hold any.

(4) The size of the board of directors (by numbers of members) is larger in Japan.

(5) In Japan, the board of directors evolves into the following hierarchy–chairman, president, managing directors, executive director, general director. In America, on the other hand, the director (chairman of the board) is the only member of the board with a distinct rank while the others are at least nominally equal. On the management side, though, the ranking follows from the chairman of the board, the president (CEO), chief operations vice president, vice president, and so on.[5]

The problems that arise from these characteristics of a Japanese company are twofold: first, policy-making and operations become indistinguishable, and second, directors double as managers. It is for this reason that outside directors in Japan are so rare. And this state of affairs becomes the cause for characteristics (3), (4) and (5).

In America, directors take charge of a trusteeship management function and decide overall company management policies by being entrusted by shareholders. The execution of these policies meanwhile is the responsibility of the executive officer or chief executive officer. In this management culture, the performance of both the executive and the directorship can be evaluated separately. And where the CEO or president is also a member of board of directors, his performance in each area is clearly defined and distinguished.

In pre-war Japan, the commercial code dictated that an executive or board member could not overrule the decisions of a general shareholders' meeting. In 1950, however, commercial law reforms distinguished between decision-making bodies and executive bodies to be more like those in America. Under this reform, the board of directors was made the supreme decision-making body with regard to corporate policy, while executives were named to represent the board in the daily operations of the company; however, this was not the case in reality whereas the two functions were separated by law. In truth, the provisions of the commercial code stipulated that representative directors were to execute company policy in accordance with the decisions of the board. As representative directors, doubling as executives, assumed the highest positions on the board, it is impossible for the board to direct and control them. As noted by A. Okumura, boards in Japanese companies have hierarchical orders based on the seniority system so the representative directors, being the highest, are also the oldest. This has more to do with social position than with function. By substituting the hierarchical concept for the functional concept that was imported from the US, the system has assumed a particularly Japanese character.

In this way, the policy-making directors and executives in Japan are not distinguished from each other, and consequently, matters that concern day-to-day operations find their way into the boardroom. This ultimately precludes the consideration of issues pertaining to corporate strategy and keeps the board from taking an industry-wide viewpoint in policy-making, preferring instead to direct the firm with a narrow, inward-looking viewpoint. In the end, this system puts policy-making and execution on the shoulders of the same people, so that when a decision is made it can be implemented immediately for the utmost effectiveness. It can also be said that this allows the company to pursue profit without undue concern over social issues.

This last point is due in part to the previously mentioned characteristic (1), which states that Japan has very few outside directors. Even where there are outside directors participating in policy-making, they either cannot or do not participate in its execution, and this, combined with their small numbers, means that policy-making bodies and executive bodies remain indistinguishable from each other. Saito, in his cross-country comparison of the UK, the US and Japan, said the following:

> In America there is a fundamental distinction between directors and executives and these two groups have their link through inside directors. In Britain, too, directors and executives are separate, but in their case executive directors are chosen from the group of inside directors. In Japan, meanwhile, executives are included in the directorship and assume responsibilities of both roles simultaneously. Then representative directors can be chosen from among the inside directors.[6]

So how have executive and directive roles in Japanese companies become so inseparable from the fact that most directors come from within? As regards this point, Saito indicates that there is a correspondence between the companies' top management structure and the state's political system. In America, the three powers of administration, legislation and judicature are separated, so that the members of congress, for example, cannot take a position in the executive branch. Corporations have followed this example and disallowed the powers of execution to members of the board. Accordingly, directors must appoint separate executives.

In Japan, by contrast, cabinet ministers are usually members of the parliament; thus the parliamentary system does not separate the powers of the executive and legislative branches; and this is mirrored in companies whereby directors also execute policy. This indicates, interestingly, that the organisation of the company mimics that of the state. However, Britain offers an obvious counter-example. Politically she is similar to Japan, but her organisation of companies is more American, rather than Japanese. The proportion of company boards in which inside directors do not have a majority is much higher in Britain than in Japan. So it is clearly not a sufficient explanation as to why Japan prefers not to distinguish between executive power and policy-making roles.

Relationship with shareholders

Executive and policy-making functions are distinguished from each other in America, so, in addition to saying that many of the policy-makers on the board of directors are appointed from the outside, we can assume that the board has been entrusted by shareholders to manage the company. This is called trustee management and it ensures that the shareholders have power over management by clearly delineating their functions. A. Okumura points out that the aim of American firms is to increase Return on Investment (ROI) and Price Earning Ratio (P/E Ratio).

This shows how US firms are constrained by the principle of 'maximising return to the shareholder'; obviously this is related to the familiar practice of having outside directors on the board. By introducing outsiders (shareholder representatives) to the board, the outsiders' interests attain priority, so shareholders and investors necessarily influence the goals of American firms.[7]

We may say conversely that in Japan there is an indistinguishable trusteeship management function resulting from a weak shareholder position. Kondo expounds this condition in the following passage:

> In a Japanese firm, the basis for coincidence of the highest executive bodies and the highest directive bodies is that the owners in the form of shareholders hold little sway over the company and managers within the company operate autonomously. There are precious few firms that view share price or dividend rate as important financial indicators. The reason for this lack of shareholder power is that there are few individual investors like in France and Germany and few purely institutional investors like there are in Britain and the US. Rather, most investors are other corporations and these type of investors look for stability in their transactions with the firm concerned, rather than its ROI. In addition, Japanese firms have a low rate of own capital to assets, and with equity playing such a small part in the total generation of funds, shareholders are bound to have less influence than their overseas counterparts.[8]

The idea that 'shareholders have little influence over a firm or its managers' may be confused with the idea that 'corporate investors are different from individual or institutional investors in that they look for stability in their transactions [with the firm in which they invest] over returns on investment'. Are executives and directors not separated in

Japan because shareholders in Japan have a weak position or because there are so many corporate investors? This is an important question. The question of whether the trusteeship management function was not established as a result of the lack of individual investors is completely different from the question of whether it was not established as a result of the lack of large corporate investors.

As Kondo said about large corporate shareholders in Japan, they are different in that they are looking for a stable relationship with the issuing company more than return or profitability on their holdings. As noted below, the shareholding facilitates the building of mutual control and trust. Like separate stars in a constellation the individual companies are drawn mutually together within a greater whole.

Large corporate shareholders issue each other blank letters of attorney for each of their shareholders' meetings. If a company does not issue such a letter, the shareholder meeting cannot proceed; when that happens, a corporation cannot manage. No matter how much a shareholder meeting may be incapacitated, it must be effectuated or else the firm cannot continue operating. That is to say, without a majority decision from the shareholders' meeting, the directors must resign. But this does not happen and the shareholders' meeting is held every period. And the suggestions of the company nearly always pass because the company possess the letter of attorney, or if present, hand in an agreement on the company's proposals.

With this situation having become typical, the shareholder representatives need not avoid separation of the trustee management from executive general management, thereby allowing executives to take on the policy-making process. In this way the corporate shareholders build mutual trust and create the Japanese style of top management structure. Of course, the historical relationship with management and administration cannot be ignored, but at the present stage the mutual trust built among large corporate shareholders has become a decidedly important factor.

Managers and share prices

American managers use share price maximisation as their number-one indicator of performance and, accordingly, push short-term gains, as investments are not made with a view to the long term. Japanese managers, in contrast, do not emphasise share price but instead take a long-term view to investing. It is suggested among economists that this is the reason for the superiority of Japanese firms *vis-à-vis* American firms. For example, in 1981, the *Economic White Paper* stated the following:

> In comparing Japan and the US, we find that, first, American firms emphasise short-term indicators such as share price and ROI to measure management's effectiveness while Japanese firms use such long-term growth indicators as market share and development of new product output.

And the above mentioned quotation from Kondo indicates that with little shareholder power, the manager need not use share price as an indicator of economic performance.

When we say that American managers extol share price as the best economic indicator, we mean that this serves as the premise for the following:

(1) Major shareholders and institutional investors require share price maximisation and so pressure the company for this. Nothing is more important to an institutional investor than getting the most out of its money. To this end they pressure the managers of the target company to push up the share price.

(2) If the share price of a company is low, they risk the possibility of takeover. If a takeover does occur, the managers are likely to lose their jobs and so they have that much more incentive to maximise the share price.

(3) Share options issued to managers make them focus on increasing share price as a means to increasing personal wealth. Share options allow a manager to buy shares in his company at a favourable price according to a predetermined condition. This method of compensation is becoming quite common in America. With a share option, as long as the market price continues to rise, the manager increases his personal wealth. In this way he becomes focused on share price maximisation.

(4) It has become a generally accepted principle in America that a corporation exists for the benefit of the shareholders, so increases in share price are for the shareholders and managers should cooperate in this endeavour.

Whether American managers came to value share price maximisation over all else cannot be corroborated here, and some of the above conditions may prove only temporary. But the premise is plausible in so far as it has been realised, and it also serves as the basis for the above conditions.

How does Japan compare on these points? On the first, in Japan institutional investors are not large shareholders like those in America. On the second point, there is very little possibility of takeover in Japan. Share options, as explained in point three, do not exist in Japan. And the general principle explained in the fourth point is weak in Japan. These differences are also reflected in the *Economic White Paper* and in the writings of Kondo. But there is one crucial item that these writings miss.

As noted in Chapter 5, Japanese firms commonly issue new equity when the price of their shares increases even slightly in order to effect what they call a shareholder stabilisation strategy. This is referred to as 'high share price management'. So managers try to increase the share price by however much they can and are willing to interfere with the price if necessary.

Of course, large corporations that hold shares in Japan differ from American institutional investors in that the former do not have the goal of profiting from a rise in the share price. Nor are takeovers or share options either expected or available in Japan. But devices which are unthinkable in the US like the 'shareholder stabilisation strategy' and 'high price share management' are used widely in Japan, and interference to achieve these devices is rarely made. So in Japan it is advantageous for a firm to raise as much funding as possible via equity finance, and it is expected that managers would cooperate in this. American managers aim to maximise share prices for their own benefit whereas Japanese managers try to raise share prices for the benefit of the corporation. This is clear evidence that 'companism' has been established in Japan. The Japanese do not increase share prices for the benefit of the shareholders: they do it for the company, because the manager is not a representative of the shareholder but of the company. Where this relationship between the manager and his company – or 'companism' – has ultimately been attained in Japan.

9
Managers and Employees

Promoting managers from within

As already stated, the top policy-making and executive functions of Japanese firms are relatively indistinguishable when compared with those of other countries, and as a consequence there are few outside directors. On this, we can refer to the previously cited Saito who compared between Japan, The US and UK following from *Tabulations of a Statistical Survey of Board of Directors – a comparative international research paper*; The Council for Economic Policy of the Japan Committee for Economic Development; and also to J. Bacon and J. K. Brown, 'The Board of Directors: Perspectives and Practices in Nine Countries', *The Conference Board Report*, No.728. Saito said in Japan:

> The average number of directors on the board is twenty-two. Most of these are inside directors and less than 10 per cent are outside. Although the majority of companies had outside directors on the board, they were all of the type where inside directors controlled the company. And of these inside directors, more than 90 per cent had been with the company throughout their careers.

Where the US is concerned, we learn that:

> The average number of directors on the board is thirteen with a mixture of inside and outside. Eighty per cent of the boards had a majority of outside directors. So boards controlled by outside directors predominate.

And where Britain is concerned:

> The average number of directors on the board is 15 and seventy per cent of executive directors spent their careers at the company. Seventy per cent of the boards consist of a majority of inside directors so most boards are controlled by insiders. Where there are outside directors, they tend to be bankers, company officers, major shareholders and the like.[9]

There are few instances in Japan of the American example. In Japan, as has been said, most of directors come from inside; outside directors are insignificant compared with those in America. As briefly mentioned before, the system of outside directors was set up to carry out trustee management functions, so it would seem natural not to have outside directors in a country where these functions are not separated from the general management function.

It should be pointed out, however, that there is a difference between inside directors and internally raised directors. The latter is a subset of the former. So, for example, a director that is dispatched to a company from its parent typically does not serve with the parent simultaneously so he is considered an inside director but not an internally raised director. Though dated, *The Toyokeizai Monthly Statistical Report* (November and December 1975) provides data on internally raised directors and inside directors. The report surveys the officers (directors and auditors) of the top 1,681 companies as of 1 July 1975. The results identified 22,235 directors and 3,815 auditors from a total of 26,165. And of that total, 30.9 per cent were brought in from outside the firm either as outside directors or quasi-outside directors, that is inside directors who started their career in other companies. And according to the report, quasi-outside directors come largely from the Ministries of Finance, Trade and Industry, Construction, and Transportation. Large numbers also come from government corporations like national rail or power utilities in a process known as *amakudari*, whereby older members of the bureaucracy serve out the remainder of their career as board members. The next biggest source of quasi-outside directors is from other companies in the family (*keiretsu*) of firms. And of these, most come from the bank around which most *keiretsu* are formed. Most of the intra-*keiretsu* appointees ended their formal role with the old company before starting with the new, but a small minority served on multiple boards. The members of this minority could hold the dual roles because of successful track-records in the parent company. So though many directors in Japan come from parent companies or affiliated banks, there is no denying that, in comparison with America, a huge number of directors are promoted from within.

Managers as workers' representatives?

So what are the consequences of having so many directors brought up from the company's own ranks of employees? Tadanori Nishiyama insists that 'since Japanese managers started as workers, they are really just workers with a supervisory function, so the capitalist has met his downfall in Japan and capitalism is no longer relevant in Japan'. Thus he suggested that Japan has 'escaped from capitalism' or 'crushed capitalism'.

According to Nishiyama, capitalism thrives in a society where the owners of capital and the means of production are at odds with the working class, which does not have capital and so sells its labour. A society without such opposing sides is not a capitalist society. Firms in a capitalist society are controlled by the owners, and when the firm becomes a joint-stock corporation they become shareholders. Since large firms in Japan do not have this type of structure and since the managers of Japanese firms are former workers, Japan can no longer be considered a 'capitalist economy'.[10]

Nishiyama's position may be extreme, but even if he is ignored, there are many who acknowledge the importance of managers starting as employees in the formation of a strong company community. The Japanese style of management views firms as a 'familial organisation' or as a 'living community', and therefore treats management and labour as one, or views management as the representatives of labour. This is premised on the fact that many directors were also employees of the company they serve. There is, however, a difference between saying that managers are from the ranks of employees and stating that they are representatives of employees.

Shichihei Yamamoto has suggested that Japanese companies resemble the military in that they have a strict vertical hierarchy with clear distinctions between employees and managers.[11] This is in marked contrast to American firms. It is the managers who decide on important human resource matters (such as dismissal and personal reshuffle) for the benefit of the company, not the employees. And in what is otherwise an employee-operated area like QC circles, the managers hold ultimate control, not the employees.

Above all, it should be noted that employees do not select their managers. That would be the minimum necessary condition for managers to truly represent the interests of the employees, but no large firms in Japan do so.

As regards this point, the political scientist Seiichi Okamoto has made a profoundly interesting comment in his *Corporate Reform* from which we quote the following:

> A company exists for the benefit of its employees and so should allow those employees to choose managers for themselves. Where employees can choose their representatives in management, they must also be able to choose whom to dismiss. So with the right to choose, employees have, for the first time, the right to know and to criticise managers and in the end determine for themselves what is best. The company will then be run in accordance with free employee decisions and the companies will constitute a completed corporate society.[12]

If employees were given the right to vote for managers, one must consider how the firm could become a vehicle for the employees and, if it did become so, would then the stronger bond between managers and employees not result in greater 'corporate egoism'? In addition, there is the suggestion that it would be extraordinarily difficult to realise such a proposal in Japan. But, as noted before, if Japanese managers are to represent the employees, the employees would require at least the right to vote for the managers. Without that, the idea that they represent the workers or are one of the workers should be rejected.

Employee participation in management

As stated, the lowest requirement for a manager to be called a representative of the employees is that he is chosen via election and this has reached a degree of realisation in Germany. Germany's 'Law on Union Decisions' cannot be explained in detail here, but it allows for manager selection as we can see in the following way. The Law on Union Decisions was enacted in 1976 for corporations, limited partnerships and limited liability corporations employing more than two thousand people. By law, the audit committee has to consist of equal numbers of auditors selected by employees and investors, respectively. When there is a tie vote on any issue, the chairperson (chosen from the investors' side) intervenes with two tie-breaking votes. The employee members of the audit committee are elected from the ranks of management, union, labour and other staff and so represent those who elected them.

This process of union decision-making can be found at other levels in the company and is known as the 'workplace cooperative' (*Betriebsrat*). This group discusses issues that deal directly with day-to-day operation of the workplace and is based on the 'management structure law'.

Japanese unions, in comparison, do not have the legal right to participate on the board of directors. First, the second article of the labour union law prohibits board members from participating in the union. So a labour union representative would have to forfeit his position in the union before joining the audit committee or board of directors. Next, according to article 276 of the commercial code, a company or its subsidiary must not have an employee on its audit committee. So a union member, as an employee, may not be on the audit committee. In this way, Japanese law, unless revised, prohibits participation of labour representatives on the board.

Then, how should non-union employees be represented on the board? In 1977 the Japan Committee for Economic Development conducted a study which found that none of the companies in the study had employee representatives on the board or on the audit committee. And of the total, two companies has responded that their boards listen to the concerns of the workers as occasion demands. It has been suggested that Japan should take up this issue in the same way as Germany, with its law on union decision-making, but the Nikkeiren and other parties on the side of employers strongly oppose such suggestions.

But at the same time, the Nikkeiren pushes what is called 'total involvement' whereby 'every level in the hierarchy can, to the same extent, make their will known through direct or indirect participation'. This is individual participation where each employee represents only himself rather than the whole. Thus it takes on a dimension similar to that of QC circles and is not actually participation in management, nor is it a substitute for participation in management.

So corporate policy is determined by the representatives of the firm in the form of managers and employees being expected to cooperate toward these ends. In this way the distinction between employees and managers is clear.

In Japan, cases where labour union members move up to the board of directors or to the audit committee and, from there, eventually reach CEO, are not at all unusual. According to the Nikkeiren report, roughly one in six of all the major posts of the companies have experienced union members assuming top executive positions. To name a few, Nisshin Steel's President Abe, Sumitomo Life's President Arai, Sumitomo Chemical's President Hijikata, Kanebo President Ito, Okamoto Riken

Rubber's President Senoo, Ohki Construction's President Tokunaga and Nikkatsu President Nemoto are some such cases. Labour union representation at the vice-president level and below is extremely common. And recently the union leader at Matsushita Electric – Takahata Keiichi – quit his union post to become a member of the board. From a cynical viewpoint, it is said that while Japanese unions do not participate in management, the members of the union act in management individually.

Here the important issue is the distinction between representation and origin. That is, originating from the union and representing the union are two different things. In Japan, joining the union can be thought of as a way of gaining promotion in the company because the company wants to have managers who can control the union. All of these issues are manifestations of 'companism' and even the union is a device for support of 'companism'. H. Hazama has the following to say:

> When the key personnels of unions in Japan go on trips abroad they are usually given parting gifts by the company and are treated on various occasions to games of golf and mah-jong in order to foster close ties with the company. It is a special characteristic of Japanese firms that key union people are promoted to positions of management within the company if they safely complete the work of the managing staff of the union. So when something like a pollution problem crops up, the union joins the company in confronting the local citizens. It is because of the union's selfish calculation that the union collaborates with the company in Japan. The union degrades itself as a parasite of the company.[13]

In this way the labour union, too, becomes 'companistic'. But this should not be reduced to individual officials of the union. It is so because 'companism' is comprehensive. Circumstances will not change even if the union participates in the management of the company. Nevertheless, it cannot do so under the system of companism.

10
Representatives of the Company

The basis of managerial authority

As indicated above, managers are neither the representatives of share-holders nor the representatives of workers. So on what basis do the managers control the company? This question pertains to the theory of managerial control. We have examined suggestions that control is based on the ownership by capitalists as well as the suggestion that it is not based on ownership. The former is called 'ownership control' and the latter 'managerial control'; most importantly, the question is whether this control is based on ownership, and if so, what type of ownership is it based upon? In order to answer this question, it is necessary to take a step back to the previous discussion:

(1) First we have the condition where control comes from the owner-ship by large individual investors. Many family firms are like this: typical cases include that of a lead investor entrusting management to a top-clerk of the firm, such as the pre-war *zaibatsu* like Mitsui and Sumitomo.
(2) Next we have control that is based on the ownership by institutional investors. There are well-known controversies over whether investors like the trust divisions of large American banks exercise a great deal of control over certain companies or not. Fitch, Oppenheimer, and Kotz maintain that banks exercise control of other companies through the shareholdings of their trust divisions, and while Herman, Sweezy and O'Connor deny their argument, they still maintain this position.
(3) There is also control based on corporate shareholders. In this area there are both unilateral ownership and mutual ownership shares.

With a unilateral purchase of shares the purchasing company can control the target company through placement of its own managers in the target company. In a mutual exchange, however, the company managers trust each other in order to guard their positions. Of course this is seldom so simple as this example suggests. There may be many companies with circular shareholdings in each other, at varying levels of ownership and control. The net of their ownerships of shares forms a system like a constellation: it is indecomposable, none of the elements being totally separate. We have already discussed this in Part II, but I must emphasise the fact that this is how managerial control can be based on corporate shareholding.

The 'ownership-based control' described above is not defined simply as control by owners, but 'non-ownership-based control' is defined popularly as control by managers. But this dichotomy is just distinguishing managers from owners. If the owners are taken out of the picture, what is the manager's control based on? We have so far not been given an explanation that is plausible. Some say that it is based on inherent power of the position, while others say it is based on the manager's conscience. The idea that the manager's control is based on his abilities is tied to the organic view of the society where people with power exercise it and those without power are controlled. But how do we determine who has legitimate powers? If proponents of the managerial control argument do not offer answers to these questions, then they are simply trying to vindicate the control by managers.

Control based on corporate shareholders

Based on the above classifications, we consider that the authority of managers in Japan is based on the last, third category mentioned – that is, managerial control based on corporate shareholders. This is not simply 'ownership control' but control by natural persons due to ownership of corporations. We must herewith regard the relationship between managers as *natural* persons and firms as *legal* persons. How can the former exercise control over the latter?

Originally a manager was a company's representative and, as such, served in an agency role. This role started even when companies gained status as corporations. With corporations, shareholders put up the funds to establish a company. And yet, the company's assets are owned by the company. If the corporation is defined as a fictitious person as the law states, then the owners are shareholders, because the company is only fictitious.

If the company accumulates a part of profits within it as a reserve fund, the owners of the assets are not shareholders but the company itself. Thus the notion has gone from the notion that 'everything which belongs to the company belongs to the shareholders' to the notion that 'the company stands on its own'.

In addition, with the company owning company shares, the idea of the ownership by the company itself becomes all the more clear. In the case of a one-way ownership by a company of shares in another company, one may say that the assets of this company are owned by big shareholders of that company. But in the case of mutual ownerships of shares of these companies, it is impossible to determine the ultimate owner of the assets of these companies.

The idea of a corporation being a fictitious person which insists that companies' assets belong to their respective owners, assumes that all shareholders are natural persons. If a corporation buys shares in another corporation, the 'fictitious person theory' must search for natural persons as the shareholders of the company. This kind of traceability of ownership to a natural person is not obtained in the case of mutual ownership of shares, as it is not so in Japan. Control is not from the ownership by individual natural persons but is exercised by managers on the basis of ownership by legal persons. This is because the former represents the latter.

Representative of the company

It is clear that managers represent neither shareholders nor employees. They are representatives of the company. In the case of the post-war Japanese economy, the relationship between company and shareholders and the relationship between company and employee are constituted in 'companism'. It is the manager who represents the company and executes as proxy its investments. In this, it is not quite what Nishiyama proposed with his 'dictatorship of the manager class', nor is it Masahiko Aoki's argument claiming the manager simply as the intermediary between employee and shareholder.[14] Both of these theories fail to explain the *raison d'être* of the manager and the basis on which he controls the company. Above all, the foundation for the manager's authority needs to be clarified. Baran and Sweezy once said:

There are many ways to describe the contrast between tycoon and modern manager. The former was the parent of the giant corporation, the latter is its child. The tycoon stood outside and above, dominating the corporation. The manager is an insider, dominated by it. The loyalty of the one was to himself and his family (which, in its bourgeois form, is essentially an extension of self); the loyalty of the other is to the organization to which he belongs and through which he expresses himself. To the one the corporation was merely a means to enrichment; to the other the good of the company has become both an economic and an ethical end. The one stole from the corporation, the other steals for it.[15]

Thus the manager is a 'company man who dedicates himself to the advancement of the company', and under corporate capitalism this is exactly the case. America's mega-companies seem to have taken a step in this direction, but in Japan the model of the company man has been fully realised. It is on this point that Nishiyama made a serious mistake. If it is true that there is a 'dictatorship of the management' as he said, the managers would be unrestrained by anything and would pursue their own benefits. In other words, the tycoons mentioned by Baran and Sweezy, i.e. the large individual capitalists, would 'steal from the company'. But today's managers would 'steal on behalf of the company'.

So what is the significance of the managers representing the company? Whenever a group of people come together, it is necessary for a few of them to represent the will of the whole. In what is called a representative democracy, each voter selects the representative of his will. But in some cases the representative fails to represent the will of his constituents; then the system deviates from a representative system, and there occurs a movement toward direct representation.

The problem here is not concerned with the case, like the above, of one person representing a group of natural persons. Rather, it is the problem of a different case where a natural person – a manager – represents a fictitious legal person – the corporation. Then the problem is bigger and more serious.

It must first be asked why it is necessary for a fictitious legal person, or corporation, to be represented by a natural person. Then we find that the necessity occurs when the corporation interacts with the outside world. It takes a natural person to sell, lend and otherwise interact with a business partner on behalf of the corporation. But it is not an interaction performed on behalf of the individual representative of the company. It is performed for the company, so the personal assets of the representative cannot be seized even if his company does not pay the money. What we discuss is a deal with a company, but since the corporation, as a fictitious person, cannot express any intent of its own, a natural person must represent the organisation. This is how the corporation works in the actual world; and from this the following problem emerges.

The company, as a legal person, has no will or ability of action and that is because it has no body. Anything which has a living body cannot escape death but those without such bodies may. Theoretically, the company does not face death. Of course, the company might go bankrupt or be dissolved, but logically speaking as a 'going concern' it can exist in perpetuity, even as shareholders may come and go. To represent a company which has a perpetual existence is entirely a different matter from representing a group of mortal natural persons. The loyalty to the company is taken as being far stronger than the one to a natural person because it exists forever. The relationship between two mortals can result in loyalty or disloyalty at a certain point of time. However, a mortal who pledges loyalty to the immortal company cannot turn his back on that company, because the pledge is eternal. In the last words of Nissho Iwai's executive director Shimada who committed suicide for his company, 'The company's life is infinite and we should serve to keep it that way.'

The manager, if he represents the shareholders, may be at constant odds with them because of opposing interests. The manager, if he represents the employees, also does not achieve a balance, as he is likely never to be trusted by the ones he represents. But such a case does not occur because the manager represents the corporation. This is the secret of how the manager encloses employees within his family circle in Japan where 'companism' has been established. He takes charge of this work as a personification of the company.

Representative directors

The duty of representing the company is, by law, the duty of the representative directors. In Japan's Commercial Code, Article 261 states, 'In accordance with the decision by the company's board of directors, it is necessary to specify a board member who will represent the company.' Dr. Imai and others interpret this as:

> Representative directors will represent the company and will constitute themselves a permanent organisation that is necessary for execution of the company's business. The title of representative director is given to the holder because he represents the company in all interactions with outside entities. As these activities of representation can take on a wide array of all external operations, the representative director is vested with executive abilities as well.[16]

So, within the role of representative, 'the representative director's role, whether *de jure* or *de facto*, includes all those management issues that relate to any form of corporate business'. And it is also said that 'recently the company's outside activities are all done through the representative director, so that representative rights have claim to everything within the purview of the company's sphere of activities'.[17]

In this way the representative director has attained executive functions and, accordingly, whether a director has representative rights has become a major issue. In the Japanese Commercial Law, there is no provision specifying the posts of company president and vice-president; but directors and representative directors are clearly defined. The board of directors is the company's decision-making body, while the representative director takes on the executive role. This distinction was made in a revision of the Commercial Code in 1950. As mentioned before, it was a distinction introduced in Japan in order to follow that in America where the decision-making and executive bodies of the company are distinguished. But in reality, this distinction has never been realised in Japan.

The system of having a representative director was originally meant to conform to the separation of execution and policy-making, but in Japan it ended up being a mere distinction in status only. In short, the most senior among the directors is the one who has become the representative director. It is characteristic of Japan that while this person is legally distinct from other directors in function, he is merely distinctive in status, so that he carries out the same function as other directors.

The representative director, as noted earlier, is the mortal representative of the legal fiction of a corporation. That is the legal concept for specifying his job function. So the nature of the corporation is such that, without a natural person to represent it, the company would not exist. But interpreting it as a concept which refers to the status of the position will create a problem. This is because it leads one to wonder who truly represents the company. As it is not concerned with the functional distinction of the representative director, it only distinguishes him from other directors in seniority. In such circumstances, any director may claim representation, so that no particular one represents the company. In terms of status, the chairman, the president, the vice-president, the managing director, and the executive director are on a straight line, in that order. The person who is highest in rank is taken as the one who represents the company, but without a clear functional definition of representation, other directors too may be regarded as representing the company. Expanding this way of thinking we may regard any employee as a representative of the company; as he gains seniority his chances of promotion to the board increase. In fact, every Japanese employee has the feeling that the company is 'my company' or 'my place', so that 'representing one's company is certainly no embarrassment'. So, in a sense, all employees represent the company. This is very much the soul of 'companism'. But while the functional concept has been replaced by the titular concept, the replacement has given rise to the paradox that a backward capitalism yields a most progressing 'companism'.

This view that all of the employees represent the company implies that there is no one person representing it. For example, if a company is guilty of polluting the environment the person in charge says that he did the work by the order of his superior officer, and the president ultimately takes the blame. But he was acting in accordance with the board of directors' stated policy. The board, in turn, was making policy based on the 'ringi' system (that is a Japanese system forwarding ideas from below to the top through a proper ladder for decision-making). In circumstances like these, there is no one person who can represent the company to the community. Moreover, in the case of someone being blamed for wrongdoing, all his colleagues support him by saying that he did it for the company. This is indeed irresponsible management, but with the company being represented by all the employees there is no individual to take the blame at times of crisis. In this respect the company after the war resembles the Japanese Army before the war. It is true that while the company is in a good condition, this system works splendidly, but in crisis it is very weak and can collapse. It is important to see that with no one in place to take the blame, incidents like financial corruption and environmental pollution are more likely to be repeated. And if, in response, public sentiment turns against the corporations, they may well concede to set up charitable foundations and contribute to various organisations until the tide of public opinion has turned, reversing their way of behaviour. When public opinion becomes calm, they bare the spirit of corporate egoism.

11

The Privilege and Position of Management

Who determines management?

The question of who chooses the manager must be separated from the question of who becomes manager. As noted before, a manager who rises from the ranks of the employees is not necessarily a representative of the employees. Managers in most companies in Japan start as employees, but clearly managers are not chosen by the employees. So let us look at who does choose the managers.

The Commercial Law makes clear that directors and auditors are appointed at the general shareholders' meeting. But the meeting is run mostly in accordance with letters of proxy passed among the various corporate shareholders, and the candidates favoured by the company are the ones who gain the positions. The shareholders' meeting is a rubber-stamp for candidates that the company has pre-selected for the various positions.

Accordingly, the person who selects the members of the board is the president and this nomination is automatically approved at the general meeting of shareholders. This is, clearly a case of one hand washing the other. The president, of course, does not recommend those who do not trust him as the members of the board but select only those who support him as the president. In effect the president is electing himself.

Looking at this alone gives the impression that the president has an unending grip on dictatorial powers. But as a mortal, there is an end to the president's power. There comes a time when a mortal gets sick or dies and, as a manager, must end his work. More importantly, opposition and betrayal may sometimes be unavoidable. So in spite of the fact that he has appointed persons who are loyal to him to the posts of managers, the president may at some point be relieved of his duties by these persons.

More importantly, there may be circumstances where, with worsening corporate performance, the president could be forced to quit by the bank or by a large shareholder. It is true that large corporations that have cross-shareholdings in each other reach mutual understandings on performance and have a system of mutual trust and control. But the system also results in a breach of trust if a company does not meet the goals agreed upon. But trust broken in one direction is broken in the other as well; so in the case of mutual shareholding of two companies it is impossible to break trust in either company. But in the case of companies forming a constellation of multiple shareholding a president may be mistrusted by a number of presidents representing shareholding of large companies.

In this way, it seems that a president essentially picks himself, and his tenure is therefore unending as far as he does not break the trust of his company's large corporate shareholders. But as soon as his business performance is found to be unsatisfactory he has to face a non-confidence resolution. In that situation, he cannot help but face dismissal.

Who becomes manager?

First, most of the directors of a given company in Japan are recruited from the ranks of that company's employees. We have already seen this proven out statistically. But let us also not forget that most of these selections are taken from among the white-collar employees. Instances of a blue-collar employee being promoted to the top are extremely rare. So to say that all employees are equal is misleading. The wage differential between white-collar and blue-collar employees has shrunk in comparison with the pre-war years, but the potential for advancement to high positions like director remains as small as ever.

Next, there are the directors who come in as outside directors from the parent firm or the affiliated bank. Of course they too are brought up from the ranks of the employees in their company or bank. There are, in addition, bureaucrats who have 'descended from heaven' towards the end of their careers to take on a directorship of the company. These groups are all white-collar. Precious little room is left for the presence of a blue-collar worker on the board.

According to the previously cited Toyo Keizai Monthly Statistical Report (November and December 1975), of all the presidents of the top-tier companies in Japan 85.3 per cent have graduated from university and college; for directors, the figure is 84.5 per cent. (These figures include graduates from the old regime professional high schools.) According to this study, presidents are on average 62-years-old, while directors are on average 57 years. This means that an overwhelming majority of the people leading these companies were born before the war. Unlike the present generation, 40 per cent of which goes to college, the number of college graduates from earlier generations is very low. This means that to become a director, one must be a member of a very select group.

And depending on their alma mater, there is also a distinction. Most presidents come from Tokyo University, and then follows, in order, graduates from Kyoto University, Keio, Hitotsubashi, Waseda, Tohoku and Kobe Universities. For directors the order is Tokyo, Kyoto, Keio, Waseda, and Hitotsubashi Universities. But since this survey was completed in 1975, it is quite old. A more recent survey (*Diamond Weekly*, 30 April 1983) bears out a different result. This survey includes results concerning the upper management (directors and auditors) of the top 1,745 companies for a total of 18,554 people surveyed. From this it is found that 5,012 people (or 27 per cent of the total surveyed) were from Tokyo University. The order from there was Kyoto, Keio, Waseda, Kyushu, Osaka, Nippon, Tokyo Institute of Technology and then Chuo University. This shows that most directors and presidents tend to hail from a select few universities and this observation is especially true for large enterprises.

There is no proof that graduates from these top universities serve any better in their roles as managers than anyone else. In fact we cannot say that graduates from top universities in these large companies necessarily perform any better than their colleagues. But the fact that these large corporations hire white-collar workers almost exclusively from the top-ranked colleges and universities means that the chances for promotion among these graduates are quite high regardless of ability. The fact is that these universities do not provide practical business training, and so the graduates have not received special training for managers. Nor does higher education forge the personalities necessary, for managers. Basically the universities serve as the large firm's recruitment screening device. As that is the case, once in a while a non-graduate will reach a managerial position and provide good results. In any case directors are selected from among employees in the way described above.

The problem of who should become a manager is an issue of social mobility. After the war, social mobility in Japan rose dramatically so that the various classes had, in a sense, all been equalised. Before the war, only those who came from the families of landholders, wealthy capitalists or high politicians could gain access to the best schools and then to the best positions. A peasant's son, no matter how bright, could not do the same and would have been likely to remain a peasant for life. But with the end of the war, the breakup of the *zaibatsu* and land reform eliminated the landholders and wealthy capitalists and the middle class was able to expand in size and wealth during the period of high-speed economic growth. Moreover, the difference between blue-collar and white-collar diminished.

This should be kept in mind when deciding who is eligible to become a manager of a large firm. However high the rate of wealthy capitalists becoming the directors of big businesses before the war, it is now much lower. As a result we see that social mobility has greatly increased in regard to managers. But the path to management of a large company is not open evenly to all.

A manager's wealth and income

The personal holdings of an individual are a secret that is not easily revealed; so those of a manager too are difficult to discover. But there is a way to indirectly guess the wealth of individuals from the statistics of properties bequeathed, published by the tax bureau. According to these reports, the top estate belongs to Taisho Pharmaceuticals' Chairman Shokichi Uehara at 669 hundred million yen, second to Kajima Construction's Chairman Morinosuke Kajima at 285 hundred million yen, third to Kajima Construction's Emeritus Chairperson Ume Kajima at 120 hundred million yen, fourth to Takeda Pharmaceutical's Vice President Shoro Takeda at 110 hundred million yen and fifth to Bridgestone Tire's Counsellor Shojiro Ishibashi at 103 hundred million yen. These people are the founders, or family members of the founders, and, as such, most of their personal wealth comes from the companies they own. The first-mentioned Shokichi Uehara holds about one hundred million shares in his company valued at 614 hundred million yen. The rest of the fortune is in real estate. As most of the wealth of these owner-managers is in share and land holdings, the typical salaried director is not in the ranking.

There are also published rankings every year from the tax bureau that indicate personal income. *The Diamond Weekly* (8 January 1983) compiled the statistics for 1981. Of the category of the top 500 in these statistics, 152 were doctors, 141 were presidents or chairmen of unlisted companies, and 58 were presidents or directors of listed companies.

Of the presidents and directors of listed companies the highest positions belonged to owner-managers like Konosuke Matsushita, Shoji Uehara, Ko Nakauchi, and Kanichiro Ishibashi. Salaried managers were not found. The same situation can be found with the unlisted companies where the wealthiest managers are also the owners. So the highest incomes in Japan go to those who own their companies.

In a review of 1982 personal reported income of the presidents and chairmen of listed companies, *The Diamond Weekly* (31 June 1983) said that, first, more than 80 per cent of the top ranked salaries came from dividend receipts. And that, next, of the 1,445 managers classified as presidents or chairmen, 201 received annual salaries between 10 and 20 million yen, 391 received between 20 and 30 million yen, and 277 received salaries in the 30 million range. Ninety of those in the survey received above 100 million yen per year. The average for chairmen was 53 million 850 thousand and the average for presidents was 42 million 870 thousand.

The fact that there are ninety owner-managers with salaries in excess of 100 million yen is rather overwhelming in contrast to the number of salaried managers with such incomes, amounting to only seven. They are Isamu Saeki (Chairman of Kinki Nippon Rail), Katsuji Kawamata (Chairman of Nissan Automobile), Hiroshi Anzai (Chairman of Tokyo Gas), Shun Ishihara (President of Nissan Automobile), Kanichi Nakayasu (Chairman of Ube Promotions), Yoshishige Ashihara (Chairman of Kansai Electric) and Tatsuji Ito (President of Mitusbishi Real Estate).

In this way, the gap in salary and estate between owner-managers and salaried managers is clear and distinct. Even the owners of small and medium-sized firms and the property owners rank higher in personal income than the salaried managers of large firms. On the other hand, those who occupy the main positions in the financial and business world are not men of wealth but salaried managers of the large firms. In this way, Japan is erasing the connection between wealth and control. Of course the salary and wealth of the salaried managers are far above those of the average wage-earner. But to say that these managers may be classified in the same category as individual investors would be a mistake. Under 'companism', the managers of the large firms attain position and power, and it could be said that they stand above wealthy individuals whose money comes from high income from their own companies, investments, land holdings or the underground economy. So in this respect, the link between wealth and power has eroded.

Before the war, this link between money and power was quite strong. In contemporary America a salaried manager from the rank of employee may become wealthy through share option plans, and their incomes are much greater than those in Japan. And owner-managers are much more common in America. So it seems that managers in Japan tend to be 'company men' while those in America are more the tycoon type.

While the Japanese manager has neither a large salary nor much wealth, his position as a manager at a large company gives him great power. He has at his disposal various company resources including entertainment funds that can be used to gain political influence or otherwise at his discretion. In addition he has a wide network of powerful contacts that may be used for things like assisting friends or family in the job hunt. And unlike the propertied *nouveaux riches* and those in the underground economy, the manager of a large firm is often the recipient of public gratitude. To sum up, the manager of a large company has a great deal of power in his position. This power, however, comes not from the individual but from the company.

But at the same time, managers in large Japanese firms cling to their positions, so that an aged top manager tends to create evil influences. His special power is due to his representation of the company for its external affairs, so when he loses his position he becomes 'just a person'. This is why, when a president quits, he so often becomes a chairman, and when a chairman quits, he so often becomes a counsellor or advisor, or an emeritus counsellor or emeritus advisor. The company is ever concocting one post more up the ladder so that their retirees will always be with the company. And for the one who does not make president in his original company there is always a higher position in a subsidiary or affiliated company.

In America, on the other hand, managers will retire at around 65 and quietly spend their remaining years on a ranch in Texas. In Japan, managers who are over 65-years-old and leave the company to spend their golden years in the countryside are extremely rare. Position and prestige as a representative of the company is the 'wealth' they have accumulated in their career and leaving the company would mean leaving behind their 'wealth'.

But with the domination of Japanese business by the elderly, this world will surely stagnate. The delay in generational change and the continuation of the old views will inevitably result in a loss of vital power within the whole society of Japan. Such an exceedingly long continuation of service of top managers is a harmful outcome of the corporate capitalism in Japan that helps to bring about 'companism'.

Notes to Part III (Chapters 7–11)

1   Wright Mills, *Power Elite*, Oxford University Press, 1956.
2   Heiwa Keizai Keikaku Kaigi, *The 1982 White Paper on Monopoly of the Nation: The Business Community* (in Japanese), Ochanomizu Shobo, 1982, p. 10.
3   T. Ohashi, *Class Composition in Japan* (in Japanese), Iwanami Shinsho, 1971.
4   F. Lundberg, *The Rich and the Super Rich*, Nelson, 1969 and P.H. Birch, *The Managerial Revolution Reassessed*, Lexington Books, 1972.
5   Akihiro Okumura, *Top Management in Japan* (in Japanese), Daiamondo-sha, 1982, pp. 26–8.
6   Tomoaki Saito, 'International Comparison of the Top Management Organization' (in Japanese), in T. Chokki, *Gendai no Keieisoshiki* (in Japanese), Yuhikaku, 1983, pp. 255–6.
7   A. Okumara, *Top Management in Japan*, 1982, p. 34.
8   Masayuki Kondo, 'Top Management in the Zero-sum Economy' (in Japanese), *Weekly Toyokeizai*, 18 June 1983.
9   T. Saito, 'International Comparison ... ', pp. 248–53.
10   T. Nishiyama, *The Structure of Management* (in Japanese), Bunshindo; and *Capitalism does not Prevail in Japan* (in Japanese), Mikasa-Shobo, 1981.
11   S. Yamamoto, *The Spirit of Japanese Capitalism* (in Japanese), Kobun-sha, 1979.
12   Seiichi Okamoto, *On a Revolutionary Change in the View of the Firm* (in Japanese), Shogakukan, 1974, pp. 78–9.
13   Asahi Shimbun Sha, *Diagnosis for the 'Japan Inc.'* (in Japanese), 1981, pp. 176–8.
14   M. Aoki, 'A Model of the Firm as a Stockholder-Employee Cooperative Game', *American Economic Review*, Sept. 1980.
15   P. A. Baran and P. M. Sweezy, *Monopoly Capital: An Essay on the American Economic and Social Order*, New York, Monthly Review Press, 1966, pp. 29–30.
16   H. Imai and Others, *Commentary: Company Law (1)* (in Japanese), Yuhikaku, 1977, p. 258.
17   Ibid, p. 260.

Part IV
Relations Between Firms

12
Fixed Relations

Problems with the inter-firm-relationship theory

Until now, economic theory has treated the firms and their relationships in the same way as it has dealt with individuals and their relationships; that is to say, it applies the idea of the market consisting of an specified number of buyers and sellers in order to explain the relationships between firms as well as those between individuals. Traditional theory does not regard firms properly and treat them as mere groupings of people. The fictitious person that is a corporation is nothing more than a group of shareholders, and it is they who own the assets of the company. This means that a corporation cannot act independently to serve its own best interests: hence there is no viewpoint that may form an inter-firm-relationship theory.

But economists who want to discuss economic mechanisms more realistically must treat firms as independent entities. As an abstraction or as a theory, they assume that the firms are not independent from individuals, but actually regard them as behaving independently. In reality, they cannot help but accommodate the interactions of firms into their theories, but there is no clear theory that can deal with the relationships between firms. These firms are personified, and concepts such as duty and sympathy, or Japanese type of groupism are used in discussing the relationships between firms in spite of the fact that they were originally devised to discuss human relationships.

But the reality of present-day Japan is that there are large problems resulting from the fact that the industrial chains (*keiretsu*) or the industrial conglomerates have made no contribution to addressing those issues. Thence a field of thought has emerged in the study of economics called intermediate area between organisations and the markets.

Since 1974, revisions to the anti-trust laws resulted in a number of problems, and consequently, economists in Japan decided to embark on such a study. In view of the fact that no significant study had been made by Japanese economists on the subject of industrial chains and conglomerates, this development was welcomed. The studies which these eonomists were mainly concerned with focussed on the economic basis upon which the firms were joined, and the functions served by *keiretsu* and conglomerates. Borrowing on the theories of Coase and Williamson, Imai and Goto made several propositions on the economic functions which *keiretsu* and conglomerates played in the intermediated area between organisation and markets. Where the transaction cost in the open market becomes very expensive, it is internalised within the system of the firm. On the other hand, in the case of very big firms, however, they are inefficient. Such firms form an enterprise group (industrial chains, conglomerates, and so on) with the purpose of avoiding the market failure and the inefficiency of the firms. The enterprise group is utilised in order to save transaction costs, especially in the area of information, intermediary goods and capital.

Here, the organisation refers to that of a firm but the market is taken as a relationship between individuals. Referring to an intermediate area between the market and the organisation, it is meant that we are concerned with the relationship between firms, but we lack a clear understanding of this inter-firm-relationship. This is so because the concept of the market is not explicit enough; and, moreover, the concept of inter-firm-relationship does not make much sense because the concept of the firm itself is unclear. Therefore, Imai and Goto's approach also does not provide an effective analysis of the reality.

Trading between firms in Japan

First and foremost, the relationship between firms is a trading relationship, which nevertheless has yet to be clearly defined. Moreover, generally speaking, the trade relationship has been a starting point of economics, so that the abstract models attributable to Walras regarded it as a most significant problem. But, in spite of this, there have been few studies and investigations regarding actual trading, so that we have to begin with very limited factual observations.

Present-day trading entities can be classified into four groups: the individuals, the firms, non-profit bodies such as governments, and foreign countries. Economic theory is based on the trade between individuals, but in reality such trade is rare. A vision of individual traders at an open-air market on the road in China comes to mind, where anyone can be a seller as well as a buyer, but in Japan such a market has disappeared.

Firms predominate among today's trading bodies and they deal with individuals, with each other, with government and with foreign countries. Figures for trade among these different bodies are not available, but we do know that trade among firms in Japan is relatively high. This is seen from an international comparison of wholesale to retail sales. The figure for Japan is 4.0; this is compared with those for America, Britain, France and West Germany, which are 1.6, 1.9, 1.2 and 1.7, respectively. In examining this result, we assume that wholesale sales are those between firms, while retail sales are those between firms and individuals. In this light we may see that trade among firms in Japan is comparatively high. In the area of assembly, for example, when a steelmaker sells to shipbuilders and automobile manufacturers, the sale is made through an intermediary trading company. In America, the trading company is not used and the sales occur directly. This is but one example of the Japanese way of trade among firms.

Generally speaking, the output of heavy and chemical industry takes a roundabout route from raw material to finished product, as inputs pass through many layers before being incorporated into the final product. It is then inevitable that a tendency towards heavy and chemical industries increases transactions between firms. After 1955, this type of industrialisation was intensified in Japan. This is one of the reasons that explains why the weight of inter-firm transaction is high in Japan.

But industrialisation was not the only reason for growth in trade among firms. It is common in Japan for large manufacturing companies, after having carried out the production work themselves, to entrust transportation of parts and semi-manufactured goods to other companies. Moreover, even for production, they use subsidiaries for producing parts and doing additional processing work. This explains how the automobile industry became so dependent on outside firms for their production. Basically, the assembly process which is broken down to a number of stages cannot perform its function unless it is associated with greater numbers of trading alliances.

Furthermore, we may mention that the lack of diversification in Japanese business also increases the need for trade among firms. Hideki Yoshihara and others showed that diversification in Japan has lagged behind America and Europe, ('Japanese Industrial Strategies for Diversification', *Nihon Keizai* newspaper). With less diversity, a firm must rely on outside suppliers for their needs. This causes increased trade among firms, and the industrial groups, which are formed for horizontal integration, further facilitate the trade.

In contrast to the horizontally integrated industrial groups, firms integrated vertically specialise in one area; this of course increases transactions between firms and discourages the group from being concerned with multiple business. Thus horizontal and vertical associations of firms result in a high level of trade among the otherwise independent firms. In this way firms become entangled in their web of relationships.

The theory behind trade among firms

According to economics textbooks, the market is a place where unspecified numbers of buyers and sellers meet each other and find out market clearing prices for goods by auction. This Walras model assumes that all the buyers and sellers are individuals. But as already stated, such a market does not exist in Japan. The closest thing to such a system in Japan is the central wholesale market where fish and the like are auctioned at an agreed price. But even there the price of the frozen fish is determined without auction. Furthermore, most buyers and sellers are not individuals but cooperatives or companies. Another example of an auction is the share market, but the prices are not necessarily determined by auction but often by face-to-face negotiation.

The theory of market transaction, i.e. that of competitive buying and selling, is concerned with trades between unspecified number of buyers and sellers, so that its essence consists of the fact that they cannot specify their opposite numbers. On the other hand, inter-firm transactions are mostly face to face, and not market transactions. Firstly, this is because the number of firms is far less that the number of individuals. So with the market being dominated by a few firms, it becomes an oligopoly and the number of potential trading partners is limited. In this atmosphere, a company must choose firstly whom to trade with, come to an agreement with that trading partner, and only then determine the terms of trade such as price, quality, and services. This is quite contrary to market trading where the terms of trade are determined before the trading partners who satisfy these terms are found.

It is often maintained that within the horizontal industrial group where face-to-face transactions are made, the regulation of the group is not tight and strict, so that one member firm prefers another only when no non-member firm can offer a less expensive price. Thus where terms and prices are the same or better within the group, a firm is obligated to buy from within. Without such an agreement among firms, the group would allow costs to go up and lose competitiveness *vis-à-vis* other groups. This is no doubt the case, but a large problem occurs in determining what 'same price' means, because it is implicitly assumed that there exists an unspecified number of sellers. However, actually no bid or auction is made in the interfirm transactions. Where a buying firm discovers a lower price; it is told to selling firms. Then they respond by lowering the price, but only to match the outside quoted price. This is not a competitive bidding process with an anonymous partner. Rather, it is favouring one company in the group over those in other groups.

This is the first characteristic of trade between firms; it then has a second characteristic that tends to be a long-term transaction relationship. For example, in the automobile industry there is hardly ever a change in partners among parts makers and assemblers. The parts maker is equipped such that it can make parts specifically for one particular assembler, and the assembler, on its side, is dependent on the supply of those parts. The long-term relationship is not only necessary for technical reasons: in America, for example, the relationship between car dealers and the producers is written in a contract, but if this relationship turns sour, the dealer or maker simply goes looking for another partner. In Japan such things never happen. In Britain, as R. Dore points out, where the inter-firm trades are mainly spot transactions, long-term relationships are few.[1] For instance, when a firm builds a factory, a British firm will first hire a consultant company who will the determine after thorough examination the best construction company and, if the firm agrees with the consultant, contract the company. But it will not consider hiring the same company to do all of its various construction projects. For if it is sued by the shareholders over something pertaining to the construction, the firm can simply be dismissed from the case by passing along the blame to the consultant. In Japan, by contrast, a firm that is constructing a factory will stay with the same construction company or select some from a list of favourite companies for its needs.

With this relationship among firms that is essentially locked up without significant flexibility, the number of trading partners has become quite limited. As noted before, big firms in Japan fix a list of regular trade-partners, and it is only from this list that the actual partner is selected. For a new company which wants to enter the market, the first thing it should do is to be accepted on the list of regular partners of some company. For this purpose, entertainment expense, rebates, and personal connections are necessary. Those new entrants who cannot be expected to offer such things are locked out of the market.

For example, Nippon Steel's sales exceed 3 trillion yen, but it sells its product to only 12 companies. This group is called the 'Tenth Day Club', consisting of selected traders (*shosha*); the only buyers outside that club are public agencies and the national railway. The Tenth Day Club dates back to before the war and so one can imagine that their trading habits are well established and inflexible.

Trading among firms is limited to a selected number of firms. This is the principle of inter-firm transactions which is most clearly observed in Japan.

The factors making relationship rigid

It is necessary for a firm to make a long-lasting inter-firm transaction relationship, in order for it to be managed rationally according to a perspective based on long-run calculations. However, if the relationship is kept unchanged, it cannot cope with rival new entries. This is the reason why spot transactions have become common in America and Britain. Therefore, to avoid a change in inter-firm relationship and to make it rigid, we need some other factors.

One of them is shareholding. It is said that the cross shareholdings between large firms that form the conglomerates help to stabilise their trading relationships and tie the firms into a group, or *keiretsu*. If it were just held together by agreements to trade on certain terms, the member firms would be free to find different trading partners, depending on terms such as prices, qualities or services. To prevent this from happening, the shareholdings are used to cement the relationship.

The relationship created by the cross-shareholdings has an effect that is entirely different from the one due to debt and credit. Under normal circumstances, a debtor will repay the loan as it comes due and the relationship will end there. But with a shareholder, unless the shares are sold off, the relationship continues unabated. So the bond between firms is very strong when they have mutual shareholdings. Corporate shareholdings in Japan are inflexible: a corporation will not sell on a rise in the share price, nor will it sell even if dividends are not paid. This is one of the ways in which Japanese corporate shareholders are different from institutional investors in the US. But it is not surprising at all because Japanese corporations hold shares in order to stabilise inter-firm relationships.

Another way of linking the firms is to provide directorships to officers and directors from other companies within the group. This is the human factor of reinforcing the bonds. In America, directors are not dispatched from one firm to another but they typically hold positions at more than one company. This phenomenon is documented in detail by a committee of the Congress. In America and Britain, and in Germany too, the top executives of large companies and banks typically sit on the board for more than one company. But the cross-shareholdings are not as common or as strong as they are in Japan, so in these three countries the fact that one person can hold several directorships in different companies is a significant factor for determining inter-firm relationships.

In Japan, sending officials to other companies as directors or appointing one person to the office of director in two or more companies, reinforces the already existing relations between the firms. So while in the West, when a director who is a member of the board at multiple companies retires or dies, the relationship between the firms also dies out, in contrast, the relationship between the firms in Japan comes first, so when a director dispatched by the parent company dies, another from the same company is likely to take his place.

In America, the power elite who serve as the upper management of the biggest companies form a small circle of social intercourse and the members connect themselves with each other through financial organisations or law firms. In contrast to this way of forming the elite circle, Japan emphasises the relationship between firms, so human interactions are based on the relationships of companies that individual members of the circle represent. Therefore, the relationships are more solid in Japan than in America and other nations.

Another way that companies strengthen their links with each other is by means of financial loan. As noted before, the credit and debt among associated firms can be disposed of more easily than shareholdings. This is a disadvantage seen from the viewpoint of maintaining stable relationships between firms. Soon after the end of the war, however, banks and industrial firms in Japan were more or less forced to form long-term arrangements and these relations became fixed. In recent years, firms have been defecting from such binding relationships with the banks, and the number of firms still reliant on bank credit has dropped. To counter this, banks have been attempting to meet the demands put upon them by industry by providing a unified service called the RM (relationship-management) system which offers a myriad of services like deposit, lending, foreign exchange, etc. collectively and adaptably. Although the relationships between the banks and industry are superficially influenced by the supply and demand for financial services, a firm, as a rule, continues to have its own main bank and the relationship with that bank never really changes. The point here is that, with banks too, firms have fixed relationships.

Lastly and recently, relationships between firms are strengthened as a result of the advances in information dissemination. The so-called firm–banking connection by which a firm and bank are linked via computer, allows the firms to instantly access and manage capital. Such an investment in technology solidifies the relations between the bank and the firm. The information age is also having a similar impact on firms who have data links with trading partners as these relationships become more intimate and that much harder to break.

So it is in these ways that the relationships among firms in Japan have solidified and industrial links have been formed, both horizontally and vertically. Compared to countries in the West, industrial links in Japan are far more advanced but create rigidity.

13
Mutual Control and Mutual Dependency

Theory on mutual trade

Reciprocal business, or mutually beneficial trade, in its simplest form, results when company A and company B agree to buy and sell from each other on mutually agreeable terms. As noted below, such trade relationships in Japan are extremely common.

Reciprocal business started to become popular in America in the 1920s, but with the move towards amalgamating conglomerates in the 1960s, it became a problem in the eyes of anti-trust lawyers. So to counter the growth of reciprocal business, article seven of the Clayton Act was applied to conclude its illegality in a number of cases. In Japan, on the other hand, reciprocal business is common, is seen as natural and does not seem to run foul of unfair trade practice laws, in spite of its accountability having to be questioned.

The first condition for reciprocal business is that the structure of the market should be oligopolistic on both sides of demanders and suppliers. Only under such a condition would the trading partners be able to decide terms like price, quality and service; otherwise, say, under perfect competition, they are determined in the market, hence there are no incentives for mutual trading. On the other hand, under monopoly too there is no meaning for making mutual trade. Thus, oligopoly is the only situation in which mutual trade is meaningful and attractive.

The next required condition is that both sellers and buyers are sufficiently diversified in business. This is because, if all firms produced only one type of goods, there would be no possibility of mutual trade where one of them buys the product of another and vice versa.

Thus, mutual trade is made in an oligopoly market between diversified firms. It will be seen below, following the argument of W. Mueller,[2] how the structure of the market affects trade.

Firstly, prices are fixed under oligopoly, resulting in the misallocation of resources. Of course, under effective competition, price, quality and service are left to be determined by market forces. But under mutual trade, transaction depends on other issues such as the condition that buying from a certain party occurs only if other purchases are made by that party, so that it cannot be effectively competitive. This kind of non-price competition is different from other usual kinds of non-price competition such as the advertising or sales facilitation which does not increase the sales across the whole industry. Rather, it gives rise to sales to one firm in the industry at the expense of another firm.

Next, participation by new entrants is deterred. In the most extreme case, if all producers specialising in one area and those specialising in another agree to buy only from each other, they can lock out new competitors. If they want to enter the market, they must seek out a partner of mutual trade. In this way, the net of mutual trade is expanded. Thus, mutual trade is an obstacle for a new firm that is a barrier caused by an element other than the scale of economy.

Third, a firm engaged in reciprocal business will increase the demand for its own products, but the relative reduction caused to competitive firms will result in greater concentration upon the oligopolistic firm within the industry.

Fourth, it is seen that all the things discussed above create structural change in the whole economy. The products are diversified, as mutual trades between firms are expanded and the comglomerate industrial structure becomes prevalent and a powerful source of economic expansion, and hence creates a further advancement of the oligopoly.

In America, markets that are controlled by anti-competitive practices like these are regarded as being in conflict with the anti-trust laws, but they are not seen in Japan as a problem. According to Mitsuko Akabori, there is a problem, 'whether the reciprocal business is considered in Japan as illegal under anti-monopoly law or not. The answer to this is probably related with the Japanese habit regarding long-standing customers more favourably'.[3] In response to this, Tetsu Negishi has the following to say:

Mutually beneficial trade that locks up the essential part of the side of sellers of the market by controlling trading partners and excluding competitors is regulated as illegal by the first part of Article 3 of the Anti-monopoly Law. Mutually beneficial trade that essentially limits competition and restricts free trade with partners is dealt with by the latter sections of the same Article, as inappropriate limitation of trade by mutual restriction on free economic behaviour.[4]

Thus in the anti-monopoly law, illegality of reciprocal trade is obvious, but there are few academics who insist on this fact and, therefore, the problem is barely recognised by the public. In spite of there being many reciprocal business arrangements in Japan, their very prevalence has resulted in a lack of consciousness about them.

Japan's reciprocal business

As noted before, reciprocal business arrangements do not arise between partners who trade in only one commodity. For a company to become both buyer and seller to a partner, it must have a variety of products to deal with. In reality this is hardly ever the case; and this is the reason why in America economists and lawyers do not give mutual transactions much serious attention. This is also used as an excuse by Japanese academics for not studying the situation.

But when there is a trading company that acts as an intermediary, the situation changes. The trading house buys goods from A to sell to some other company; similarly, for company B. Then both A and B make two mutual trades concerning goods, one and two with the trading company. This is especially significant in view of the fact that the trading house in Japan deals in a wide variety of products and can therefore be a buyer as well as a seller for any company.

In Japan, most of the trade between companies take place through these trading houses, and it is these houses that have allowed reciprocal trade to flourish. For example, Nippon Steel can sell its products to Mitsubishi Heavy Industries for use in their ships and trains, etc., but there is no product of M.H.I. for Nippon Steel to buy. However, if Mitsubishi Corporation acts as the intermediary, Nippon Steel can sell its steel product and buy at the same time iron ore and coke for its mills from Mitsubishi Corporation. And on the other side of the fence, Mitsubishi Heavy Industry can buy steel at the same time as it sells ships and machinery from and to Mitsubishi Corporation. It is in this way that the general trading houses facilitate and encourage mutual tradings in Japan.

On this point, the following statement was made by an affiliate of the Mitsubishi group:

> The steel-maker decides the amount of the deal of rolled steel in view of the availability of its raw materials, so that if a steel-maker has a powerful merchant house which can supply a large amount of the latter, then it can offer a large amount of rolled steel.

In free market trading, if terms of trade are favourable, buyers will buy the goods from whichever sellers offering them at the prescribed terms. But such is not the case in the situation described above. In this economy, even if an agent looking to sell a certain amount of rolled steel has only a limited amount of dealing of iron ore, then he cannot deal with that amount of rolled steel. This fact fixes the trade links between it and its partners and so shuts out any new entrants to the market. In America a steel-maker can sell directly to a machine-maker without the assistance of a trading house. In Japan such direct buying and selling is extremely rare and everything goes through comprehensive merchant houses. Therefore, mutual trade is much more widely prevalent in Japan than in America.

Reciprocal business also occurs between banks and industry. As banks are also firms, so this link can also be regarded as a relationship between firms. In Japan, though, most borrowers from banks are non-bank firms and most depositors are corporations. Most foreign exchange is also similarly conducted. Because the banking functions are carried on entirely in the same way, we may say that most trades are made between firms, so that mutual trade is most significant in the banking area too.

When a bank provides financing to a company, it is usual that the company is asked to keep its deposits there. Where the reciprocity in loans and deposits becomes stronger, then the deposits should be regarded as restricted deposits which are contrary to the anti-monopoly laws. Regardless of whether the firm considers these deposits as restricted or not, it is obvious that lending and borrowing are closely related with each other and form a mutual trade, by which relationships between banks and firms are fixed so that new entry is checked.

As noted before, Japanese big banks have recently introduced the R.M. (relationship management) system, according to which various services of deposits, lending and foreign exchanges so far dealt with by different sections are gathered companywise and treated by a single section. This is a systematisation of mutual dealings such as sales of government securities which is made possible recently by virtue of the revision of the banking law, as well as those concerning deposits, loan and foreign exchanges.

This represents a structural expansion of the reciprocal business practice among large corporations and among them and big banks in dealings of both goods and money. Mutual relationships of firms make their appearance, first of all, in these aspects of dealings. We concentrate our attention, in the next section, upon systematic mutual tradings within enterprise groups.

Trading within the industrial group

In 1983 the Fair Trade Commission issued two reports: *A Survey of Actual Trade Practices among Comprehensive Trading Companies* and *The Realities of Industrial Groups*. These are the first two reports on the internal trading practices of these enterprise groups, on which there have been no substantial studies at all. These reports, however, are rather superficial and only statistical and do not go deep enough into the subject-matter. But they may be regarded as the first research on trade practices within industrial groups.

In *The Realities of Industrial Groups* it is reported that firms (excluding banks) in the six largest industrial groups have a dependency of 10.8 per cent of sales and 11.8 per cent of purchases on other members of the own groups. If firms are confined to manufacturers only, the dependency is 20.4 per cent and 12.4 per cent, respectively. According to *A Survey of Actual Trade Practices among Comprehensive Trading Companies*, as far as the largest six industrial groups are concerned, sales to group members through a group's trading house was 11 per cent, and purchases from the trading house of the group was 5.8 per cent.

The Fair Trade Commission stresses that these numbers, on the whole, are not high. But this assessment should be queried. We cannot decide whether the figures of internal trades within industrial groups are high or low, unless we clearly define 'outside' firms. In this survey, only those firms whose presidents are members of the industrial group's meeting of presidents are defined as internal group members, so that a subsidiary of a firm whose president is not a member of the group is not defined as a group member. For example, most of Sumitomo Industries' metals purchases come from the subsidiary Sumitomo Metal Trading. But these purchases would not be counted as internal transactions; and other trades between parent and subsidiary are not regarded as internal.

Taking these shortcomings in data collection into account, from the observation that the dependence of manufacturing on sales within the group is at an average of 20.4 per cent for the top six conglomerates and 29.0 per cent for the top three groups of the pre-war *zaibatsu* origin, we cannot conclude that the dependence is low. In view of the fact that each of the industrial groups has 20 or 30 member companies, the obtained figures of 20–30 per cent may be considered as very high.

It is especially unfortunate that the Fair Trade Commission has not investigated how much the comprehensive trading houses facilitate and promote the intra-group trade. In spite of the report being quite detailed in other respects, the role of the trading houses is passed over. Rather than knowing what percentage of trade is internal to the groups, it is more important to confirm or reject whether the overwhelming majority of trade within the groups is conducted by the trading house, and concrete explanations of how reciprocal business is developed and handled by the houses and how that affects the group's structure would be most insightful.

Mutual shareholdings

Behind the reciprocal business relationships there are mutual shareholdings: this is the way of fixing trade relations. In their simplest form, mutual shareholdings are an exchange of shares by two companies.

The next level up is where company A holds shares in company B, company B holds shares in company C and company C holds shares in company A. This is circular, but not direct mutual shareholdings. However, a chain of one-way holdings makes a system of mutual holdings.

The situation described above is the company from the viewpoint of individual firms, but from that of an industrial group as a whole we may obtain a different view to the effect that mutual shareholdings can be expressed in terms of an indecomposable matrix including that of circularity. On the other hand, in the case of independent companies there is a large corporation in the centre, around which there are numerous companies, and thus the group makes a radial formation, like spokes from a hub. The large central company itself is independent.

In the case of the simple form with only two companies exchanging shares, it is usual that the rate of cross-holdings is low and so it is not very significant. The simple triangle illustrated above tends to have higher overall cross-ownership levels, but the extent of each one is still not high. It is the matrix forms which have the highest overall rates – perhaps greater than 30 per cent – and therefore allow for levels which are significant for controlling the target company. Then the presidents' meeting of the industrial group becomes powerful and makes decisions such as instalment or replacement of presidents of member companies.

But it must also be remembered that those corporations which are controlled by other members in the industrial group are also companies that control some others in the group. Thus the mutual control emerges from mutual shareholdings. It is not a one-to-one control between firms. They are members of a conglomerate and controlled by the entire group, which is connected to the whole by trust between members. When one link in the chain of trust is broken, the entire presidents' meeting becomes ill-trusting and the group cannot sustain itself. To avoid such a situation, the group must exercise strict control.

In the case of the independent corporation in the radial formation, the success of the group does not depend on mutual trust and control, but if a firm performs badly, the large central shareholder will force it to accept an agreement. In this way mutual trust and dependence is eventually established in the radial formation as well. Furthermore, independent large firms and conglomerates will make mutual shareholdings, and in this way mutual control and dependence will expand themselves in the sector of large firms. Thus a firm which is a member of a certain controlling group is controlled by the group itself. This is of course neither unilateral control nor simple mutual dependence, but we may characterise it as a system of mutual control and mutual dependence.

Elements which support 'companism'

In order for a system of 'companism' to persist, it is necessary to prevent the possibility of takeover. It has been seen that the strategy for establishing stable shareholdings will clearly prevent any trial of takeover. There is the case of unilateral holdings of shares, but more often it is a multilateral exchange of shares that accomplishes the strategy. This is because, although it would be fine for a parent company to have unilateral shareholdings in its subsidiary, a large firm that buys shares in another large firm in order to stabilise its shareholders wants the favour returned by that company. In the case of industrial groups, mutual shareholdings are made in a systematic way, so that they become more prevalent.

Thus one of the benefits of mutual shareholding is to prevent takeovers. This, in turn, provides security to companies and makes 'companism' possible. Whereas mutual dependence and mutual control are enhanced, threats from the outside are minimised.

The reciprocal business enables the companies to maintain fixed trade relations for a long period; this sustains the oligopoly and also blocks out new entrants. As trade partners are fixed for a long period, every company can make decisions of long-term investment in trust of its trade partners. The long-term plans of the companies are well adjusted to those of the partners. The fact that business is carried out on the basis of long-term views is very important in order for the system of companism to be maintained.

Finally, mutual control and mutual dependence have the benefit of reducing risks for each of the parties. It is generally observed that in the case of a slump in operations, the firms of the same industrial groups serve to support each other. On this topic, Iwao Nakatani has made an interesting point in his 'Research on Industrial Groups' to the effect that, in comparison with independent firms, the firms belonging to an industrial group have lower profit and growth rates. But, at the same time, growth and profit rates for members of a group do not differ much from one firm to another. This is because when a firm in the group falls on hard times, the other members come to its aid, which brings down their performance as well as enhancing the ailing firm's performance. Nakatani calls this system 'the mutual insurance system' or 'risk sharing', and finds the economic function of the industrial groups.[5]

This so-called risk sharing also promotes 'companism' in that, when a firm is at risk of failing, it can be assured that assistance is on the way to rescue it. This enhances faith that the company will continue to exist in the long term.

14
Externalisation and Formation of *Keiretsu*

Externalisation by large firms

It has been pointed out that large manufacturers in Japan entrust their buying and selling functions and transportation to a separate company and subcontract the manufacture and processing of parts, so they concentrate solely on the function of assembly of the main body of products. This was first found by Rodney Clark. In *The Japanese Company* he mentioned the high degree of specialisation in a Japanese company. He states that 'many firms limit themselves to one industry even to the extent of production or distributing only one item'.[6] He further details the situation as follows:

> The second aspect of the functional specialisation of the Japanese company is the way in which a firm will farm out what in the West would be considered essential parts of its business to other companies. A great number of Japanese firms, and especially smaller ones, sell through trading companies and wholesalers, and rely on haulers to carry their goods to their customers. The companies thereby leave themselves free to concentrate on manufacture. Yet they do not even undertake the complete process of manufacture, but rely instead on subcontractors. Thus the activities that are carried out by a large Western company, activities ranging from gathering raw materials, refining them, turning them into parts, assembling components, marketing the product and carrying it to the customer, may in Japan all be undertaken by separate companies, specialised in a particular task.[7]

In America, for example, a steel-maker is concerned with production of the ore and coal from the time it is mined, then processes them into the steel or coil and delivers the final products to the customer. In Japan, by contrast, most of the process, even the part which is considered as the mainstay of the industry (that is to say, the work to convey ingot iron from blast furnace to revolving furnace), is subcontracted. This is a very sharp observation which highlights the fact that big firms in Japan externalise a substantial part of their business. In the case of the automobile industry, it has been said that the rate of reliance on the parts produced by outside factories is more than 70 per cent in Japan, while it is about 52 per cent, 41 per cent and 40 per cent for GM, Ford and Chrysler, respectively. Another example is in the manufacture of colour televisions. In Japan, TV manufacturers rely on outside sources for 60 to 70 per cent of the parts, excluding the IC and the Braun tube. A similar figure in the West is comparatively low at 50 to 60 per cent.[8]

There is a problem here in that the current system has not resulted from division of labour, but from the fact that parts are supplied by subsidiaries which are under the control of parent companies. We may thus conclude that externalisation is made possible only in the form of the *keiretsu*.

The realities of industry's *keiretsu*

The term '*keiretsu*' came out during the Second World War, so it is a relatively new concept which is hard to translate into foreign languages. Of course it includes subsidiaries and affiliated firms, but the meaning is greater than that. A subsidiary is usually more than 50 per cent owned by the parent while an affiliate is more than 10 per cent owned by its parent. But such levels of ownership do not define a company as a *keiretsu* because it includes companies which have no equity at all held by the parent.

In 1982, the Fair Trade Commission conducted a survey of the top 100 non-bank firms. These top one hundred had 8,529 affiliations (more than 10 per cent of equity) within Japan and served as parent companies (holding more than 50 per cent of equity) to 2,995 companies. Most of the affiliates are connected to general trading houses, electrical parts manufacturers, and auto and steel-makers. Another important point is that below all these firms are the subcontractors, forming a pyramid of layers, ultimately controlled by the parent company at the top. According to the 1982 White Papers on Small and Medium Enterprises, among the small and medium manufacturers, 66.5 per cent were subcontractors for other firms; and the figure is increasing from year to year. For this reason, Japan is sometimes referred to as the '*keiretsu* archipelago'.

Masataka Ikeda states that, in spite of the lower dependency that Western automobile companies have on outside firms, the number of subcontractors is still very high. For example, in 1964 West Germany's Daimler Benz had 18,000 separate subcontractors. The dependency of Japanese firms on subcontractors is higher on a percentage of content, but the number of contractors is markedly fewer. Toyota and Nissan each have about 200 direct subcontractors. He says:

> This is because in Japan the subcontractors form a vertical hierarchy. At the top is the automobile manufacturer. The topmost layer of sub-contractors is directly controlled by the firm and then the lower levels of subcontractors are handled by the layers immediately above them. In the West, where subcontractors are not put into a system, the automobile maker has to deal directly with all the necessary sub-contractors, but cannot influence those subcontractors which are not directly supplying parts.[9]

This shows that in Japan the relationship between a parent and a *keiretsu* member firm is top down, while in the West companies involved are more equal. The large Japanese firm serves as a hub around which all else gathers and through which most of its activity is externalised. This provides these firms with a favourable edge and is said to be a source of great advantage in the international marketplace.

The aim of forming a *keiretsu*

There are several different types of *keiretsu*. The first is the type with a vertical, top-down structure, in which the raw materials or the semi-finished goods that its subsidiaries make are supplied to the parent. In the West, cases of vertical integration are either when a parent company itself advances into the business or it merges with another existing company. In Japan, subcontracts are formed by the parent company in such cases.

The second type of *keiretsu* is the type of horizontal structure that has firms specialising in one area. Here the parent operates in conjunction with the other firms in its speciality. Toyota, with its affiliates Hino Motors and Daihatsu Industries, is such a case. The industries commonly forming such *keiretsu* are found in the areas of banking, securities, trading and transport rather than those of general manufacturing. The parent of these *keiretsu* has managed to strengthen its control over the market through this type of partnership.

The third type of *keiretsu* favours diversification, as the parent always ventures into new areas and spins off new companies for those new businesses. The fourth type is the sales *keiretsu*. In Japan, electric and automobile manufacturers establish subsidiaries for selling their products; these have, under the umbrella, companies specialising in sales for a particular geographic area.

The fifth type is formed especially for the purpose of advancement into foreign markets. A new company is formed in the target country as a 100 per cent owned foreign venture or as a joint venture financed by a domestic firm or the government of that country. Since the 1970s the Japanese have increasingly ventured overseas in this manner.

There are several reasons why big companies do not carry out the entire work by themselves and externalise so many of their functions to other firms. The first is to take advantage of wage differentials. As has been said before, the formation of *keiretsu*, as well as the use of the term, became popular after the Second World War. In the 1950s, when the Korean War was fought, the wage differential between large firms and small or medium-sized enterprises was quite wide, so large companies formed *keiretsu* with smaller firms to take advantage of their lower wages. Then, in the so-called period of high-rate growth (1950–70) when new entrants to the labour market were scarce, the wage differentials for those new labourers narrowed. But for middle-aged and older workers, the wage gap was still substantial, and in view of other labour conditions we must say that wage differentials between the large and small firms remained unchanged.

The second aim for forming a *keiretsu* is for the parent to shift risks away from itself to subsidiaries. For example, when entering a new industry or a new field of business, the parent company would bear a great deal of risk if it entered on its own. By pushing one of the *keiretsu* member firms into the new business, the parent itself is not unduly harmed, even if the venture is a failure. In the area of liability for environmental pollution and workforce health and safety welfare, risks are minimised, as blame for an incident that is the responsibility of another firm or subcontractor does not accrue to the parent.

Thirdly, a parent company forms *keiretsu* in order to avoid too much expansion of its organisation and to guard against inefficiency due to scale. For this purpose, the various functions of the firm are separated and entrusted to an independent company. Hitachi and Matsushita follow this model under which they have established many subsidiaries to deal with the work specified.

Thus the aims of forming a *keiretsu* range from taking advantage of wage differentials, to spreading risks and invigorating the management of the organisation. As time goes on, the weight moves from the former to the latter. The *keiretsu* which had once been regarded as an old-fashioned organisation has now become the source of Japan's competitiveness. The *keiretsu*, therefore, is an indispensable pillar of 'companism'.

The tools of the *keiretsu*

The first tool of the *keiretsu* is the shareholdings by the parent in the subsidiary. The structural characteristics of Japan's corporate shareholders have already been noted, along with their aim of linking with other companies, so that shareholding has been used for forming *keiretsu*. Shares are either bought from existing firms in order to make them its own subsidiaries, or held by the parent when it establishes a new subsidiary by separating its part as an independent organisation.

By saying that the parent firm controls the *keiretsu* firm through its shareholdings, I mean that it controls the latter by becoming a major shareholder. But it must be remembered that the parent firm is of course a legal person, not a capitalist as a natural person. Needless to say, legal persons cannot attend the shareholders' meeting; they are represented by the managers of the respective companies. Although these do not have shares, as the representatives of the parent they can exercise the right of shareholding of the parent and by this means control the *keiretsu* firm.

Although it is the parent who usually owns equity in the subsidiary unilaterally, the subsidiary can sometimes own shares in the parent as well. This is a case of mutual shareholding. But owning shares in one's parent in this way is like owning shares in one's own company and the latter is forbidden by commercial law. In 1981, however, a revision was made to the laws which clarified the limitations of shareholding between parent and subsidiary. The new law stated that parents who own more than 50 per cent of the shares of a subsidiary could not allow the subsidiary to own a share in the parent.

Another important tool for the *keiretsu* is the dispatch and assignment of directors. It is suggested that the so-called 'control by managers' separates management from ownership, resulting in control without ownership. However, parent firms exercise control via their ownership, so this statement is not entirely true. And the fact that the parent dispatches its own employees to fill the top spots in its subsidiaries means that there are not many subsidiaries whose president posts are filled by its own employees.

According to the *Statistical Report on Management Participation by Shareholders* issued by the Fair Trade Commission, the number of managers dispatched to subsidiaries correlates strongly with the degree of shareholdings the parent has in the subsidiaries. We may say that in *keiretsu* there is a clear link between shareholding and dispatched managers. The decision-makers and action-takers are human managers, not the fictitious person that is the parent company. So for the parent to install its own managers in the subsidiary allows for better influence and control than if the firm is left to run its own affairs.

In addition to the tools described above, there is the lending of funds by the parent to subsidiaries, as well as the assurance by the former regarding the debts made by the latter. In Japan, bills are often used and inter-firm trust and credit play an important role in inter-firm transactions. There are cases in which the parent controls subsidiaries by offering inter-firm credit to them. With the development of computerisation, information technology and data links are likely in the future to be used as weapons for controlling *keiretsu*.

The relationship between a parent and subsidiary is not merely a one-way street in which the parent takes and the subsidiary gives. The *keiretsu* provides a stable trading environment to the subsidiary, which obtains support from the parent through financing and other means. But the relationship is also not an equal one and the subsidiary is not just a freelancer. Trade partners are fixed and the subsidiary is controlled by the parent, so its transactions are restricted.

Logic of externalisation

We have seen that large companies in certain industries in Japan have externalised most of their operations. The externalisation gives birth to organisations outside of the main body of the large firm; they have not, however, run freely. In America we have seen that manufacturers like General Motors have a relatively high internal content, but of course they still have parts sourced from the outside. In this case the contractor and the subcontractor are placed on an equal footing as long as the latter produces according to the terms of the contracting firm. But if either of the two does not satisfy the conditions offered by the opposite number, it can switch to another contractor or subcontractor.

In Japan, on the other hand, it would be inconceivable to have a parts-maker for Toyota which sells its product to Nissan. As already explained, Japanese makers have fixed their trading partners within the *keiretsu*, so that externalisation is very restrictive. This externalisation by forming *keiretsu* has been judged in recent years to be Japanese industry's competitive edge. The famous British sociologist Ronald Dore said that the give-and-take relationship among Japanese firms (called 'obligated relational contracting' by him) allowed them to ride out the oil crisis and regain their high level of performance. The stable, long-term trading relationship enables the firm to make investment on the basis of a long-term perspective. In order to maintain a long-term relationships with the contractor, the subcontractor must keep the quality of their products at a high level. This is the reason why Japan has performed well. Then Dore concludes that British and American firms have to learn from Japan seriously in this respect.

On the other hand, the trading relationships among the *keiretsu* have been blamed by the American government and Congress and EC Commissioners for closing the Japanese market to foreign goods. But Yoshio Sato disagrees. According to him, the subcontracting system is set up for the sake of the parent company, to save capital, to obtain low wage labour, to establish more effective labour management, and for the purpose of shock absorption in times of crisis. Expounding these points he continues:

> In economic terms the *keiretsu* is a 'vertical integration'. First, it plays the same role as all *keiretsu* firms when they are integrated into one company. Secondly, transactions they make have a market relationship. Thirdly, the competitive principle is realised effectively in the *keiretsu*. So as the industry or company expands, and social division of labour is in progress, the specialisation among firms is deepened. Those that have started as subcontractors, later grow up to become independent companies with high-level skill and technique which they have acquired and learned from their ex-parent companies.[10]

I disagree with Sato's view, particularly on his point of the *keiretsu* having the same function as the market. We have seen above that the trade relations of the *keiretsu* are fixed, so it cannot be equated to the market, as has been pointed out by Dore.

It has been seen that the parent firm benefits from the inter-firm relationship, and, at the same time, the subcontractors also benefit to some degree. Although this fixed structure is more or less consented to by both sides in the partnership, we cannot say that it is equivalent or alternative to a free-market system.

Thus the parent and subsidiaries form a hierarchy and the latter are ranked according to their position within it. In parallel to this, the employees of these companies are ranked. In this way, the rank of the company determines the rank of human beings. Where 'companism' becomes a caste system, equality in human relations is cast aside.

15
Exclusionary Character

Trade friction

As serious trade frictions have emerged in succession between Japan on the one hand and America and Europe on the other, Japan's relationship with these countries has deteriorated, as voices there that used to praise the Japanese economy have now been drowned out by those who blame it. The trade debate started with textiles and moved on to steel, consumer electronics and automobiles. At first the problem was dealt with and was settled by each of these industries as it imposed export control on itself. Then it was found that this did not lead to a satisfactory solution and the problem was regarded as a general one related to the Japanese government's industrial policy, or a basic problem accruing from malfunctions of the mechanism of circulation of commodities in Japan. In these environments, ex-*zaibatsu* groups, or simply industrial groups and *keiretsu* were said to be ringleaders of those who had set non-tariff barriers.

Analysing the foreign trade of the US, the Gibbons Report expresses the following view:

> While many Japanese would argue that the pre-war holding companies or *zaibatsu* have not been recreated, they are clearly in close contact. As one American scholar has written (and as was confirmed to The Delegation): There is nevertheless, close contact. For the largest combinations, this contact has traditionally taken place in monthly clubs.[11]

These monthly meetings are Nimokukai of the Mitsui Group, Kinyokai of Mitsubishi and Hakusuikai of Sumitomo, for example.

In *Business and Society in Japan*, Professor Albert Keidel of Ohio State University has this to say about Japanese company structure:

> In fact, the most important form of Japanese business combination is not centered around control of a single market, but rather around oligopolistc influence in an entire range of related industries and markets. Hence, to understand the economic power of business groupings in Japan, one must be familiar with a tangle of intercorporate ownership, market, and credit relationships.

This observation by Keidel is extremely important. In the past, the problems of concentration of firms and of new entry have been discussed from the viewpoint of the theory of industrial structure directly imported from America. But according to Keidel, it is not this, but the relationship between firms that is the problem.

As pointed out by the Gibbons Report, Mr. Olmer, US Under-Secretary for Trade, has said the following about US–Japan trade in 1982: 'The *keiretsu* formed on the basis of vertical and horizontal relationships between firms and banks results in a closed system which often closes its eyes to open competition and stimulates the mentality of "buy Japanese" ' (*Nihon Keizai Shimbun*, 1 July 1982).

The EC has issued condemnations of the *keiretsu* similar to the American criticisms. At the GATT conference in Geneva in May 1982, the EC representative exclaimed, 'The ringleader of Japan's closed market is the *keiretsu*'. The top six industrial groups – Mitsui, Mitsubishi, Sumitomo, Fuyo, Sanwa and Daiichi Kangin – were all responsible for the closedness of the Japanese economy. It is a typical social and economic barrier preventing the market from opening (*Nihon Keizai Shimbun*, 29 May 1982).

After that, the EC brought action on this issue under GATT Article 23, and the confrontation continues to this day.

The Japanese government's response

At the second session of the GATT meeting held in July of the same year in which criticism was made against Japan by the EC, the Japanese government had the following response:

> If Japanese firms were plants grown in a hot-house such as the *keiretsu*, as the EC maintains, then Japanese industry would not have had such dynamic international competitiveness. Success overseas is an

outcome of hard work at home. We believe that the EC charges are fundamentally incorrect. The fact that foreign companies are finding it difficult to compete with Japanese firms in Japan is just proof of world-beating capabilities of Japanese industries. If the EC wants companies that are competitive and exportable enough to beat Japanese companies, it is up to the EC to cultivate them. (*Nihon Keizai Shimbun*, 10 July 1982)

As a rebuttal against the EC, the Ministry of Foreign Affairs formed a research committee with Professor Uekusa of Tokyo University as its chairman, and this committee issued a report called *Industrial Characteristics of Japanese Industry and Trade Friction*. This report was a response to the EC's insistence that Japan violated GATT Section 23, Chapter I, paragraph C, on the following points: first, the industrial groups effectively controlled industry; second, the principal firms formed alliances (subcontracting) with small and medium enterprises that locked out newcomers; third, there existed associations of enterprises and the effective regulatory control of them was absent; fourth, industry had intimate links with the financial sector; and fifth, principal firms of specific industries were favoured by industrial policy.

The committee's report concluded:

Concerning the publication issued by the EC condemning Japan, the accusation that the *keiretsu* do not abide by the reciprocal agreement insisted by GATT should be considered to be a subjective one. First, the EC statement makes sweeping generalisations based on fragmentary information. Second, to some degree or other, Western Europe too has all the characteristics for which the EC criticises Japan: industrial groupings, subcontracting, locked distribution chains and industrial policies that favour certain firms. It is true that some of the Japanese systems have special characteristics which are not found in the US and the EC, but it must be considered one-sided to say that those systems common through the West and Japan play the role of barrier to trade and direct international investment.[12]

The Fair Trade Commission also contributed to the debate by saying in two reports issued in 1983 that trade within the industrial groups of Japan was comparatively low, thereby contradicting the accusations from abroad.

But the Japanese government's response (other than via Fair Trade Commission) was not empirical, their points lacking persuasion. There is no doubt that the ties, trade and agreements among firms in Japan, have brought it international competitive strength so they have drawn criticism in the trade debates. In truth, the US and Europe have been too quick to take the problem as a simple matter of the trade barrier. Indeed they have missed the crux of the problem.

Opposition to financial liberalisation

The US government and Congress, along with the EC commission, have assumed that the problem is in non-tariff barriers resulting from the *keiretsu* and industrial groups. But if one takes a closer look, they will see that the problem of financial liberalisation follows it.

According to the Gibbons Report:

> One easy way of entering The Japanese market would be to purchase an on-going business – but such acquisitions run against Japanese culture since one is in essence buying the people who work in the company.

Also, in the *Wall Street Journal* (23 March 1982), J. C. Abegglen points out: 'A Western firm cannot buy-out a Japanese company and this fact is the biggest barrier to trade. It is an issue that should take centre-stage in any trade debates from here on out.'

The *Nihon Keizai Shimbun* also reported that in September 1983 President Reagan emphasised that the US government would remove any barrier to investment and promote trade with other countries, whilst simultaneously demanding that foreign governments should also remove the barriers to an increase in investment by US firms. It says: 'Today the President released a statement pressing for the removal of limitations on foreign investment in Japan by US companies. He said that the investment issue is of such importance that it could become the focal point of Japanese/US relations' (10 September 1983). So it is restriction of investment that is sparking the trade debate.

The Japanese government takes the attitude that it is significantly liberalising in the area of investments and that foreign firms are free to buy Japanese companies if they so desire. Since the 1960s, investment liberalisation measures have been progressing, so that by 1980, the foreign investment law was abolished and replaced with the Foreign Exchange and Trade Control Law which is said to have fully liberalised the market for investing. But the United States Trade Representative said that, according to the report on Japan's trade barriers with the US and on the Japanese government's recent policy for opening the markets even under the new law, in the industries of mining, petroleum, leather and leather goods, agriculture, forestry, fisheries and for eleven specified companies the market is as closed as ever to foreign investors. Japan reserves ample rights to check and obstruct the advances of the foreign capital which may put Japanese competitors and other domestic economies in danger. The ability of incumbents in Japan to exclude new entrants makes the reservations that much greater. The Ministry of Finance should issue a detailed plan on investment and have any other ministries concerned examine that plan. The Bank of Japan also examines direct investment issues but these investigations have been criticised as lacking clarity in the extreme.

But as the US Trade Representative has said, while the Japanese government is liberalising on the surface, it cannot be denied that they are in reality preventing liberalisation. This is illustrated most effectively by the fact that foreign direct investment has been negligible since 1965 despite steps towards liberalisation. Foreign direct investment means that foreigners' investment aims to obtain the right of control of businesses and so is distinguished from portfolio investment in the country. Yoshikazu Miyazaki[13] pointed out that, in 1975, no more than 3.3 per cent of Japan's top 300 companies had some form of foreign direct investment and this figure reaches 8.3 per cent if those jointly managed by foreign and Japanese companies are included.

Moreover, we find that the Japanese firms with foreign investment links are many of the old-established companies – like NCR, Yamatake-Honeywell, Toa Energy, Nippon Light Metals, Showa Petroleum, Mitsubishi Petroleum, Kyowa Petroleum and so on – that took on foreign investments before and shortly after the war. It was only after the 1960s that Japanese firms became an attractive investment target among foreigners; therefore those made during the decade should be regarded as true foreign investment. American investment in Europe over the same period increased noticeably while remaining very poor in Japan.

Another important point is that foreign capital makes direct investment in Japan, in the form of an increase in third party equity, except for the case of establishing new firms. But recently, large direct investments have been undertaken by GM in Isuzu, Ford in Mazda and Merck in Banyu Pharmaceuticals. But these companies increased their level of third party equity in order to accommodate the investments by the foreign companies. So in these cases Japanese companies were willing to accept foreign funds in the form of third party equity, so that they cannot be regarded as takeovers.

Most typical participations in direct investment are either to call for takeover bids, as are usually made in the US and Europe, or to buy shares issued by the target companies in the market. There is no such case having happened in Japan, except for the single example of a takeover bid carried out by Bendix, although even this cannot be considered to be on a full scale.

The trade friction that is apparent between Japan and the US or Europe is a result of the competitive strength of the Japanese auto and consumer electronics industries. So it would seem that European and American firms would want to invest directly in these competitive Japanese firms and to take them over. It is of course true that the imbalance of the trade surpluses would not disappear between Japan on one side and the US and Europe on the other. However, takeover bids are the easiest way for the capital of the US and Europe to solve the problem because they make use of the management resources efficiently. There is no such advance of foreign capital into Japan.

It is not for this reason alone that Japanese firms oppose foreign investment. Shareholder stabilisation policies more or less prohibit foreign firms from taking over a Japanese company. So no matter how much the government liberalises the investment climate on the surface, countermeasures are taken behind the scenes and buy-outs are prevented.

The shareholder stabilisation policy also contributes to the exclusion of direct foreign investment and is quite xenophobic in nature. It is to the degree where, for example, Toyota Motors' articles of incorporation expressly states that a foreigner cannot be a member of the board of directors. The offending article was recently removed, but it is a systematic way of thinking that is instilled in the national universities that have no foreign professors.

As mentioned previously, the shareholding among firms can be mutual or unilateral, but the resulting mutual dependence between domestic firms and the *keiretsu* control system lock out foreign investment.

Competition among firms

The exclusionary methods are not intended to keep only foreigners out; they are also aimed at domestic rivals. We have hitherto pointed out that there are connections between Japanese firms that are spread widely, but it should be recognised that there prevails severe competition between rival Japanese firms. This domestic competition is cut-throat, and Japanese economists cite it as one of the main factors in the forging of high growth and international competitiveness among Japanese companies. Japanese orthodox economists call it excessive and insist that the principle of competition is accomplished in the economy.

These statements, however, fail to capture the realities of the situation; they are rather academic and heavily favour the imported theories. They also result from the attitude that regards the competition between firms in the same way as we do the competition between individuals. But as has been stated previously, interactions among firms and among individuals are fundamentally different. To apply the framework of a market consisting only of individuals to oligopolistically behaving big firms is misleading and confuses the issue.

The fact that inter-firm trading is usually made by direct face-to-face negotiation does not necessarily mean that a new firm that wants to start up in business is locked out. A firm which is growing must find a new trading partner to satisfy its own increased demand. According to the standard theory of competition, the way for a seller to attract new partners is to lower the price of goods being sold. In the case of face-to-face dealings, however, a trading partner has to be found first and the price is negotiated afterwards, as we discussed earlier. So if company B wants to sell to company A, but the new entrant C offers a lower price than B, then B is told of that fact. At that point, if B does not meet or beat the price offered by C, B loses the trading partner A. In order to prevent this, he will change only the price. The traditional competition argument supposes that the trading relationship is changed by a change in the price.

But if a firm decides to expand its trading arrangement, it has means other than a price strategy to attract a new trading partner. Various tools are at its disposal, from shareholdings and financial assistance to rebates and entertainment expenses. Of course, price can also be used to oppose a rival firm, even to the point of pricing below cost. This is because the competition is localised to a certain industry or product and the group as a whole can afford to ignore profitability until the firm itself becomes profitable again. The competition is very severe because it is localised, as economists call it excessive competition.

Although inter-firm tradings are stable, as a whole, they have to expand in order for existing firms to grow and for new firms to be established. Thus, while stable transactions are constantly made on the one hand, severe competition has to be carried out on the other in order to secure new trading partners. The balance between stable trans-actions and competitive acquisition of new partners of trade is essen-tially important for the business success of Japanese firms.

The above is the competition that results from trading between firms. It is not the same as the competition that occurs in trading with individuals and foreign countries. The actual inter-firm competition may be describe as follows. The one aspect is fierce and often criticised as excessive compared with the other in which the market share is stable. Successful growing firms acquire many new trade partners and fiercely compete with each other in order to expand their shares in the market between individuals and firms.

Here a rival firm is considered as the enemy, so, as Haniya says, one works in order to 'kill the enemy'. The attitude of shutting out the rival also promotes 'companism'. The supposition that one's own firm must be made stronger than the rival firm in order to beat it effects a sense of camaraderie and patriotism which is the spirit of 'companism'. This gives the Japanese company a vitality and enables Japanese firms to grow.

16
Institutional Framework

Relationships between companies

Ronald Dore, who was introduced in the last chapter, has said that the long-term relationships between firms in Japan depend on trust rather than on contracts. Long-term relationships are traditional in Japan. For instance, in past times, Japanese homeowners would occasionally thatch their roofs; this was not a job for one man so a neighbour collaborated in the work. Of course the favour would be returned when it came time to fix the neighbour's roof in his son's generation. This resulted in a long-term relationship among neighbours. The same sense of community is projected on to today's firms in Japan.

It is important to mention the fact that even though this tradition has changed, the feeling between Japanese as individuals is said to persist today. But the relations between two firms are logically different from the relations between two people. The above-described analogy does have some merit, but the parallels should not be overstated.

Ryushi Iwata, who believes that the relations between firms and between people are more or less the same, says that the style of 'Japanese management' originates from the individual relationships in Japan:

> The belief that views harmonious and perpetual relationship as being important in Japan is not only confined within firms. It is also relevant to the relationships between firms and the relationships of firms with consumers, i.e. their customers. Since the olden days we have had a saying – 'Avoid one-time only'. In other words, Japanese avoid doing business with anyone other than regular customers.[14]

In relations with banks and trade partners, Japanese firms maintain harmonious and perpetual relationships with their regular partners, providing a great deal of cooperation on a regular basis. Kohei Hisaeda thinks of it as a tacit understanding and an insurance network. He points out that in North America business is opened only after investigation by a specialist company and having effected appropriate insurances. But in Japan, by contrast, enough time is spent on maintaining communication with the partner of the trade until the parties know each other well.[15]

In this way, Iwata describes how firms become familiar with each other.

In the same vein, Masumi Tsuda, an adherent to the 'Japanese-style management', who insists that its idea originates from the Japanese community life, has the following to say concerning industrial groups:

> The formation of the industrial groups cannot be explained as a simple pursuit of economic benefit. The character of Japanese-style management that it puts its root in the community life is expanded into the community of business.[16]

He also states in another passage that group management within a firm extends its practice to industrial groups.[17]

In fact it was Naohiro Amaya who first personified the relationship between firms. According to him:

> The relationships between firms and their trading partners are not the cold relations that are performed with an abacus and contract documents. The cool and dry character of company relations is cemented with human emotions of love and duty. While the usual acquaintance would not provide feelings of assurance, firms have to obtain the added benefit of stable mutual shareholdings and the dispatch of directors from one company to another. Stable shareholdings and dispatch of directors have a variety of consequences but in Japanese society the ownership of shares means that the relationship is not of a between-strangers type but between family members.[18]

So the relationships between firms in Japan tend to be thought of as obligations, long-term relationships, groupism, and other characteristics that define human relations in Japan. But if this is the case, it is more or less arbitrary, so that it is no more than an analogy that establishes no logical connection between institutional and personal relationships. It cannot be said to be a theoretical explanation of the matter.

When firms are thought as being the same as people, the relations between firms tend also to be personified. Although the inter-firm relationships are held by the members of the companies, it does not mean that humanness should be extended to the whole firms. The firms and their relationships are a system and they should be judged by the laws that govern them. Before arguing that the relationships among firms are the same as the relationships among people, we should examine the systematic framework of those company relationships. Relationships between firms have histories which have been influenced by and are reflected in their respective countries' cultures, but to take the cultural explanation unthinkingly is a mental shortcut that is harmful to understanding.

Anti-monopoly law

The primary law that regulates tie-ups among firms is the anti-monopoly law. The meaning of tie-ups among firms can be widely interpreted and includes organisations from cartels to conglomerates. The Japanese law legislates on all of them, but it does not contain any sections pertaining to the *keiretsu* or industrial groups.

The criticisms of the major trading houses that resulted from the oil crisis in 1973 prompted calls for reform of the anti-monopoly law. The main point of these calls was to strengthen the anti-monopoly law by allowing it to break up monopolistic corporations and strengthen regulations against cartels (on cooperative pricing, etc.). Also called for were regulations on industrial groups. The first two were to include specifically the detailed regulations into the revised version of the law, and the third was only to strengthen limitations on corporate shareholding in order to regulate industrial groups. Public opinion stated that the industrial groups and the *keiretsu* should be regulated, but when the time came to put these proposals into law, it was not to be.

In fact, the anti-monopoly law was at first equipped with a provision that forbids the existence of holding companies. This kind of law did not exist in Europe or the US and was unique to Japan. The law was the consequence of the break-up of the *zaibatsu* by the American occupation and was meant to ensure that the *zaibatsu* could not be rebuilt. The anti-monopoly law of 1947 has been reformed three times and the provisions have changed markedly. However, this provision forbidding holding companies remains unchanged. Thus we may remember that the Japanese regard it, together with the ninth article of the Constitution, as the symbol of Japan's responsibility for the war. In the same way as the Constitution is impaired by establishing the force of self-defence, the anti-monopoly law is also ruled by its reformulations. Its original spirit has now disappeared, because holding companies that have other businesses are then allowed (only pure holding companies being prohibited) in spite of the fact that they were the target of the original law, and *zaibatsu's* holding companies were, in fact, the companies with some other businesses.

The next shareholding regulation governs the non-banking sector (industry). Although the original law of 1947 prohibited shareholding, by industry, it was reformed in 1949 so that if the essence of competition between firms is diminished or if the essence of competition is restricted in one area of trade, shareholdings by firms in firms of the same area of trade will be disallowed. Firms that have their business outside of the market area in question, however, were able to buy shares in firms within that market. Then the 1953 reform made the restriction apply 'only to specific markets where trade has been essentially restricted', thereby eliminating the part about diminished competition between firms. The reforms had the effect on firms so as to put them under no substantial regulation concerning shareholdings. Those firms not covered by the legislation bought up shares of other firms and the process contributed to the formation of the *keiretsu* and industrial groups.

The previously mentioned criticisms of the trading houses did result in some strengthening of the anti-monopoly law. In the third reform to the law, non-financial companies with more than ten billion yen in capital or more than thirty billion yen in net assets could not own more in another domestic company than their own worth measured in equity or net assets, whichever was higher. But there are many exceptions to this provision, so only a few, other than big comprehensive trading houses, conflict with it.

The next reform, for financial institutions, was to the original law which restricted equity ownership to no more than 5 per cent of the target company's total issue of shares. In 1953, in order for banks to be able to hold shares of other companies, the limit was lifted to 10 per cent, only to be rolled back in 1977 to the original ceiling. The ownership limit for life insurance companies, meanwhile, remains at 10 per cent.

The major push of the third reform, as noted, was to regulate the industrial groups. To accomplish this, the sole method used was to strengthen limitations on the shareholding of the mega-firms and financial institutions. The move was ineffective due to its weakness and bore no fruit at all. First of all the implementation of the law was delayed by ten years so that firms would have time to build up their equity or assets to meet the law's requirements. Second, there was no stipulation on how to dispose of shares if the requirements were not met. For example, it is legitimate for a trading company to dispose of its shares only to have a manufacturing company from the same group pick up the shares, or for a bank to make a similar disposal to a trust bank or an insurance company of the same group. This type of intra-group share trading was not touched upon.

In addition to the limitations on shareholding by industrial com-bines, Article 13 of the anti-monopoly law addresses directorships. But as we discussed earlier, the dispatching of directors in Japan is quite common and so the law in this regard is too ineffective. Another area prohibits unfair trade practices, and it regulates the industrial com-bines in a wider sense as well. In particular, where a prominent posi-tion has been misappropriated against a *keiretsu* company, the case is treated as a matter of unfair trade practices. But these cannot be seen at all to be useful regulations of conduct against the *keiretsu* and indus-trial groups.

Japan's large corporation systems

So why is Japan's anti-monopoly law so ineffective against its *keiretsu* and industrial groups? One reason is that the regulation of cartels is the pillar of Japanese anti-monopoly law and strategy. Cartels are an organisation of companies from one sector that collude to control price and output. The law is quite strict in this regard and so there have been many incidents of transgression. But they have been mostly committed by small to medium enterprises so the law has been seen as a tool for intimidating small businesses.

But, of course, in times of recession, large firms form cartels which control the scale of production. But these instances are rare and except for a few examples, competition between large firms is fierce. So to look at Japanese industry from the viewpoint of cartels is to downplay the significance of competition between large firms and also to ignore collusions between large firms.

Another main thrust of Japanese anti-trust laws is against mergers. But under the Japanese commercial code, a merger is defined as multi-ple companies forming a single company in the sense as defined by the commercial law. In America's antitrust legislation, the merger is defined the same as the above but it also includes cases of acquisition of substantially large numbers of shares. Nowhere in Japanese law does such a definition seem to exist. To date Japan has seen several large mergers so it is true that they have contributed in strengthening the oligopolistic system in Japan. But, as has been stated earlier, takeovers common to the US and UK are scarcely observed in Japan. Mergers in Japan are always mutually agreed ones. When firms intend to advance into a new area or to make an expansion in their own fields they will form appropriate new *keiretsu*.

Mergers have a significance for Japan's large corporation system. There are many cases where the firms within an industrial group or *keiretsu* make a merger, but there are few cases of mergers which are made between the companies belonging to different groups. Also rare are cases in which *keiretsu* is disturbed. It would be a mistake to see that in spite of these, the merger is the main target of the regulation. Nevertheless, we may ask why the core of Japan's anti-monopoly law concentrates on regulation of cartels and mergers. It has a lot to do with the fact that Japan imported it from America directly. Japan's anti-monopoly policy is based on Bain's and Caves' theory of industrial organisation.[19] Originally the laws were imported from America lock, stock and barrel, so they were based on the American experience with business. It had no meaning to the Japanese since they themselves did not disband the *zaibatsu* and did not impose the anti-monopoly law. But academics in Japan could be blamed as they did not form their own theory based on the experiences and observations in Japan.

In the Bain and Caves type of industrial organisation theory, it is formulated in terms of market structure, market behaviour and market conduct. In the discussion of market structure, market share is emphasised and barriers to entry are discussed. This theory which emphasises the degree of concentration does not entirely deal with the problem of fusion of firms. We may therefore say that it completely ignores the problems of industry groups and *keiretsu* which have a great significance in Japan. The American theory of industrial organisation, especially the abstract version of Bain and Caves, has been directly imported and applied to Japan. This is the defect of the Japanese anti-monopoly law.

It is reasonable that in America, the Bain and Caves type of industrial organisation theory has become mainstream. The theory and the laws, which are based upon the anti-monopoly sentiment as was seen in the populist movement and have been created from the investigation of monopoly in the period of the New Deal, are firmly based on the reality in America. It is very reasonable there to take merger and cartel seriously.

Unlike Japan's *keiretsu*, the equality in relationships among American firms is based on tradition. Instead of forming a *keiretsu*, US firms would prefer a unification by merger. It is partly for this reason that US companies have a high internal sourcing rate. Unlike Japan, America has no habit of holding shares mutually between two firms; therefore, in America more than in Japan, combines are not seen as a problem. More threatening is the merger or cartel. Although there are industrial combines in America too, the historical sentiment in Japan is substantially different. It is indeed a great mistake that Japan imported the American theory and produced her own industry laws, neglecting the difference between the two countries.

Viewed in this light, one can see the significance of the industrial combines, *keiretsu* and industrial groups in Japan. These arrangements and structures of firms have, more than anything else, made 'companism' possible in Japan and allowed the establishment of belief in 'corporate capitalism'.

Regulation of mutual shareholding

So far we have seen that the Japanese commercial law does not have a single provision that regulates industrial combines. This is considered its major flaw. Before the reform of the commercial code in 1981, the only provisions that pertained to combines concerned parent firm auditors and their rights in auditing the subsidiary. This lack of regulation on industrial combines in a country where they have had such a profound and overwhelming presence, is astonishing.

In 1981 the code was reformed to address and regulate mutual shareholding in addition to simple shareholding procedures. An advisory body of the Ministry of Finance found that the dispersion of individual shareholders was a problem and, to combat this, regulations should be imposed on mutual corporate shareholding.

In spite of mutual shareholding reaching full bloom in Japan, there were no laws in place to govern it. Ken'ichiro Osumi, Professor of Commercial Law, claimed that, when looked at from a point of logic, there seems no rational reason for mutual corporate shareholding. It seems to act against the principle of efficient use of capital and promotes a hollowing-out of capital. For two companies to raise capital, if they exchange equity with each other the value of the companies grows. The two exercise control over each other without any real investment and so distort the control of the real investors. So there is no rhyme or reason in promoting mutual corporate shareholding.

It was long in coming but in 1981 reform of the commercial code was finally enacted. It stated that a company could buy shares in another publicly traded company, and if the sum was more than 25 per cent of the target company's total issued shares, the target could not have a say in the general shareholders assembly of the investing company even if it had shares of its own in that company.

Upon examination, it becomes clear that this does not regulate mutual corporate shareholding itself. It means that this is permitted subject to the rule set for mutually held shares, saying that the exercise of their right of voting is put under a certain control. It is a lukewarm regulation, much more loose compared with the one in Europe. In fact, existing parent companies that own more than 25 per cent of their subsidiary are few, so most parents will be unfazed by the reform.

That said, it seems that the legislators would have no reasonable argument on which to base their work. It is just the expediency of form over function. The superficial reforms have flourished, but among the substantial changes is the stipulation that a subsidiary cannot buy equity ownership in its parent. The reason is that for a subsidiary to do so would be the same as the parent owning shares in itself, a practice which is against the law. This practice has been overlooked until now but it has finally been addressed with an effective regulation. This regulation, however, means that a subsidiary is allowed to buy shares of its parent, provided that the latter owns less than 50 per cent of the shares of the former. There is no good reason for this allowance, except for benefiting the parent by pushing up the value per share as some of the floated shares are drawn back off the market by the hand of the subsidiary.

Because this round of reform resulted in so many weak regulations, it has been suggested that new laws should be made in order to regulate the industrial combines. But because such an act is likely to be far off, a reform on mutual shareholdings has hastily been made. I hope that this book can clarify the background of the problem for the next round of reform.

Notes to Part IV (Chapter 12–16)

1 Ronald Dore, 'Goodwill and the Spirit of Market Capitalism', *British Journal of Sociology*, 34, iv, 1983; *Flexible Rigidities*, The Athlone Press, 1986; *Taking Japan Seriously*, The Athlone Press, 1987.
2 Willard F. Mueller, 'The Rising Economic Concentration in America: Reciprocity, Conglomeration and the New American "Zaibatsu" System', *Antitrust Law and Economics Review*, vol. 4, no. 3–4; 'Economic Concentration', *Hearings before the Subcommittee on Antitrust and Monopoly of the Committee of the Judiciary*, US Senate, 1969, Part 8 A.

3 M. Akaboshi, 'Restriction on Competition that Reciprocal Contracts Bring Forth' (in Japanese), *Kosei Torihiki*, December 1969, p. 15.
4 T. Negishi, 'Regulation of Reciprocal Contracts by Means of the Anti-Monopoly Law' (in Japanese), *Kokusai Shogyo*, November 1974, p. 160.
5 I. Nakatani, 'The Japanese Economy from the Viewpoint of Risk Sharing' (in Japanese), *Osaka Daigaku Keizaigaku*, vol. 32, no. 2–3, 1982.
6 Rodney Clark, *The Japanese Company*, pp. 62–3.
7 Ibid.
8 M. Ikeda, 'The Production System of Subcontract and the Japanese Management' (in Japanese), *Nippon no Kagakusha*, June 1983, p. 10.
9 Ibid, p. 12.
10 Y. Sato, 'Subcontract System' (in Japanese), *Nihon Sangyo no Seidoteki Tokucho to Boeki Masatsu*, ed. by Ministry of Foreign Affairs, Japan, 1983, p. 69.
11 The Gibbons Report Subcommittee on Ways and Means, US House of Representatives, *Report on Trade Mission to Far East*, US Government Printing Office, 1981, pp. 15–17.
12 Ministry of Foreign Affairs, Japan, ibid, p. 3.
13 Y. Miyazaki, *Contemporary Capitalism and Multinational Firms* (in Japanese), Iwanami, 1982, p. 280.
14 R. Iwata, *Natural Features of Management in Contemporary Japan* (in Japanese), Nihon Keizai Shimbun Sha, 1978, p. 94.
15 Ibid, p. 96.
16 M. Tsuda, *The Logic of Japanese Management* (in Japanese), Chuo Koronsha, 1977, p. 279.
17 M. Tsuda, *Defense for Japanese Management* (in Japanese), Toyo Keizai Shimposha, 1976, p. 20.
18 N. Amaya, *Drifting Japanese Economy* (in Japanese), Mainichi Shimbun Sha, 1975, p. 128.
19 J. S. Bain, *Industrial Organisation*, Wiley, 2nd edn, 1968, and R. Caves, *American Industry*, Prentice-Hall, 1964.

Index